With deepest affection
or something like that -
Henri

THE BATTLE-PIECES OF
HERMAN MELVILLE

THE BATTLE-PIECES OF
HERMAN MELVILLE

Edited with Introduction and Notes by **Hennig Cohen**

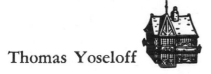

Thomas Yoseloff   New York • London • Toronto

New material © 1963 by A. S. Barnes and Company, Inc.
Library of Congress Catalog Card Number: 62-14910

Thomas Yoseloff, *Publisher*
11 East 36 Street
New York 16, N. Y.

Thomas Yoseloff, Ltd.
123 New Bond Street
London W.1, England

9793
Printed in the United States of America

For a band of brothers:
David, Mark, Jonathan

Acknowledgments

The text for this edition of *Battle-Pieces* follows a copy of the original edition published by Harper & Brothers (New York, 1866) in the University of Pennsylvania Library. The illustrations to the poems, except where otherwise credited, are from the Waud Collection of the Library of Congress. Assistance relating to the illustrations accompanying the notes to the poems was given me by the National Academy of Design and the Frick Art Reference Library, both in New York, the Berkshire Athenaeum in Pittsfield, Massachusetts, and the Joslyn Art Museum in Omaha, Nebraska.

I would like to record my gratitude to Milton Kaplan and the late Vincent L. Eaton, of the Library of Congress, and Jesse Mills and Mrs. Delphine Richardson, of the University of Pennsylvania Library, for guidance and interest far beyond their professional obligation. For providing me with information which I might otherwise have missed and for turning me from the path of error I am grateful to Peter D. Murray, John Bernstein, James Murnik, Maurice Johnson, Sidney Kaplan, Nathalia Wright, John Seelye, and Merton Sealts.

The preparation of this edition took place in 1960 while I was the recipient of a Guggenheim Fellowship. Further assistance was provided by the Graduate Research Committee of the University of Pennsylvania.

H. C.

Contents

Introduction

On August 12, 1866 the New York *Herald,* in a column called "The Book World," mentioned the publication of Herman Melville's *Battle-Pieces,* adding, as though it had been an afterthought, that "for ten years the public has wondered what has become of Melville." There was reason for speculation. Beginning auspiciously in 1846 with *Typee,* a narrative of personal adventure in the South Seas, moving on in 1851 to *Moby-Dick,* a strange novel about the pursuit of a white whale, and ending in 1857 with an even stranger book, *The Confidence-Man,* Melville had published ten prose works in eleven years; had successively delighted, puzzled, and alienated the literary world; and then had not been heard from for almost a decade.

In the interval two things had occurred. The first was that Melville, to use the words of his wife Elizabeth, had "taken to writing poetry." The second was that as the Civil War dragged on month after month, it had begun to occupy his mind and to set it off into paths which had many curious twistings and turnings. Melville in an elegy to Sherman's men had written that "battle can heroes and bards restore." A restoration was forthcoming. At first he saw the war as a struggle between North and South, Union and Secession, Freedom and Slavery, and—according to his own firm conviction—between Right and Wrong. Eventually however, the war became a metaphor of conflict in general—whether within a single consciousness, among the angels of heaven, on the plains of Tewksbury and Barnet Heath, or at Malvern Hill. What concerned him most were those conflicts which led to the disruption of order, and the problem of how they were to be resolved. The central theme of *Battle-Pieces* is one of opposition and reconciliation.

The raw materials for his poetic speculations on opposition and reconciliation came from a variety of sources. These include the Bible, especially the Old Testament; Milton, particularly his treatment of the revolt of Satan; and Shakespeare, notably, crucial passages from the tragedies. They also include personal experiences such as a visit to a cousin at the war front, the feats and personalities of certain army officers he had known, stories of the war he had got first hand, things he had observed on the streets of New York, and matters of such common knowledge as to be routinely discussed among acquaintances or read about in the newspapers. Another source, and one pertinent to the nature of his metaphor, consisted of the paintings in the great collections of Europe which he had seen on his trips abroad, the art exhibitions he attended in New York, the prints which he found such pleasure in collecting, and the sketches of military life which he saw in *Harper's Weekly*. Besides such casual sources there was one which Melville used in a deliberate and calculated way, a periodical called *The Rebellion Record*. Its purpose, according to an introductory note, was "to give a comprehensive history of this struggle; sifting fact from fiction and rumor, presenting the poetical and picturesque aspects, the noble and characteristic incidents, separated from the graver and more important documents." For Melville it provided a variety of subject matter and detail, as well as a device for assuring scope and orderly arrangement.

Melville used more biblical references than did Emerson, the ordained minister, or even Hawthorne, the friend who shared his concern with sin, salvation, and the fallen state of man. As he grew older and dealt with more complex subjects, biblical allusion increased. Among his own works, *Clarel,* the narrative poem set in the Holy Land, not surprisingly contains the highest proportion of biblical allusions; but *Battle-Pieces* is not far behind, ranking in this respect with *Moby-Dick, The Confidence-Man,* and even with *Billy Budd,* his last prose work. From the Bible Melville drew the comparison of the battlefield to a wilderness, a place of testing and purification as it had been for Christ, for John the Baptist, and for the Children of Israel. Likewise of biblical origin is his portrayal of God as the militant, thunderous Jehovah and his association of the Union cause with the fate of the Israelites. Such biblical imagery lends an exalted tone to the discourse.

So closely related to the biblical sources as at times to be indistinguishable from them are the Miltonic materials. The principal Miltonic elements are the War in Heaven and the Fall of Man. Members of the satanic host of *Paradise Lost* who appear in *Battle-Pieces* include Lucifer, Moloch, Belial, Mammon, and Dagon. Associated with the South in the earthly counterpart of the War of the Angels, they outnumber and indeed all but overpower Michael and Raphael. Often the angels of light and darkness are as flat as figures from a medieval morality play, though as the fortune the North improves the dark angels become lost creatures to whom sympathy may be shown and who sometimes seem, like Milton's Lucifer, to possess a perverted magnificence. The theme of the Fall of Man is so persistent in Melville's work that it is more accurate to describe it as an interest shared with Milton than as a borrowing. Yet Melville's treatment of this great myth is re-enforced by his knowledge of the work of Milton. Milton begins his epic with the statement that its subject is the "loss of Eden" and the consequences of that loss. Melville, who saw America as "man's fairest hope," a second Eden grown corrupt, indicates his concern with "man's latter fall" at the outset of *Battle-Pieces* and returns to it at the end. Thus he makes clear the importance for him of the concept of the Fall of Man, at the same time manipulating it in such a manner as to give his cycle of poems a greater degree of structural unity. Equating the Civil War with the Miltonic version of the War in Heaven amplified the earthly conflict and infused it with meaning.

That *Battle-Pieces* is studded with Shakespearean echoes is no surprise, for Shakespeare, as Leon Howard states, gave Melville "the most important direction he received during his journey in the world of the mind." Shakespeare is the only writer referred to in the poems—or for that matter in the notes, aside from the mention of the historians Plutarch and Froissart. It is the dramatist's tragic vision of history that Melville finds so provocative, his perception of the incursion of evil into a green and orderly world, the disruption of historical processes to the detriment of human achievement and thereafter the need for restoration. As the last paragraph of the "Supplement" informs us, the Civil War for Melville was a "terrible historic tragedy." One of the things Melville was attempting in *Battle-Pieces* was historic portrayal. To this Shakespeare's view of history contributed.

Melville's own participation in the "historic tragedy" was limited. He was touched by the news that the frigate "United States"—the "Neversink" of *White-Jacket*—on which he had served for a year, had been destroyed at Norfolk to prevent her capture by the Confederacy. He enrolled with the Pittsfield militia in 1861 and attended drills until late in the summer of 1863, when he began to arrange for his move to New York. He visited the New York Navy Yard in July 1861, perhaps to offer himself for naval service, but if the offer was made nothing seems to have come of it. The truth is that Melville was out of joint with the times. He could not commit himself to anything. He was not physically well and he was no longer young, though it is true that his shipmate of *Typee* days, Toby Greene, like Melville born in 1819, was fighting Rebels in Mississippi, and Walt Whitman, born the same year, was working in the Washington hospitals and writing *Drum-Taps*. Melville thought of himself as an old man. Wars, like going to sea, were the business of youth. His youthful characters White-Jacket, Redburn, and Ishmael had experienced an initiation as sailors, and now boy soldiers were facing an equivalent experience. Melville at forty-two was an onlooker, sensitive and compassionate, but personally remote.

His sense of his own superannuation appears in "The March into Virginia," "Ball's Bluff," and "The Stone Fleet," poems near the beginning of the collection. "Senior wisdom suits not now,/ The light is on the youthful brow" we are told in "The Conflict of Convictions," and the theme persists to "A Scout Toward Aldie" at the end, with its contrast between the seasoned major and the youthful colonel. In this poem Melville writes that "command is a boyish thing," and in still others he scrutinizes the actions of such boyish commanders as Worden of the "Monitor," and Cushing, who sank a Confederate ram with a torpedo lashed to a spar.

At Pittsfield in August 1863 Melville joined his fellow townspeople in honoring the twenty-three-year-old colonel, William Bartlett, just returned from Louisiana at the head of his regiment, a leg missing and his arm in a sling; and when Melville visited his cousin, Colonel Henry Gansevoort, at the battlefront in Virginia in the spring of 1864, he met doomed young heroes like Charles Lowell. From them he heard tales of the exploits of the partisan leader, John C. Mosby, and absorbed details of the landscape and atmosphere which he was to incorporate into "A Scout Toward Aldie." He was a youth himself for a few hours, borrowing horse and equipment and accompanying a calvary detachment on a "scout." The episode was reminiscent of a voyage to England in 1849 when he performed "feats in the rigging" of his packet ship, recapturing moments from the days when he had served on whalers, merchantmen, and a frigate.

Gradually his sense of participation increased. He felt sympathies and he saw analogies. Naval operations seem to have moved him most, especially when they involved oaken ships, anachronisms in an age of iron and steam. The shameful draft riots, an example of the disruption of civil order, set him to speculating on the shackles and deceits which man seemed to require. The battles in dense Virginia forests he saw as counterpart to the trials of saints and prophets in biblical wildernesses. An oil sketch of a Negro street vendor became a portrait of a benign sibyl foreseeing in the distant future a peace of which she herself could not partake.

"With few exceptions, the Pieces in this volume originated in an impulse imparted by the fall of Richmond," Melville states in the introductory note to *Battle-Pieces.* Richmond fell on April 3, 1865. At some time during that month, in a state of mind quite different from the staleness and lack of purpose which had characterized him four years before, he attended the annual exhibition of the National Academy of Design. He was more than casually interested, for his brother, Allen Melville, was one of the sponsors and Mrs. Allen Melville, in recognition of a gift of $500 to the Academy, was listed in its catalogue as a "Fellow for Life." The paintings shown included cavalry charges, foraging parties, soldiers departing for the front, drummer boys, and idealized slave women. There was also a landscape darkened by an approaching storm, and a scene of Niagara Falls at sunrise. Melville absorbed what he saw, adding it to the store of visual images of the Civil War which he got from illustrated news magazines like *Leslie's* and *Harper's.* The exhibition reminded him of paintings by Salvator Rosa and others, in the genre known as "battle-pieces," which he had seen in

European museums and which he had found interesting enough to note in his travel journals. Prior to this, in *Moby-Dick* (Chap. 56), he had spoken of the melodramatic whaling pictures of Ambroise Louis Garneray as "sea battle-pieces."

The figurative use of *battle-pieces* as a literary term is now more common than its use to indicate a genre of painting, but when Melville took it as the title for his collection of war poems, he did so with an awareness of its primary meaning. In fact, he may have chosen it deliberately on that account. Its visual connotation was important to him, and to make certain that his readers were apprised that he was presenting a series of pictures, he added the subtitle "Aspects of the War." His pictorial intention is further confirmed in the "Supplement" essay when he refers to the poems individually as "the battle-pieces in the foregoing collection," and in the dedication. At any rate, he found in the pictures at the National Academy an important source, and they led to the recollection of paintings that had impressed him, such as Titian portraits and Constable seascapes. These also went into the poems.

The ingredients of *Battle-Pieces,* ranging as they did from a Renaissance portrait to participation in a cavalry raid, were diverse in the extreme but scarcely representative of what Melville called the "varied amplitude" of the war. Much had to be filled in. Impressions wanted corroboration, and realistic detail was needed. Hence, as he had done on previous occasions, Melville sought a book which would help him flesh out impressions, which would assist him in seeing his object whole, and which would contribute a degree of order. He found such a book in *The Rebellion Record*. Despite Melville's statement in his introductory note that he served as a "harp in the window, and noted the contrasted airs which wayward winds have played," the poems are frequently specific, detailed, and selective in terms of subject. They were not often the product of white heat generated by immediacy, but rather of the cool calculation which the passage of time makes possible.

The Rebellion Record was a periodical designed to present a history of the Civil War in "a digested and systematic shape," through selected newspaper accounts and official reports interspersed with verse and anecdotes. The material was cumulated in a series of eleven volumes and a supplement. Each volume contained a "Diary of Events," a section of "Documents and Narratives" and a section of "Poetry, Rumors and Incidents." On the whole the quality of the writing was adequate but prosaic, unpretentious except for the poems, which were of indifferent quality. The first eight volumes, covering the years 1860 to 1864, were available to Melville in time to have been of use to him for *Battle-Pieces*.

There is no evidence that Melville owned a set of *The Rebellion Record,* but in his note to the poem, "Rebel Color-bearers at Shiloh," he states that the "incident upon which this piece is based is narrated in a newspaper account of the battle to be found in the 'Rebellion Record,'" and the quotation which he gives is accurate. "The Rebel Color-bearers at Shiloh" is, in the order of the poems in the volume, probably the last for which *The Rebellion Record* is a source. In all, Melville drew upon *The Rebellion Record* for at least twenty poems, a majority of those which deal with military events. Eighteen concern events before 1863, and of this number twelve contain material which can be traced to *The Rebellion Record.* Not only did Melville need *The Rebellion Record* for the nudge it gave his muse but he also depended upon it for raw facts, especially concerning the first years of the war, when his interest had been relatively slight, and which were then as much as five years in the past.

The poem "Donelson," the longest of those for which he drew upon *The Rebellion Record,* reveals three principal ways in which Melville used the various newspaper dispatches and official reports in this compendium. For narrative purposes, he would follow closely a number of different sources, choosing facts and incidents and weaving them together with little embellishment or expansion. For intensifying drama or mood, he would take a single source and strip it to its essence. Finally, to suggest larger implications and relationships than narrative, drama, or mood alone could provide, he would use his source material as the starting point for a cluster of imagery weighted with moral significance.

An example of diverse sources fused into a unified narrative is the account of the Thursday morning fight (lines 59ff.). Within some fifty lines Melville employs material from articles reprinted from the New York *Times, Missouri Democrat,* Charleston *Courier,* and Richmond *Dispatch.* He took items unique to a single newspaper and also information available in several. In the latter case it is sometimes hard to ascertain the exact source. Thus the *Courier* and the *Dispatch* report the use of distinctive arm bands to identify the tatterdemalion Confederate troops (lines 99–101), and only the *Times* notes a "great profusion of gold lace" worn by Confederate officers (line 104). Both the *Times* and the *Missouri Democrat* mention the expertise of the Federal sharpshooters (lines 82–83) and the death of Colonel Morrison (line 80), but only the *Times* describes the injuries caused by falling tree limbs which had been struck by artillery (line 78) or compares the Union riflemen to hunters at a salt lick in ambush for deer (lines 86–88).

Melville took the description of Thursday night at Donelson (lines 136–51) from one newspaper, the *Missouri Democrat,* adhering to the order of the dispatch and echoing its language, but pruning and refining to create a sense of grim determination in the face of icy misery and danger. An extract from this account shows how closely he followed the original:

The night of Thursday will long be remembered by the troops surrounding Donelson. The weather . . . toward the close of the afternoon became chilly and lowering. About six o'clock a heavy rain set in. During the warmth of the day before . . . whole regiments had cast aside their overcoats and blankets, and without tents, and in a great majority of cases, occupying positions rendering a fire a sure mark for the enemy's batteries, with nothing to eat but cold rations, their condition was deplorable indeed.

To add to their discomfort, when thoroughly saturated with rain, a pelting snow-storm set in, continuing all night. As can be imagined, with an enemy in front, continually annoying and annoyed, but little sleep was indulged in. The only demonstration of importance on the part of the rebels, during the night, was a formidable attempt on the right wing to obtain Taylor's battery. . . .

But, cold and hungry, with garments stiff with frost, the soldiers were still hopeful and firm. . . . The universal sentiment was, as blunt Col. Oglesby expressed it, "We came here to take that fort, and *we will take it*. . . ." (See "Donelson," p. 51.)

The passage in "Donelson" which describes the duel between the Union gunboats and the Confederate water batteries (lines 207-22) illustrates how Melville took a prosaic newspaper article, in this case from the New York *Times* of February 15, 1862 (*Rebellion Record*, IV, 172), and reworked it in such a way that it becomes not merely terse, effective narrative but narrative with moral significance. The newspaper account relates how the gunboat "Louisville" was damaged:

At this time the boats were within some four hundred yards, and were on the point of using grape-shot, when a shot disabled the steering apparatus of the Louisville, by carrying off the top of the wheelhouse, and knocking the wheel itself into fragments. There was a tiller aft, and this was instantly taken possession of by the pilot—but he had scarcely reached it, ere the rudder was carried away by a shot from the Tyler. Of course the boat became instantly unmanageable, and swung around, receiving a shot in the woodwork towards the stern, which, I believe, wounded several seamen. Under this circumstance, it was thought best to retire, and accordingly the whole fleet fell back to the position it had occupied in the morning. The most serious damage sustained during the action was from one of those monster one hundred and twenty-eight-pound shots, which passed through a bow-port of the Louisville and dismounted the second gun on the starboard quarter, killing three men and wounding six others. A captain of one of the guns was cut completely in two, and spattered his brains over Captain Dove, who stood by him, and otherwise so mangled him that scarcely a resemblance of humanity remained. (See "Donelson," p. 51.)

For the "Louisville" passage Melville winnows out journalistic wordiness and compresses details; for example, the number of damaging shots which the vessel received is reduced to one. This increases the pace of the narrative and heightens the drama. Moreover, it provides a focal situation which may be invested with cosmic implications. The projectile from the Confederate battery is a planet, a malign and fateful wanderer in the skies. When it destroys the steering mechanism of the ship, the ship drifts uncontrolled, "lawless," itself useless and a danger to the fleet. The figurative language drawn from astronomy and the law underscores two ideas which recur in *Battle-Pieces*: the role of Fate in the lives of men and the need for mechanisms of control by individuals and society.

A final point should be made about the way Melville used *The Rebellion Record*. In the deliberate choice of certain material Melville contributed to the thematic and structural unity of his book. I have suggested that opposition and reconciliation constitute the principal theme of *Battle-Pieces*. Melville's use of a sentence from the New York *Times* of February 17, 1862 is a minor but telling instance of the ramifications of this theme: "In some cases, a few of our wounded were cared for by the rebels, although they were without fire, and could give them but little valuable assistance." The sentence is the basis for this passage in "Donelson":

> Some of the wounded in the wood
>   Were cared for by the foe last night,
> Though he could do them little good,
>   Himself being all in shivering plight. (Lines 254–57)

The function of this passage is to portray the universality of suffering and the compassion of the enemy. Melville's view that the Union was right on the issues of the war is quite clear. Du Pont's fleet "warred for the Right," Stonewall Jackson "Stoutly stood for wrong," and the defeat of the Confederacy was "Treason thrown." Therefore the use of an incident which reveals such a curious display of generosity raises questions. The explanation is that Melville took the first opportunity to speak out for compassion and humanity, the foundation, as he saw it, upon which the opposition of North and South could be reconciled. The irony of the war was rooted in the fact that men were dehumanized by the very ideas that they fought for. In order to attain a reconciliation, principles would have to be subordinated to individuals. Melville could make his point best by emphasizing individuals, common soldiers trapped in a common misery, and by playing down the abstract issues of a "war of Wrong and Right"—to quote the words of "Look-out Mountain." "Donelson" happens to be one of the more ambitious poems in *Battle-Pieces* and the first in the sequence to have as its subject a military engagement in which the Union was victorious. Hence Melville could afford the luxury of depicting the humanity of the foe.

The nature of the ingredients which went into the making of *Battle-Pieces*—the Bible, Milton, Shakespeare, personal experiences and impressions, paintings, the illustrated weeklies, newspaper articles and official reports from *The Rebellion Record*—indicates Melville's distance from the actual events of the war. This was not entirely a disadvantage. Melville had long been uneasy about his dependence upon personal experience, sensing a danger in "immediate literary success, in very young writers" (to quote from *Pierre*), because of his memories of the days of *Typee* and *Omoo*. Nor could "mere reading" of *The Rebellion Record* or anything else serve as a substitute. His solution was not the recording of a "rich and peculiar experience" nor the skillful retelling of a tale once told. Instead, in the best of the *Battle-Pieces,* he distilled the essence of the experiences of war, pointing out their symbolic significance, universal application, and complexity. At a distance Melville could see the lineaments of the fundamental.

In his introductory statement Melville's explanation of the impulsive origins of *Battle-Pieces* and the almost involuntary derivation of the individual poems obscures the structural unity he achieved for the sequence. Unity was always a consideration, and in his prose he had justified and explained disgressions partly to show that they did not interfere with unity. In *Battle-Pieces* the chronological arrangement, a progression of subjects from the darkly prophetic hanging of John Brown to the dream vision of the mother goddess in "America" which holds forth a prospect of order and serenity, argues for structural unity. The spatial range of the poems—North and South, land and sea, soldiers from Maine dying in Louisiana—suggests that Melville was attempting to encompass and unify the geographical totality of the war. The sociological range is likewise wide; there are poems deal with officers of the highest rank and with enlisted men of both armies, with Negroes and whites, with civilians as well as soldiers, and with both men and women. This, too, appears to be an effort to achieve a comprehensive portrayal. It might even be submitted that the inclusion of a number of inferior poems may be explained by Melville's desire for his collection to be rounded out and filled in, a structural whole, and the remarkable range of verse forms, none of which is used more than once, is perhaps a formal principle, intended to show unity in diversity, and to reflect the "varied amplitude" of the war.

Melville sought unity in other and more significant ways. These include the use of introductory and terminal groups of poems as a framing device, the grouping together of poems on related subjects, the repetition of major themes, the interweaving of certain images, and chiefly the infusing of the total historic experience of the Civil War, delineated in its many aspects and complexities, with symbolic import.

The four poems which begin the sequence—"Misgivings," "The Conflict of Convictions," "Apathy and Enthusiasm," and "The March into Virginia"—have points in common. Stressing prophecy, they are filled with forebodings; they are relatively lacking in topical allusion; and they are patterned in a series of contrasts between age and youth, winter and spring, dark and light, doubt and faith, Lucifer and God, with greater weight given to age, winter, dark, doubt, and Lucifer. These poems have special relationships with the group of poems which terminates the sequence. For example, the raging tempest of "Misgivings" recurs in "The Coming Storm," one of the poems near the end, as though to justify the apprehensions expressed in the earlier poem. "The Conflict of Convictions" and "A Canticle," a hymn of thanksgiving with hints that evil is never really overcome, are both heavily Miltonic and have essentially the same theme. "Apathy and Enthusiasm" and "The Fall of Richmond" have historical ties as well as Miltonic imagery in common, since the former originates in the fall of Fort Sumter to the Confederacy at the beginning of the war and the latter has as its subject the fall of the fortress city, Richmond, to the Union. "The March into Virginia" of the untried boy soldiers has a logical consequence in the elegiac "On the Slain Collegians." "Weird" John Brown, portent of war, is linked to "Sibylline" Jane Jackson, formerly a slave, whose "reverie takes on prophetic cheer," and to the visionary mother goddess in "America," the final poem of the end group and of *Battle-Pieces* proper. At intervals between are other poems of prophecy such as "Misgivings" with its omens of nature, "Apathy and Enthusiasm" with its "forebodings," "Lyon," which has a "seer" as its hero, and "Aurora-Borealis," in which the northern lights are seen as "portent and promise." Further interrelationships may be noted between "The Conflict of Convictions" and "America," the latter of which contains the fully developed theme of the "foundations" revealed and repeats the image of the Capitol dome.

In addition to the initial and end groups which together frame the sequence, *Battle-Pieces* has other poems which are linked to each other and therefore tend to increase the coherence of the whole. These groups consist of poems which derive from a common historic event or personage. The naval engagement between the "Monitor" and the "Merrimac" provoked "The Cumberland," "In the Turret," "The Temeraire," and "A Utilitarian View of the Monitor's Fight," while the Tennessee Campaign of 1863 inspired "Look-out Mountain" and "Chattanooga." Sherman's exploits led to "The March to the Sea" and "The Frenzy in the Wake." The final Confederate defeat produced "The Fall of Richmond," "The Surrender at Appomattox," and "A Canticle." "Malvern Hill," about "McClellan's men," prepares the way for the poem which follows immediately, "The Victor of Antietam," which is about McClellan himself.

Melville felt that almost mystical influences emanated from great men, Nelsons and Wellingtons, Lincolns and Lees, drawing individuals together and leading them into accomplishments beyond normal expectations. In *White-Jacket* he had observed, "One large brain and one large heart have virtue sufficient to magnetise a whole fleet or an army." Thus his many poems in praise of famous men serve as a unifying force simply through the persistence of their theme. Lyon, Sheridan, McClellan, Worden, Cushing, the corps commander, the college colonel, and the anonymous sailor in "Commemorative of a Naval Victory" are such heroes of the Union. Lincoln himself is the subject of two poems. The Southern leaders, however, posed a special problem because Melville found it hard to reconcile heroic qualities and error. Stonewall Jackson is seen in one poem from a Northern and one from a Southern perspective, while Lee appears principally in the role of the defeated leader.

Two themes which are allied with the basic theme of opposition and reconciliation are of such importance and recur so often as to warrant discussion. The first is, inevitably, the theme of death. The section consisting of "Verses Inscriptive and Memorial" is elegiac by definition, but many other poems belong in this category—"The Portent," "Lyon," "Ball's Bluff," "Sheridan at Cedar Creek," "A Dirge for McPherson," "On the Slain Collegians," and in special ways "Shiloh," "Malvern Hill," "Chattanooga," and "The Scout Toward Aldie." Sometimes death seems so overwhelming and so final, especially where the dead are juxtaposed with vibrant creatures like the swallows of "Shiloh" and the fish of "A Requiem for Soldiers Lost in Ocean Transports"—that consolation is at best remote. But ultimately even death may be overcome. In *Pierre,* an ambiguous work in almost every other respect, Melville wrote unequivocally: ". . . the most mighty of Nature's law is this, that out of Death she brings Life," and the mother goddess of the poem "America" survives both the mortal strife between her children and her own death sleep to emerge with "Law on her brow and empire in her eyes."

A second recurrent theme closely associated with that of opposition and reconciliation is the integrity of the law, for Melville an institution which, buttressed by religion, preserves order in society. The rebellion against the Union is a disruption of order and an opposition to the law. Reconciliation comes with the restoration of law. So sacred is the law that the use of the phrase "such the law," in "The Portent," to explain why John Brown's body hangs from a beam, is not entirely ironical. Admiral Du Pont's victory at Port Royal is a "victory of Law"; the investment of Richmond by Grant is an instance where "Right through might is Law"; and Lee himself "His doom accepts" and informs the Reconstruction Committee that the South wants "quiet law again."

The mere recurrence of such themes as those of death and the sanctity of the law in itself contributes to the unity of *Battle-Pieces*. However, when it is seen that this recurrence is not random but focuses directly upon the main theme of opposition and reconciliation their considerable importance to the structure of the work is evident.

The thematic concern with aspects of the law is accompanied by much legal imagery and wordplay, and such figurative language is another device which increases unity. In "The March into Virginia" no "lets and bars" dampen the ardor of the young soldiers on their way to First Manassas. In "The House-top" the Athenian lawgiver "Wise Draco comes" to restore order to a city torn by riot with a "code corroborating Calvin's creed." It is the Northern view in "Stonewall Jackson" that "Justly his fame we outlaw." "The Swamp Angel," a great siege gun shelling Charleston, "dooms by far decree." In "The Conflict of Convictions" the wrought-iron dome of the Capitol, beneath which originates the law which orders American society, first ominously shows streaks of rust but then becomes the symbol of future greatness. McClellan in "The Victor of Antietam" is lauded for having "propped the Dome." Cavalrymen pursuing the Virginia guerrilla, Mosby, find it strange that he should dare to "prowl where the Dome was seen." And before he meets with the Reconstruction Committee, where he will appeal for "re-established law," Lee muses on "the looming Dome," a white temple.

Important as are the unifying devices which have been discussed, they are secondary in comparison to Melville's use of symbol for the same purpose. One of his major achievements was to create an awareness of the generic implications of a specific event. Melville saw that in the great stream of history the Civil War was merely another war. But he was no less aware that it was likewise a projection of the suffering and internal conflict of all men, an interruption of the orderly progress of his own country, a battle in the endless struggle between powers of light and darkness.

In spite of Melville's virtual withdrawal from the literary market place, Harper was willing to publish *Battle-Pieces* because of his former popularity and the potential appeal of his subject. Publication of the Civil War poems was a last attempt to obtain a popular hearing, and a half-hearted attempt at that, for in them Melville was writing more to please himself than anyone else. Around 1865 he bought Ruskin's *Modern Painters* and in it marked a passage in the essay "Of Vulgarity": "By the very acuteness of his sympathy he knows how much of himself he can give to anybody. . . . Whatever he said, a vulgar man would misinterpret: no words that he could use would bear the same sense to the vulgar man that they do to him. . . ." Melville's misgivings about the possibility of his communicating satisfactorily were confirmed. The book was not a critical success, and his account with

Harper on February 13, 1868 showed a total sale of only 486 copies. It appears not to have mattered very much. In the winter of 1866, only a few months after the volume of poems had appeared, Melville obtained an appointment as an inspector of customs at New York. For all practical purposes his literary career had ended.

Years before Melville had written to Hawthorne that what he felt "most moved to write, that is banned,—it will not pay." When he saw no possibility of earning a living with his writing and he resigned himself to reaching no audience other than the few whose sensibilities corresponded to his own, he could write with full freedom, and for the remaining twenty-five years of his life he chose to write mainly verse. His most ambitious work was *Clarel: A Poem and Pilgrimage in the Holy Land.* The pilgrimage once more was among opposing forces and led into strange byways. Consisting of 18,000 lines divided into four parts and 150 cantos, it was published by Putnam in 1876. Melville paid the entire cost with funds given him by his uncle, Peter Gansevoort. In a brief introductory statement he wrote of *Clarel* that he was "content beforehand with whatever future awaits it." The book was scarcely noticed. Late in his life he published privately, in editions of only twenty-five copies, two more volumes of poetry: *John Marr and Other Sailors* (1888), based largely upon his own memories of life as a seaman, and *Timoleon* (1891), which recalls his travels to Europe and the Levant. Between 1888 and 1891 he wrote but did not publish *Billy Budd,* a short novel of quality comparable to his best prose of forty years before. In the last months of his life he turned once more to the preparation of a volume of verse, this one especially for his wife. He gave it the title "Weeds and Wildings, with a Rose or Two." It was discovered among his literary remains after his death on September 28, 1891.

ON THE ILLUSTRATIONS

The relation between Melville's poems and the drawings of Alfred and William Waud is tenuous, in that there is no record of the poet's having associated with the artists, or of any recognition on either side of the other's work. Yet Melville and the Wauds both produced "battle-pieces," Melville figuratively and somewhat pretentiously and the Wauds quite literally. In comparison, Melville was more the artist, for he wrote for a limited public and his impact depended upon the subtle and the remote. The Wauds were craftsmen producing for the mass following of the illustrated weeklies, and their force derived from simplicity and directness.

Whether the Wauds had read Melville's novels is not known. Melville

could hardly have escaped knowing their war sketches. In 1861 he sub-
scribed to *Harper's Weekly*, on whose staff they served, and having in
December 1865 purchased bound volumes for that year and the four preceding as Christmas presents for his wife and children, he had a file of
the magazine in his house when he was writing *Battle-Pieces*. He also
bought a copy of Nichols' *The Story of the Great March*, which had illustrations by the Wauds and others, and found in it material which he could
use. It cannot be said that the Waud drawings are the principal source of
any particular Melville poems, but Melville was visually receptive, and
they form part of the matrix of *Battle-Pieces*. It seems reasonable to sup-
pose that he absorbed what he saw of the Civil War through the drawings
by the *Harper's Weekly* combat artists in much the same way as he did
the dispatches of the newspaper correspondents and the reports of the army
officers published in *The Rebellion Record*. Verbal parallels make the latter
conclusion unquestionable. It is much more difficult to trace a transformation of the visual to the verbal.

Alfred and William Waud were Englishmen who came to the United
States in the 1850's. Alfred had studied art at the Royal Academy and
William had worked as an architect with Sir Joseph Paxton, serving in
1851 as one of his principal assistants in designing the Crystal Palace. After
several years in Boston as an engraver and illustrator, Alfred was employed
as a staff artist by the New York *Illustrated News*. Here he remained until
February 1862, when he joined *Harper's Weekly*, thus beginning an association which lasted until his death. William found a position with *Leslie's
Illustrated Newspaper*, and one of his notable successes was an assignment
in Charleston on the eve of the Secession, where his British passport and
his accommodating nature stood him in good stead. In 1863 he too became
a *Harper's* artist. In covering the Civil War Alfred Waud spent most of
his time in Virginia, Maryland, and Pennsylvania with various units of
the Army of the Potomac. William travelled more widely. He went west
with Admiral Farragut and south with Sherman, in addition to following
the campaigns of McClellan and Grant in Virginia. Alfred was so highly
regarded by Federal authorities that he is said to have been several times
offered a commission; and William, during the march through Georgia and
the Carolinas, was treated almost as a member of Sherman's staff. Neither
of the brothers was wounded, but both, being somewhat older than most
of the artists and correspondents, suffered severely from the rigors of
campaigning. Alfred was once captured, but protected by his passport,
civilian clothes, and sketchbook (in which he drew pictures of his captors),
he was promptly released.

G. A. Sala, an English journalist and contributor to *Harper's*, met
Alfred Waud in January 1864 and wrote a memorable description of
him in *My Diary in America in the Midst of War* (London, 1865):

There had galloped furiously by us, backwards and forwards during our journey, a tall man, mounted on a taller horse. Blue-eyed, fair-bearded, strapping and stalwart, full of loud, cheery laughs and comic songs, armed to the teeth, jack-booted, gauntleted, slouch-hatted, yet clad in the shooting-jacket of a civilian. I had puzzled myself many times during the afternoon and evening to know what manner of man this might inwardly be. He didn't look like an American; he was too well dressed to be a guerrilla. I founded him out at last, and struck up an alliance with him. The fair-bearded man was the "war artist" of *Harper's Weekly*. He had been with the Army of the Potomac, sketching, since its first organization, and doing for the principal pictorial journal of the United States that which Mr. Frank Vizetelly, in the South, has done so admirably for the *Illustrated London News*. He had been in every advance, in every retreat, in every battle, and almost in every reconnoissance. He probably knew more about the several campaigns, the rights and wrongs of the several fights, the merits and demerits of the commanders, than two out of three wearers of general's shoulder-straps. But he was a prudent man, who could keep his own counsel, and went on sketching. (I, 303-4.)

Major Nichols in *The Story of the Great March* was probably referring to William Waud when he wrote: "There is, by the way, a most excellent artist accompanying the expedition, who is working for Harper's. His sketches are artistically executed, and he has the genuine spirit of an artist in his choice of subject." (p. 71.)

William P. Campbell, who arranged the exhibition of Civil War drawings at the National Gallery of Art in 1961, states in its catalogue that Alfred Waud published 344 pictures during the war, by far the largest number by any "special artist." He has identified 115 by William Waud.

After the war William Waud continued to work as an illustrator, but he did not portray military subjects. When he died on November 10, 1878, *Harper's Weekly* described him as "one of the foremost artists in the United States." Alfred Waud went south for *Harper's* in April 1866, and later the same year became one of the first artist-correspondents to tour the Western plains. He contributed forty illustrations to A. D. Richardson's *Beyond the Mississippi* (Hartford, 1867), and with William and others illustrated William Cullen Bryant's *Picturesque America* (New York, 1872–74). His drawings also appear in *Battles and Leaders of the Civil War* (New York, 1887) and a number of other publications. He seems to have retired around 1882, for after this year his contributions to *Harper's* are infrequent.

Although the illustrations in this book were intended for publication, in a certain sense most of them are here published for the first time. Many were redrawn from the field sketches onto blocks of boxwood, often by several engravers simultaneously working from the same sketch. Sometimes considerable liberties were taken, and always there was a loss in quality and tone. At best the *Harper's* woodcuts lack the freshness, intensity, and freedom of the Waud drawings. This the *Harper's* editors unwittingly acknowledged when, in an effort to pay tribute to the skill of the engravers, they explained that the "rough sketches of battles and incidents hastily sent from the field or the deck, have been faithfully and skillfully elaborated . . ." (June 3, 1865). W. Fletcher Thompson in *The Image of War* (New York, 1960) explains the relation of original sketch to wood engraving in this way:

> The engraving for *Harper's Weekly* was at first abominably bad. Illustrations in the *Weekly* were monotous, lacking in detail, and often marred by bad perspective. When Alf Waud submitted an admittedly hurried sketch of a bayonet charge at the battle of Fair Oaks, Harper's engravers reproduced it as an illustration showing nearly five hundred men in a perfect line, each man a mirror replica of the man on either side, every man running with the same leg forward, each bayonet poised at exactly the same height. When that particular issue of the *Weekly* reached the Army of the Potomac, the soldiers greeted it with shouts of derision . . . . Most of Harper's engravers never got closer to the war than the east bank of the Hudson River, but they did not hesitate to "improve" the composition and appearance of sketches made by artists right on the scene. They moved and eliminated figures and added others . . . . Without exception their alterations failed to improve upon the original sketches. (pp. 83–84.)

Another group of drawings appearing in this book was never intended for publication. It consists of the quick sketches and detail notes which were made for future incorporation into a more ambitious picture or, in some instances, simply because the subject was irresistible. A third group includes sketches which *Harper's* did not use because of space limitation and similar considerations. With the exception of the *Harper's* woodcuts, an effort has been made to present here only sketches which have not been published previously.

Attribution accompanying the illustration by Alfred or William Waud is made on the basis of the signature or, if that is lacking, of such evidence as there is apart from style. Among the unattributed drawings there may be several by other *Harper's* artists. In the captions to the illustrations, the quotation marks enclosing a title indicate that it is taken from the artist's notes in the margin or on the back of the sketch. The punctuation and the order of the phrases of these notes have occasionally been changed. Titles not in quotes are supplied from captions in *Harper's* and from information provided by the curators of the several collections.

Thompson's *The Image of War,* cited above, is an excellent study of the pictorial reporting of the Civil War and contains much material on the Wauds. Robert Taft in *Artists and Illustrators of the Old West,* 1850–1900 (New York, 1953) devotes part of a chapter to Alfred Waud. Both books are admirably documented and contain bibliographical information. Two catalogues are important for information on the Wauds and other artists who portrayed the war. Hermann Warner Williams Jr. of the Corcoran Gallery of Art prepared *The Civil War: The Artists' Record* (Boston, 1961). The National Gallery of Art has issued *The Civil War: A Centennial Exhibition of Eyewitness Drawings* (Washington, 1961). It is generously illustrated and authoritative.

Unless otherwise specified it may be taken for granted that the subjects of the drawings are Northern. This was inevitable. Yet the Wauds were remarkably detached. While this detachment was perhaps a result of their English origin, it was also in keeping with a professional point of view.

Contemporary critics sometimes dealt severely with the work of the combat artists. For example, William J. Hoppin wrote in the *U. S. Army and Navy Journal* (1863–64):

It is true that the illustrated newspapers are full of sketches, purporting to be pictures of important scenes; but the testimony of parties engaged shows that these representations are, when not taken from photographs, not always reliable. The desire of producing striking effects sometimes overcomes all other considerations, and the truth is now and then sacrificed to the demand for dramatic action or pleasing play of light and shadow. Many of these designs are of little value, excepting as studies of costume. Some of them are positively lying and fabulous. (Vol. I, p. 350.)

A more balanced view appears in *Harper's Weekly*. In the issue for June 3, 1865 is an article entitled "Our Artists during the War." Self congratulations aside, it provides an estimate of their accomplishment and the conditions under which they work:

We may be pardoned for special pride in our artists who have gone through all the long and stirring campaigns of this war, commemorating its most interesting incidents and noted men, so that the volumes of the *Weekly* are really a vivid history of the struggle. Messrs A. R. Waud, Theodore R. Davis, William Waud, Robert Weir, Andrew M'Callum, A. W. Warren and others have been not less busy and scarcely less imperilled than the soldiers. They have made the weary marches and dangerous voyages. They have shared the soldiers' fare; they have ridden and waded, and climbed and floundered, always trusting in lead pencils and keeping their paper dry. When the battle began, they were there. They drew the enemy's fire as well as our own. The fierce shock, the heaving tumult, the smoky sway of battle from side to side, the line, the assault, the victory—they were a part of all and their faithful fingers, depicting the scenes, have made us a part also.

The *Harper's* statement strikes exactly the right note. The combat artists (and foremost among them the accomplished and prolific Wauds) made possible a vicarious participation in a momentous conflict for an immense number, including a few perceptive and compassionate individuals like Herman Melville who were seeking to comprehend the meaning of the war.

Battle-Pieces
and
Aspects of the War

by

HERMAN MELVILLE

THE BATTLE-PIECES

IN THIS VOLUME ARE DEDICATED

TO THE MEMORY OF THE

THREE HUNDRED THOUSAND

WHO IN THE WAR

FOR THE MAINTENANCE OF THE UNION

FELL DEVOTEDLY

UNDER THE FLAG OF THEIR FATHERS.

WITH few exceptions, the Pieces in this volume originated in an impulse imparted by the fall of Richmond. They were composed without reference to collective arrangement, but, being brought together in review, naturally fall in to the order assumed.

The events and incidents of the conflict—making up a whole, in varied amplitude, corresponding with the geographical area covered by the war —from these but a few themes have been taken, such as for any cause chanced to imprint themselves upon the mind.

The aspects which the strife as a memory assumes are as manifold as are the moods of involuntary mediation—moods variable, and at times widely at variance. Yielding instinctively, one after another, to feelings not inspired from any one source exclusively, and unmindful, without purposing to be, of consistency, I seem, in most of these verses, to have but placed a harp in a window, and noted the contrasted airs which wayward winds have played upon the strings. [Melville's note]

The Portent.

(1859.)

Hanging from the beam,
   Slowly swaying (such the law),
Gaunt the shadow on your green,
   Shenandoah!
5   The cut is on the crown
   (Lo, John Brown),
And the stabs shall heal no more.

Hidden in the cap
   Is the anguish none can draw;
10   So your future veils its face,
   Shenandoah!
But the streaming beard is shown
   (Weird John Brown),
The meteor of the war.

"Harper's Ferry." By Alfred R. Waud.

Misgivings.

(1860.)

WHEN ocean-clouds over inland hills
 Sweep storming in late autumn brown,
And horror the sodden valley fills,
 And the spire falls crashing in the town,
5 I muse upon my country's ills—
The tempest bursting from the waste of Time
On the world's fairest hope linked with man's foulest crime.

Nature's dark side is heeded now—
 (Ah! optimist-cheer disheartened flown) —
10 A child may read the moody brow
 Of yon black mountain lone.
With shouts the torrents down the gorges go,
And storms are formed behind the storm we feel:
The hemlock shakes in the rafter, the oak in the driving keel.

The Conflict of Convictions.

(1860–1).

ON starry heights
 A bugle wails the long recall;
Derision stirs the deep abyss,
 Heaven's ominous silence over all.
5 Return, return, O eager Hope,
 And face man's latter fall.
Events, they make the dreamers quail;
Satan's old age is strong and hale,
A disciplined captain, gray in skill,
10 And Raphael a white enthusiast still;
Dashed aims, at which Christ's martyrs pale,
Shall Mammon's slaves fulfill?

"8th N. Y. V. Rifles." By Alfred R. Waud.

(Dismantle the fort,
Cut down the fleet—
15   *Battle no more shall be!*
While the fields for fight in æons to come
Congeal beneath the sea.)

The terrors of truth and dart of death
   To faith alike are vain;
20   Though comets, gone a thousand years,
      Return again,
Patient she stands—she can no more—
And waits, nor heeds she waxes hoar.

(At a stony gate,
25   *A statue of stone,*
Weed overgrown—
Long 'twill wait!)

But God his former mind retains,
   Confirms his old decree;
30   The generations are inured to pains,
   And strong Necessity
Surges, and heaps Time's strand with wrecks.
   The People spread like a weedy grass,
   The thing they will they bring to pass,
35   And prosper to the apoplex.
The rout it herds around the heart,
   The ghost is yielded in the gloom;
Kings wag their heads—Now save thyself
   Who wouldst rebuild the world in bloom.

40   *(Tide-mark*
And top of the ages' strife,
Verge where they called the world to come,
The last advance of life—
Ha ha, the rust on the Iron Dome!)

45   Nay, but revere the hid event;
   In the cloud a sword is girded on,
I mark a twinkling in the tent
   Of Michael the warrior one.
Senior wisdom suits not now,
50   The light is on the youthful brow.

(Ay, in caves the miner see:
His forehead bears a blinking light;
Darkness so he feebly braves—
A meagre wight!)

55   But He who rules is old—is old;
Ah! faith is warm, but heaven with age is cold.

(Ho ho, ho ho,
The cloistered doubt
Of olden times
60   *Is blurted out!)*

The Ancient of Days forever is young,
    Forever the scheme of Nature thrives;
I know a wind in purpose strong—
    It spins *against* the way it drives.
65   What if the gulfs their slimed foundation bare?
So deep must the stones be hurled
Whereon the throes of ages rear
The final empire and the happier world.

(The poor old Past,
70   *The Future's slave,*
She drudged through pain and crime
To bring about the blissful Prime,
Then—perished. There's a grave!)

    Power unanointed may come—
75   Dominion (unsought by the free)
    And the Iron Dome,
Stronger for stress and strain,
    Fling her huge shadow athwart the main;
But the Founders' dream shall flee.
80   Age after age shall be
As age after age has been,
(From man's changeless heart their way they win);
And death be busy with all who strive—
Death, with silent negative.

85   Yea and Nay—
Each hath his say;

BUT GOD HE KEEPS THE MIDDLE WAY.
NONE WAS BY
WHEN HE SPREAD THE SKY;
90   WISDOM IS VAIN, AND PROPHESY.

"Moving into Action at Cedar Creek, Va., Oct. 19, 1864." By Alfred R. Waud.

Apathy and Enthusiasm.

(1860–1.)

I.

O THE clammy cold November,
   And the winter white and dead,
And the terror dumb with stupor,
   And the sky a sheet of lead;
5   And events that came resounding
   With the cry that *All was lost,*
Like the thunder-cracks of massy ice
   In intensity of frost—
Bursting one upon another
10   Through the horror of the calm.
   The paralysis of arm
In the anguish of the heart;
And the hollowness and dearth.

The appealings of the mother
15   To brother and to brother
Not in hatred so to part—
And the fissure in the hearth
    Growing momently more wide.
Then the glances 'tween the Fates,
20   And the doubt on every side,
And the patience under gloom
In the stoniness that waits
The finality of doom.

II.

So the winter died despairing,
25   And the weary weeks of Lent;
And the ice-bound rivers melted,
    And the tomb of Faith was rent.
O, the rising of the People
    Came with springing of the grass,
30   They rebounded from dejection
    After Easter came to pass.
And the young were all elation
    Hearing Sumter's cannon roar,
And they thought how tame the Nation
35   In the age that went before.
And Michael seemed gigantical,
    The Arch-fiend but a dwarf;
And at the towers of Erebus
    Our striplings flung the scoff.
40   But the elders with foreboding
    Mourned the days forever o'er.
And recalled the forest proverb,
    The Iroquois' old saw:
Grief to every graybeard
45   *When young Indians lead the war.*

The March into Virginia,
Ending in the First Manassas.

(JULY, 1861.)

DID all the lets and bars appear
    To every just or larger end,

"Spring on the R. R.," detail from a panel of "Scenes near Richmond."
By Alfred R. Waud. *Harper's Weekly,* July 26, 1862.

    Whence should come the trust and cheer?
    Youth must its ignorant impulse lend—
5   Age finds place in the rear.
      All wars are boyish, and are fought by boys,
    The champions and enthusiasts of the state:
      Turbid ardors and vain joys
        Not barrenly abate—
10   Stimulants to the power mature,
        Preparatives of fate.
    Who here forecasteth the event?
    What heart but spurns at precedent
    And warnings of the wise,
15   Contemned foreclosures of surprise?

The banners play, the bugles call,
The air is blue and prodigal.
      No berrying party, pleasure-wooed,
No picnic party in the May,
20   Ever went less loth than they
      Into that leafy neighborhood.
In Bacchic glee they file toward Fate,
Moloch's uninitiate;
Expectancy, and glad surmise
25   Of battle's unknown mysteries.
All they feel is this: 'tis glory,
A rapture sharp, though transitory,
Yet lasting in belaureled story.
So they gayly go to fight,
30   Chatting left and laughing right.

But some who this blithe mood present,
      As on in lightsome files they fare,
Shall die experienced ere three days are spent—
      Perish, enlightened by the vollied glare;
35   Or shame survive, and, like to adamant,
      The throe of Second Manassas share.

Union Evacuation and Firing of Manassas Junction. By Alfred R. Waud.
Harper's Weekly, March 29, 1862.

Lyon.
Battle of Springfield, Missouri.

(AUGUST, 1861.)

SOME hearts there are of deeper sort,

Prophetic, sad,
Which yet for cause art trebly clad;
        Known death they fly on:
5   This wizard-heart and heart-of-oak had Lyon.

"They are more than twenty thousand strong,
        We less than five,
Too few with such a host to strive."
        "Such counsel, fie on!
10 'Tis battle, or 'tis shame;" and firm stood Lyon.

"For help at need in vain we wait—
        Retreat or fight:
Retreat the foe would take for flight,
        And each proud scion
15 Feel more elate; the end must come," said Lyon.

By candlelight he wrote the will,
        And left his all
To Her for whom 'twas not enough to fall;
        Loud neighed Orion
20 Without the tent; drums beat; we marched with Lyon.

The night-tramp done, we spied the Vale
        With guard-fires lit;
Day broke, but trooping clouds made gloom of it:
        "A field to die on,"
25 Presaged in his unfaltering heart, brave Lyon.

We fought on the grass, we bled in the corn—
        Fate seemed malign;
His horse the Leader led along the line—
        Star-browed Orion;
30 Bitterly fearless, he rallied us there, brave Lyon.

There came a sound like the slitting of air
        By a swift sharp sword—
A rush of the sound; and the sleek chest broad
        Of black Orion
35 Heaved, and was fixed; the dead mane waved toward Lyon.

"General, you're hurt—this sleet of balls!"
        He seemed half spent;

With moody and bloody brow, he lowly bent:
    "The field to die on;
40   But not—not yet; the day is long," breathed Lyon.

For a time becharmed there fell a lull
    In the heart of the fight;
The tree-tops nod, the slain sleep light;
    Warm noon-winds sigh on,
45   And thoughts which he never spake had Lyon.

Texans and Indians trim for a charge:
    "Stand ready, men!
Let them come close, right up, and then
    After the lead, the iron;
50   Fire, and charge back!" So strength returned to Lyon.

The Iowa men who held the van,
    Half drilled, were new
To battle: "Some one lead us, then we'll do,"
    Said Corporal Tryon:
55   "Men! *I* will lead," and a light glared in Lyon.

On they came: they yelped, and fired;
    His spirit sped;
We leveled right in, and the half-breeds fled,
    Nor stayed the iron,
60   Nor captured the crimson corse of Lyon.

This seer foresaw his soldier-doom,
    Yet willed the fight.
He never turned; his only flight
    Was up to Zion,
65   Where prophets now and armies greet brave Lyon.

Ball's Bluff.
A Reverie.

(OCTOBER, 1861)

ONE noonday, at my window in the town,
    I saw a sight—saddest that eyes can see—
Young soldiers marching lustily

"The 164th N. Y. V. charging. Col. killed." By Alfred R. Waud. "McMahon's regiment is in [John] Gibbon's division wears a zouave uniform dark green— the colonel's last words were 'Now boys we' ve got 'em.' 7 bullets reached him and he fell over the rifle pit dead." [Note on back of sketch.]

           Unto the wars,
5   With fifes, and flags in mottoed pageantry;
         While all the porches, walks, and doors
     Were rich with ladies cheering royally.

     They moved like Juny morning on the wave,
       Their hearts were fresh as clover in its prime
10   (It was the breezy summer time),
         Life throbbed so strong,
     How should they dream that Death in a rosy clime
       Would come to thin their shining throng?
     Youth feels immortal, like the gods sublime.
15   Weeks passed; and at my window, leaving bed,
       By night I mused, of easeful sleep bereft,
       On those brave boys (Ah War! thy theft);
         Some marching feet
     Found pause at last by cliffs Potomac cleft;

20   Wakeful I mused, while in the street
          Far footfalls died away till none were left.

"Portion of the Rebel battery at Wynn's mill {Va.}. The Gun which wounded
Lieut. Wagner, Topographical Engineer." By Alfred R. Waud. *Harper's Weekly*,
May 10, 1862.

Dupont's Round Fight.

(NOVEMBER, 1861.)

In time and measure perfect moves
     All Art whose aim is sure;
Evolving rhyme and stars divine
     Have rules, and they endure.

5   Nor less the Fleet that warred for Right,
     And, warring so, prevailed,
In geometric beauty curved,
     And in an orbit sailed.

      The rebel at Port Royal felt
10   The Unity overawe,
And rued the spell. A type was here,
      And victory of LAW.

The Stone Fleet.
An Old Sailor's Lament.

(DECEMBER, 1861.)

I HAVE a feeling for those ships,
      Each worn and ancient one,
With great bluff bows, and broad in the beam:
      Ay, it was unkindly done.
5   But so they serve the Obsolete—
      Even so, Stone Fleet!

You'll say I'm doting; do but think
      I scudded round the Horn in one—
The Tenedos, a glorious
10   Good old craft as ever run—
             Sunk (how all unmeet!)
      With the Old Stone Fleet.
An India ship of fame was she,
      Spices and shawls and fans she bore;
15   A whaler when her wrinkles came—
      Turned off! till, spent and poor,
             Her bones were sold (escheat)!
      Ah! Stone Fleet.

Four were erst patrician keels
20   (Names attest what families be),
The Kensington, and Richmond too,
      Leonidas, and Lee:
             But now they have their seat
      With the Old Stone Fleet.

25   To scuttle them—a pirate deed—
      Sack them, and dismast;
They sunk so slow, they died so hard,
      But gurgling dropped at last.
             Their ghosts in gales repeat

"Pioneers, 8th N. Y., German Rifles, 1861." By Alfred R. Waud.

30   *Woe's us, Stone Fleet!*
      And all for naught. The waters pass—
      Currents will have their way;
      Nature is nobody's ally; 'tis well;
      The harbor is bettered—will stay.
35   A failure, and complete,
          Was your Old Stone Fleet.

"Capture of the Forts at Hatteras inlet. First Day, fleet opening fire and troops landing in the Surf. Ships identified above left to right Minnesota. Harriet Lane Cumberland. Wabash. Susquehannah." By Alfred Waud. *New York Illustrated News*, September 16, 1861.

Donelson.

(FEBRUARY, 1862.)

      THE bitter cup
        Of that hard countermand
      Which gave the Envoys up,
      Still was wormwood in the mouth,
5   And clouds involved the land,

When, pelted by sleet in the icy street,
  About the bulletin-board a band
Of eager, anxious people met,
And every wakeful heart was set
10   On latest news from West or South.
"No seeing here," cries one—"don't crowd"—
"You tall man, pray you, read aloud."

IMPORTANT.

We learn that General Grant,
15   *Marching from Henry overland,*
And joined by a force up the Cumberland sent
  (Some thirty thousand the command),
On Wednesday a good position won—
Began the siege of Donelson.

20   *This stronghold crowns a river-bluff,*
  A good broad mile of leveled top;
Inland the ground rolls off
  Deep-gorged, and rocky, and broken up—
A wilderness of trees and brush.
25   *The spaded summit shows the roods*
Of fixed intrenchments in their hush;
  Breast-works and rifle-pits in woods
Perplex the base.—
          The welcome weather
30   *Is clear and mild; 'tis much like May.*
The ancient boughs that lace together
Along the stream, and hang far forth,
  Strange with green mistletoe, betray
A dreamy contrast to the North.

35   *Our troops are full of spirits—say*
  The siege won't prove a creeping one.
They purpose not the lingering stay
Of old beleaguerers; not that way;
  But, full of vim *from Western prairies won,*
40   *They'll make, ere long, a dash at Donelson.*

Washed by the storm till the paper grew
Every shade of a streaky blue,
That bulletin stood. The next day brought
A second.

45   LATER FROM THE FORT.

   Grant's investment is complete—
     A semicircular one.
   Both wings the Cumberland's margin meet,
   Then, backward curving, clasp the rebel seat.
50   *On Wednesday this good work was done;*
     But of the doers some lie prone.
   Each wood, each hill, each glen was fought for;
   The bold inclosing line we wrought for
   Flamed with sharpshooters. Each cliff cost
55   *A limb or life. But back we forced*
   Reserves and all; made good our hold;
   And so we rest.

        Events unfold.
   On Thursday added ground was won,
60   *A long bold steep: we near the Den.*
   Later the foe came shouting down
    In sortie, which was quelled; and then
   We stormed them on their left.
   A chilly change in the afternoon;
65   *The sky, late clear, is now bereft*
   Of sun. Last night the ground froze hard—
   Rings to the enemy as they run
   Within their works. A ramrod bites
   The lip it meets. The cold incites
70   *To swinging of arms with brisk rebound.*
   Smart blows 'gainst lusty chests resound.

   Along the outer line we ward
    A crackle of skirmishing goes on.
   Our lads creep round on hand and knee,
75   *The fight from behind each trunk and stone;*
    And sometimes, flying for refuge, one
   Finds 'tis an enemy shares the tree.
   Some scores are maimed by boughs shot off
    In the glades by the Fort's big gun.
80   *We mourn the loss of Colonel Morrison,*
    Killed while cheering his regiment on.
   Their far sharpshooters try our stuff;
   And ours return them puff for puff:
   'Tis diamond-cutting-diamond work.
85   *Woe on the rebel cannoneer*

Who shows his head. Our fellows lurk
*   Like Indians that waylay the deer*
By the wild salt-spring.—The sky is dun,
Foredooming the fall of Donelson.
90   *Stern weather is all unwonted here.*
*   The people of the country own*
We brought it. Yea, the earnest North
Has elementally issued forth
*   To storm this Donelson.*
95   FURTHER.

*   A yelling rout*
Of ragamuffins broke profuse
*   To-day from out the Fort.*
*   Sole uniform they wore, a sort*
100   *Of patch, or white badge (as you choose)*
Upon the arm. But leading these,
Or mingling, were men of face
And bearing of patrician race,
Splendid in courage and gold lace—
105   *   The officers. Before the breeze*
Made by their charge, down went our line;
But, rallying, charged back in force,
And broke the sally; yet with loss.
This on the left; upon the right
110   *Meanwhile there was an answering fight;*
*   Assailants and assailed reversed.*
The charge too upward, and not down—
Up a steep ridge-side, toward its crown,
*   A strong redoubt. But they who first*
115   *Gained the fort's base, and marked the trees*
Felled, heaped in horned perplexities,
*   And shagged with brush; and swarming there*
Fierce wasps whose sting was present death—
They faltered, drawing bated breath,
120   *   And felt it was in vain to dare;*
Yet still, perforce, returned the ball,
Firing into the tangled wall
Till ordered to come down. They came;
But left some comrades in their fame,
125   *Red on the ridge in icy wreath*
And hanging gardens of cold Death.
*   But not quite unavenged these fell;*

Our ranks once out of range, a blast
Of shrapnel and quick shell
130   *Burst on the rebel horde, still massed,*
Scattering them pell-mell.
(This fighting—judging what we read—
Both charge and countercharge,
Would seem but Thursday's told at large,
135   *Before in brief reported.—Ed.)*
Night closed in about the Den
Murky and lowering. Ere long, chill rains.
A night not soon to be forgot,
Reviving old rheumatic pains
140 *And longings for a cot.*
No blankets, overcoats, or tents.
Coats thrown aside on the warm march here—
We looked not then for changeful cheer;
Tents, coats, and blankets too much care.
145   *No fires; a fire a mark presents;*
Near by, the trees show bullet-dents.
Rations were eaten cold and raw.
The men well soaked, came snow; and more—
A midnight sally. Small sleeping done—
150   *But such is war;*
No matter, we'll have Fort Donelson.
        "Ugh! ugh!
'Twill drag along—drag along,"
Growled a cross patriot in the throng,
155 His battered umbrella like an ambulance-cover
Riddled with bullet-holes, spattered all over.
"Hurrah for Grant!" cried a stripling shrill;
Three urchins joined him with a will,
And some of taller stature cheered.
160 Meantime a Copperhead passed; he sneered.
    "Win or lose," he pausing said,
"Caps fly the same; all boys, mere boys;
Any thing to make a noise.
    Like to see the list of the dead;
165 These 'craven Southerners' hold out;
Ay, ay, they'll give you many a bout."
    "We'll beat in the end, sir,"
Firmly said one in staid rebuke,
A solid merchant, square and stout.

170   "And do you think it? that way tend, sir?"
    Asked the lean Copperhead, with a look
    Of splenetic pity. "Yes, I do."
    His yellow death's head the croaker shook:
    "The country's ruined, that I know."
175   A shower of broken ice and snow,
      In lieu of words, confuted him;
    They saw him hustled round the corner go,
      And each by-stander said—Well suited him.

    Next day another crowd was seen
180   In the dark weather's sleety spleen.
    Bald-headed to the storm came out
    A man, who, 'mid a joyous shout,
    Silently posted this brief sheet:

    GLORIOUS VICTORY OF THE FLEET!

185   FRIDAY'S GREAT EVENT!

    THE ENEMY'S WATER-BATTERIES BEAT!

    WE SILENCED EVERY GUN!

    THE OLD COMMODORE'S COMPLIMENTS SENT
    PLUMP INTO DONELSON!

190   "Well, well, go on!" exclaimed the crowd
    To him who thus much read aloud.
    "That's all," he said. "What! nothing more?"
    "Enough for a cheer, though—hip, hurrah!
    "But here's old Baldy come again—
195   "More news!"—And now a different strain.

    (Our own reporter a dispatch compiles,
      As best he may, from varied sources.)

    Large re-enforcements have arrived—
      Munitions, men, and horses—
200   *For Grant, and all debarked, with stores.*

    The enemy's field-works extend six miles—
    The gate still hid; so well contrived.

Yesterday stung us; frozen shores
  Snow-clad, and through the dread defiles
205 And over the desolate ridges blew
A Lapland wind.
             The main affair
  Was a good two hours' steady fight
Between our gun-boats and the Fort.
210   The Louisville's wheel was smashed outright.
A hundred-and-twenty-eight-pound ball
Came planet-like through a starboard port,
Killing three men, and wounding all
The rest of that gun's crew,
215 (The captain of the gun was cut in two);
Then splintering and ripping went—
Nothing could be its continent.
  In the narrow stream the Louisville,
Unhelmed, grew lawless; swung around,
220   And would have thumped and drifted, till
All the fleet was driven aground,
But for the timely order to retire.

Some damage from our fire, 'tis thought,
Was done the water-batteries of the Fort.

225 Little else took place that day,
Except the field artillery in line
Would now and then—for love, they say—
  Exchange a valentine.
The old sharpshooting going on.
230 Some plan afoot as yet unknown;
So Friday closed round Donelson.

LATER.

  Great suffering through the night—
A stinging one. Our heedless boys
235   Were nipped like blossoms. Some dozen
  Hapless wounded men were frozen.
During day being struck down out of sight,
And help-cries drowned in roaring noise,
They were left just where the skirmish shifted—
240 Left in dense underbrush snow-drifted.
Some, seeking to crawl in crippled plight,

So stiffened—perished.
                              Yet in spite
Of pangs for these, no heart is lost.
245   *Hungry, and clothing stiff with frost,*
Our men declare a nearing sun
Shall see the fall of Donelson.

    And this they say, yet not disown
The dark redoubts round Donelson,
250   *And ice-glazed corpses, each a stone—*
        A sacrifice to Donelson;
They swear it, and swerve not, gazing on
A flag, deemed black, flying from Donelson.
Some of the wounded in the wood
255   *Were cared for by the foe last night,*
Though he could do them little needed good,
        Himself being all in shivering plight.
The rebel is wrong, but human yet;
He's got a heart, and thrusts a bayonet.
260   *He gives us battle with wondrous will—*
This bluff's a perverted Bunker Hill.

The stillness stealing through the throng
The silent thought and dismal fear revealed;
        They turned and went,
265   Musing on right and wrong
        And mysteries dimly sealed—
Breasting the storm in daring discontent;
The storm, whose black flag showed in heaven,
As if to say no quarter there was given
270   To wounded men in wood,
        Or true hearts yearning for the good—
All fatherless scemed the human soul.
But next day brought a bitterer bowl—
        On the bulletin-board this stood:

275   *Saturday morning at 3 A.M.*
        A stir within the Fort betrayed
        That the rebels were getting under arms;
            Some plot these early birds had laid.
        But a lancing sleet cut him who stared
280   *Into the storm. After some vague alarms,*
        Which left our lads unscared,
        Out sallied the enemy at dim of dawn,

With cavalry and artillery, and went
In fury at our environment.
285   *Under cover of shot and shell*
Three columns of infantry rolled on,
Vomited out of Donelson—
Rolled down the slopes like rivers of hell,
Surged at our line, and swelled and poured
290   *Like breaking surf. But unsubmerged*
Our men stood up, except where roared
The enemy through one gap. We urged
Our all of manhood to the stress,
But still showed shattered in our desperateness.
295   *Back set the tide,*
But soon afresh rolled in;
And so it swayed from side to side—
Far batteries joining in the din,
Though sharing in another fray—
300   *Till all became an Indian fight,*
Intricate, dusky, stretching far away,
Yet not without spontaneous plan
However tangled showed the plight:
Duels all over 'tween man and man,
305   *Duels on cliff-side, and down in ravine,*
Duels at long range, and bone to bone;
Duels every where flitting and half unseen.
Only by courage good as their own,
And strength outlasting theirs,
310   *Did our boys at last drive the rebels off.*
Yet they went not back to their distant lairs
In strong-hold, but loud in scoff
Maintained themselves on conquered ground—
Uplands; built works, or stalked around.
315   *Our right wing bore this onset. Noon*
Brought calm to Donelson.

The reader ceased; the storm beat hard;
  'Twas day, but the office-gas was lit;
  Nature retained her sulking-fit,
320   In her hand the shard.
Flitting faces took the hue
Of that washed bulletin-board in view,
And seemed to bear the public grief
As private, and uncertain of relief;

325 Yea, many an earnest heart was won,
       As broodingly he plodded on,
     To find in himself some bitter thing,
     Some hardness in his lot as harrowing
                As Donelson.
330 That night the board stood barren there,
       Oft eyed by wistful people passing,
       Who nothing saw but the rain-beads chasing
     Each other down the wafered square,
     As down some storm-beat grave-yard stone.
335 But next day showed—

                         MORE NEWS LAST NIGHT.

       STORY OF SATURDAY AFTERNOON.

       VICISSITUDES OF THE WAR.

            The damaged gun-boats can't wage fight
340   *For days; so says the Commodore.*
        Thus no diversion can be had.
        Under a sunless sky of lead
            Our grim-faced boys in blackened plight
        Gaze toward the ground they held before,
345   *And then on Grant. He marks their mood,*
        And hails it, and will turn the same to good.
        Spite all that they have undergone,
        Their desperate hearts are set upon
        This winter fort, this stubborn fort,
350   *This castle of the last resort,*
                This Donelson.

        1 P.M.
                An order given
            Requires withdrawal from the front
355   *Of regiments that bore the brunt*
        Of morning's fray. Their ranks all riven
        Are being replaced by fresh; strong men.
        Great vigilance in the foeman's Den;
        He snuffs the stormers. Need it is
360   *That for that fell assault of his,*
        That rout inflicted, and self-scorn—

Immoderate in noble natures, torn
By sense of being through slackness overborne—
The rebel be given a quick return:
365 *The kindest face looks now half stern.*
Balked of their prey in airs that freeze,
Some fierce ones glare like savages.
And yet, and yet, strange moments are—
Well—blood, and tears, and anguished War!
370 *The morning's battle-ground is seen*
In lifted glades, like meadows rare;
The blood-drops on the snow-crust there
Like clover in the white-weed show—
Flushed fields of death, that call again—
375 *Call to our men, and not in vain,*
For that way must the stormers go.

3 P.M.
The work begins.
Light drifts of men thrown foward, fade
380 *In skirmish-line along the slope,*
Where some dislodgments must be made
Ere the stormer with the strong-hold cope

Lew Wallace, moving to retake
The heights late lost—
385 *(Herewith a break.*
Storms at the West derange the wires.
Doubtless, ere morning, we shall hear
The end; we look for news to cheer—
Let Hope fan all her fires.)

390 Next day in large bold hand was seen
The closing bulletin:

VICTORY!
Our troops have retrieved the day
By one grand surge along the line;
395 *The spirit that urged them was divine.*
The first works flooded, naught could stay
The stormers: on! still on!
Bayonets for Donelson!
Over the ground that morning lost

400   *Rolled the blue billows, tempest-tossed,*
            Following a hat on the point of a sword.
        Spite shell and round-shot, grape and canister,
        Up they climbed without rail or banister—
            Up the steep hill-sides long and broad,
405   *Driving the rebel deep within his works.*
            'Tis nightfall; not an enemy lurks
                In sight. The chafing men
                    Fret for more fight:
                "To-night, to-night let us take the Den!"
410   *But night is treacherous, Grant is wary;*
        Of brave blood be a little chary.
        Patience! the Fort is good as won;
        To-morrow, and into Donelson.

LATER AND LAST.

THE FORT IS OURS.

            A flag came out at early morn
        Bringing surrender. From their towers
            Floats out the banner late their scorn.
        In Dover, hut and house are full
420   *Of rebels dead or dying.*
                The National flag is flying
        From the crammed court-house pinnacle.
        Great boat-loads of our wounded go
        To-day to Nashville. The sleet-winds blow;
425   *But all is right: the fight is won,*
        The winter-fight for Donelson.
                    Hurrah!
        The spell of old defeat is broke,
            The habit of victory begun;
430   *Grant strikes the war's first sounding stroke*
                At Donelson.

        For lists of killed and wounded, see
        The morrow's dispatch: to-day 'tis victory.

    The man who read this to the crowd
435   Shouted as the end he gained;
            And though the unflagging tempest rained,

They answered him aloud.
And hand grasped hand, and glances met
In happy triumph; eyes grew wet.
440   O, to the punches brewed that night
Went little water. Windows bright
Beamed rosy on the sleet without,
And from the deep street came the frequent shout;
While some in prayer, as these in glee,
445   Blessed heaven for the winter-victory.
But others were who wakeful laid
    In midnight beds, and early rose,
    And, feverish in the foggy snows,
Snatched the damp paper—wife and maid.
450   The death-list like a river flows
And there the whelming waters meet.

        Ah God! may Time with happy haste
        Bring wail and triumph to a waste,
455   And war be done;
        The battle flag-staff fall athwart
        The curs'd ravine, and wither; naught
            Be left of trench or gun;
        The bastion, let it ebb away,
460   Washed with the river bed; and Day
            In vain seek Donelson.

The Cumberland.

(MARCH, 1862.)

SOME names there are of telling sound,
    Whose voweled syllables free
Are pledge that they shall ever live renowned;
    Such seems to be
5   A Frigate's name (by present glory spanned) —
    The Cumberland.

                Sounding name as ere was sung,
                Flowing, rolling on the tongue—
                Cumberland! Cumberland!

"Making parallels." By Alfred R. Waud. *Harper's Weekly,* August 6, 1864.

10   She warred and sunk. There's no denying
        That she was ended—quelled;
      And yet her flag above her fate is flying,
        As when it swelled
      Unswallowed by the swallowing sea: so grand—
15   The Cumberland.

               Goodly name as ere was sung,
               Roundly rolling on the tongue—
               Cumberland! Cumberland!

What need to tell how she was fought—
20   The sinking flaming gun—
The gunner leaping out the port—
        Washed back, undone!
Her dead unconquerably manned
        The Cumberland.

25   Noble name as ere was sung,
                           Slowly roll it on the tongue—
                           Cumberland! Cumberland!

Long as hearts shall share the flame
        Which burned in that brave crew,
30   Her fame shall live—outlive the victor's name;
        For this is due.
Your flag and flag-staff shall in story stand—
        Cumberland!

                           Sounding names as ere was sung,
35   Long they'll roll it on the tongue—
                           Cumberland! Cumberland!

"U.S. Ship Cumberland."

In the Turret.

(March, 1862.)

Your honest heart of duty, Worden,
   So helped you that in fame you dwell;
You bore the first iron battle's burden
   Sealed as in a diving-bell.
5   Alcides, groping into haunted hell
To bring forth King Admetus' bride,
Braved naught more vaguely direful and untried.
   What poet shall uplift his charm,
Bold Sailor, to your height of daring,
10   And interblend therewith the calm,
And build a goodly style upon your bearing.

Escaped the gale of outer ocean—
   Cribbed in a craft which like a log
Was washed by every billow's motion—
15   By night you heard of Og
The huge; nor felt your courage clog
At tokens of his onset grim:
You marked the sunk ship's flag-staff slim,.
   Lit by her burning sister's heart;
20   You marked, and mused: "Day brings the trial:
   Then be it proved if I have part
With men whose manhood never took denial."

A prayer went up—a champion's. Morning
   Beheld you in the Turret walled
25   By adamant, where a spirit forewarning
   And all-deriding called:
"Man, darest thou—desperate, unappalled—
Be first to lock thee in the armored tower?

I have thee now; and what the battle-hour
30   To me shall bring—heed well—thou'lt share;
This plot-work, planned to be the foeman's terror,
    To thee may prove a goblin-snare;
Its very strength and cunning—monstrous error!"

"Stand up, my heart; be strong; what matter
35   If here thou seest thy welded tomb?
And let huge Og with thunders batter—
    Duty be still my doom,
Though drowning come in liquid gloom;
First duty, duty next, and duty last;
40   Ay, Turret, rivet me here to duty fast!"—
    So nerved, you fought, wisely and well;
And live, twice live in life and story;
    But over your Monitor dirges swell,
In wind and wave that keep the rites of glory.

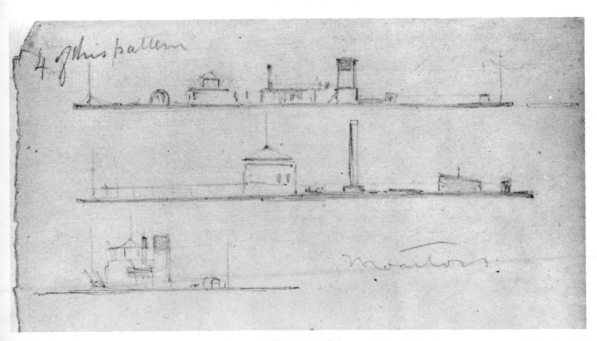

"Monitors."

The Temeraire.

(Supposed to have been suggested to an Englishman of the old order by the fight of the Monitor and Merrimac.)

THE gloomy hulls, in armor grim,
   Like clouds o'er moors have met,
And prove that oak, and iron, and man
   Are tough in fibre yet.

5   But Splendors wane. The sea-fight yields
   No front of old display;
The garniture, emblazonment,
   And heraldry all decay.

Towering afar in parting light,
10   The fleets like Albion's forelands shine—
The full-sailed fleets, the shrouded show
   Of Ships-of-the-Line.

The fighting Temeraire,
   Built of a thousand trees,
15   Lunging out her lightnings,
   And beetling o'er the seas—
O Ship, how brave and fair,
   That fought so oft and well,
On open decks you manned the gun
20   Armorial.
What cheerings did you share,
   Impulsive in the van,
When down upon leagued France and Spain
   We English ran—
25   The freshet at your bowsprit
   Like the foam upon the can.
Bickering, your colors
   Licked up the Spanish air,
You flapped with flames of battle-flags—

30   Your challenge, Temeraire!
The rear ones of our fleet
   They yearned to share your place,
Still vying with the Victory

Throughout that earnest race—
35   The Victory, whose Admiral,
With orders nobly won,
Shone in the globe of the battle glow—
The angel in that sun.
Parallel in story,
40   Lo, the stately pair,
As late in grapple ranging,
The foe between them there—
When four great hulls lay tiered,
And the fiery tempest cleared,
45   And your prizes twain appeared,
Temeraire!

But Trafalgar is over now,
The quarter-deck undone;
The carved and castled navies fire
50   Their evening-gun.
O, Titan Temeraire,
Your stern-lights fade away;
Your bulwarks to the years must yield,
And heart-of-oak decay.
55   A pigmy steam-tug tows you,
Gigantic, to the shore—
Dismantled of your guns and spars,
And sweeping wings of war.
The rivets clinch the iron-clads,
60   Men learn a deadlier lore;
But Fame has nailed your battle-flags—
Your ghost it sails before:
O, the navies old and oaken,
O, the Temeraire no more!

A Utilitarian View of the Monitor's Fight.

PLAIN be the phrase, yet apt the verse,
More ponderous than nimble;
For since grimed War here laid aside
His Orient pomp, 'twould ill befit
5   Overmuch to ply
The rhyme's barbaric cymbal.

Navy stoker

Hail to victory without the gaud
    Of glory; zeal that needs no fans
Of banners; plain mechanic power
Plied cogently in War now placed—
    Where War belongs—
    Among the trades and artisans.

Yet this was battle, and intense—
    Beyond the strife of fleets heroic;
Deadlier, closer, calm 'mid storm;
No passion; all went on by crank,
    Pivot, and screw,
    And calculations of caloric.

Needless to dwell; the story's known.
    The ringing of those plates on plates
Still ringeth round the world—

The clangor of that blacksmith's fray.
    The anvil-din
Resounds this message from the Fates:

25   War shall yet be, and to the end;
        But war-paint shows the streaks of weather;
        War yet shall be, but warriors
        Are now but operatives; War's made
            Less grand than Peace,
30   And a singe runs through lace and feather.

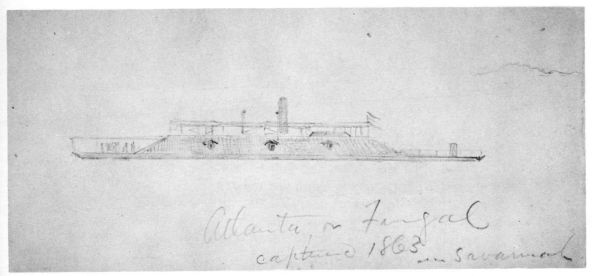

"Atlanta or Fingal captured 1863 in Savannah."

Shiloh.
A Requiem.

(APRIL, 1862.)

SKIMMING lightly, wheeling still,
  The swallows fly low
Over the field in clouded days,
  The forest-field of Shiloh—
5   Over the field where April rain
Solaced the parched ones stretched in pain
  Through the pause of night

That followed the Sunday fight
Around the church of Shiloh—
10   The church so lone, the log-built one,
That echoed to many a parting groan
And natural prayer
Of dying foemen mingled there—
Foemen at morn, but friends at eve—
15   Fame or country least their care:
(What like a bullet can undeceive!)
But now they lie low,
While over them the swallows skim.
And all is hushed at Shiloh.

The Battle for the Mississippi.

(APRIL, 1862.)

WHEN Israel camped by Migdol hoar,
Down at her feet her shawm she threw,
But Moses sung and timbrels rung
For Pharaoh's stranded crew.
5   So God appears in apt events—
The Lord is a man of war!
So the strong wing to the muse is given
In victory's roar.

Deep be the ode that hymns the fleet—
10   The fight by night—the fray
Which bore our Flag against the powerful stream,
And led it up to day.
Dully through din of larger strife
Shall bay that warring gun;
15   But none the less to us who live
It peals—an echoing one.

The shock of ships, the jar of walls,
The rush through thick and thin—
The flaring fire-rafts, glare and gloom—
20   Eddies, and shells that spin—
The boom-chain burst, the hulks dislodged,
The jam of gun-boats driven,

"Mounted Rifleman." By Alfred R. Waud.

Or fired, or sunk—made up a war
   Like Michael's waged with leven.

25   The manned Varuna stemmed and quelled
     The odds which hard beset;
The oaken flag-ship, half ablaze,
     Passed on and thundered yet;
While foundering, gloomed in grimy flame,

30   The Ram Manassas—hark the yell!—
  Plunged, and was gone; in joy or fright,
    The River gave a startled swell.

  They fought through lurid dark till dawn;
    The war-smoke rolled away
35 With clouds of night, and showed the fleet
    In scarred yet firm array,
  Above the forts, above the drift.
    Of wrecks which strife had made;
  And Farragut sailed up to the town
40   And anchored—sheathed the blade.

  The moody broadsides, brooding deep,
    Hold the lewd mob at bay,
  While o'er the armed decks' solemn aisles
    The meek church-pennons play;
45 By shotted guns the sailors stand,
    With foreheads bound or bare;
  The captains and the conquering crews
    Humble their pride in prayer.

  They pray; and after victory, prayer
50   Is meet for men who mourn their slain;
  The living shall unmoor and sail,
    But Death's dark anchor secret deeps detain.
  Yet Glory slants her shaft of rays
    Far through the undisturbed abyss;
55 There must be other, nobler worlds for them
    Who nobly yield their lives in this.

Malvern Hill.

(JULY, 1862.)

YE elms that wave on Malvern Hill
  In prime of morn and May,
Recall ye how McClellan's men
    Here stood at bay?
While deep within yon forest dim
  Our rigid comrades lay—

"Jones' Neck from Gen. R. S. Foster's Head Quarters Deep Bottom between 3 & 4 miles from Malvern Hills and on the same side of the James River showing the Pontoon Bridge & the Double end Gun Boats protecting his flanks." By William Waud. *Harper's Weekly,* July 23, 1864.

> Some with the cartridge in their mouth,
> Others with fixed arms lifted South—
>   Invoking so
10   The cypress glades? Ah wilds of woe!
>
> The spires of Richmond, late beheld
>   Through rifts in musket-haze,
> Were closed from view in clouds of dust
>   On leaf-walled ways,
15   Where streamed our wagons in caravan;
>   And the Seven Nights and Days
> Of march and fast, retreat and fight,

Pinched our grimed faces to ghastly plight—
Does the elm wood
20   Recall the haggard beards of blood?

The battle-smoked flag, with stars eclipsed,
    We followed (it never fell!)—
In silence husbanded our strength—
    Received their yell;
25   Till on this slope we patient turned
    With cannon ordered well;
Reverse we proved was not defeat;
But ah, the sod what thousands meet!—
    Does Malvern Wood
30   Bethink itself, and muse and brood?

            We elms of Malvern Hill
                Remember every thing;
            But sap the twig will fill:
            Wag the world how it will,
35   *Leaves must be green in Spring.*

The Victor of Antietam.

(1862.)

When tempest winnowed grain from bran,
And men were looking for a man,
Authority called you to the van,
            McClellan:
5   Along the line the plaudit ran,
As later when Antietam's cheers began.

Through storm-cloud and eclipse must move
Each Cause and Man, dear to the stars and Jove;
Nor always can the wisest tell
10   Deferred fulfillment from the hopeless knell—
The struggler from the floundering ne'er-do-well.
A pall-cloth on the Seven Days fell,
            McClellan—
Unprosperously heroical!
15   Who could Antietam's wreath foretell?

"Birney's Quartermaster, 1861." By Alfred R. Waud.

Authority called you; then, in mist
And loom of jeopardy—dismissed.
But staring peril soon appalled;
You, the Discarded, she recalled
20   Recalled you, nor endured delay;
And forth you rode upon a blasted way,
Arrayed Pope's rout, and routed Lee's array,
          McClellan:
Your tent was choked with captured flags that day,
25   McClellan.
Antietam was a telling fray.

Recalled you; and she heard your drum
Advancing through the ghastly gloom.
You manned the wall, you propped the Dome,

30   You stormed the powerful stormer home,
                McClellan:
        Antietam's cannon long shall boom.

        At Alexandria, left alone,
                McClellan—
35   Your veterans sent from you, and thrown
        To fields and fortunes all unknown—
        What thoughts were yours, revealed to none,
        While faithful still you labored on—
        Hearing the far Manassas gun!
40   McClellan,
        Only Antietam could atone.

        You fought in the front (an evil day,
                McClellan)—
        The fore-front of the first assay;
45   The Cause went sounding, groped its way;
        The leadsmen quarrelled in the bay;
        Quills thwarted swords; divided sway;
        The rebel flushed in his lusty May:
        You did your best, as in you lay,
50   McClellan.
        Antietam's sun-burst sheds a ray.

        Your medalled soldiers love you well,
                McClellan:
        Name your name, their true hearts swell;
55   With you they shook dread Stonewall's spell,
        With you they braved the blended yell
        Of rebel and maligner fell;
        With you in shame or fame they dwell,
                McClellan:
60   Antietam-braves a brave can tell.

        And when your comrades (now so few,
                McClellan—
        Such ravage in deep files they rue)
        Meet round the board, and sadly view
65   The empty places; tribute due
        They render to the dead—and you!
        Absent and silent o'er the blue;

The one-armed lift the wine to *you,*
          McClellan,
70   And great Antietam's cheers renew.

"McClellan entering Frederick." By Alfred R. Waud.

Battle of Stone River, Tennessee.
A View from Oxford Cloisters.

(JANUARY, 1863.)

WITH Tewksbury and Barnet heath
    In days to come the field shall blend,
The story dim and date obscure;
    In legend all shall end.
5   Even now, involved in forest shade

A Druid-dream the strife appears,
The fray of yesterday assumes
    The haziness of years.
        In North and South still beats the vein
10   Of Yorkist and Lancastrian.

Our rival Roses warred for Sway—
    For Sway, but named the name of Right;
And Passion, scorning pain and death,
    Lent sacred fervor to the fight.
Each lifted up a broidered cross,
15   While crossing blades profaned the sign;
Monks blessed the fratricidal lance,
    And sisters scarfs could twine.
        Do North and South the sin retain
20   Of Yorkist and Lancastrian?

But Rosecrans in the cedarn glade,
    And, deep in denser cypress gloom,
Dark Breckinridge, shall fade away
        Or thinly loom.
25 The pale throngs who in forest cowed
    Before the spell of battle's pause,
Forefelt the stillness that shall dwell
    On them and on their wars.
        North and South shall join the train
30   Of Yorkist and Lancastrian.

But where the sword has plunged so deep,
    And then been turned within the wound
By deadly Hate; where Climes contend
        On vasty ground—
35 No warning Alps or seas between,
    And small the curb of creed or law,
And blood is quick, and quick the brain;
    Shall North and South their rage deplore,
    And reunited thrive amain
40   Like Yorkist and Lancastrian?

Bugler

Running the Batteries,
As observed from the Anchorage above Vicksburgh.

(APRIL, 1863.)

A MOONLESS night—a friendly one;
  A haze dimmed the shadowy shore
As the first lampless boat slid silent on;
  Hist! and we spake no more;
5   We but pointed, and stilly, to what we saw.

We felt the dew, and seemed to feel
  The secret like a burden laid.
The first boat melts; and a second keel
  Is blent with the foliaged shade—
10   Their midnight rounds have the rebel officers made?

Unspied as yet. A third—a fourth—
  Gun-boat and transport in Indian file
Upon the war-path, smooth from the North;
  But the watch may they hope to beguile?
15   The manned river-batteries stretch for mile on mile.

A flame leaps out; they are seen;
  Another and another gun roars;
We tell the course of the boats through the screen
  By each further fort that pours,
20   And we guess how they jump from their beds on those
    shrouded shores.

Converging fires. We speak, though low:
  "That blastful furnace can they thread?"
"Why, Shadrach, Meshach, and Abed-nego
  Came out all right, we read;
25   The Lord, be sure, he helps his people, Ned."

How we strain our gaze. On bluffs they shun
  A golden growing flame appears—
Confirms to a silvery steadfast one:
  "The town is afire!" crows Hugh: "three cheers!"
30   Lot stops his mouth: "Nay, lad, better three tears."

A purposed light; it shows our fleet;

        Yet a little late in its searching ray,
      So far and strong, that in phantom cheat
      Lank on the deck our shadows lay;
35   The shining flag-ship stings their guns to furious play.

        How dread to mark her near the glare
        And glade of death the beacon throws
      Athwart the racing waters there;
          One by one each plainer grows,
40   Then speeds a blazoned target to our gladdened foes.

        The impartial cresset lights as well
        The fixed forts to the boats that run;
      And, plunged from the ports, their answers swell
        Back to each fortress dun:
45   Ponderous words speaks every monster gun.

        Fearless they flash through gates of flame,
        The salamanders hard to hit,
      Though vivid shows each bulky frame;
        And never the batteries intermit,
50   Nor the boats huge guns; they fire and flit.

        Anon a lull. The beacon dies:
        "Are they out of that strait accurst?"
      But other flames now dawning rise,
        Not mellowly brilliant like the first,
55   But rolled in smoke, whose whitish volumes burst.

        A baleful brand, a hurrying torch
        Whereby anew the boats are seen—
      A burning transport all alurch!
        Breathless we gaze; yet still we glean
60   Glimpses of beauty as we eager lean.

        The effulgence takes an amber glow
        Which bathes the hill-side villas far;
      Affrighted ladies mark the show
        Painting the pale magnolia—
65   The fair, false, Circe light of cruel War.

        The barge drifts doomed, a plague-struck one.

Shoreward in yawls the sailors fly.
But the gauntlet now is nearly run,
The spleenful forts by fits reply,
70   And the burning boat dies down in morning's sky.

All out of range. Adieu, Messieurs!
Jeers, as it speeds, our parting gun.
So burst we through their barriers
And menaces every one:
75   So Porter proves himself a brave man's son.

"Gunboat on the Appomattox at Port Walthall. The nearest point to Petersburg approached by the Gun Boats. The one shown in the sketch is the Commodore Perry commanded by Captain Amos P. Foster." By William Waud. *Harper's Weekly*, July 23, 1864.

Stonewall Jackson.
Mortally wounded at Chancellorsville.

(MAY, 1863.)

THE Man who fiercest charged in fight,
  Whose sword and prayer were long—
      Stonewall!
  Even him who stoutly stood for Wrong,
5 How can we praise? Yet coming days
  Shall not forget him with this song.

Dead is the Man whose Cause is dead,
  Vainly he died and set his seal—
      Stonewall!
10 Earnest in error, as we feel;
  True to the thing he deemed was due,
    True as John Brown or steel.

Relentlessly he routed us;
  But *we* relent, for he is low—
15   Stonewall!
  Justly his fame we outlaw; so
  We drop a tear on the bold Virginian's bier,
    Because no wreath we owe.

"Near Falmouth [Va.] Jany. 1863."

Stonewall Jackson.
(Ascribed to a Virginian.)

ONE man we claim of wrought renown
  Which not the North shall care to slur;
A Modern lived who sleeps in death,
  Calm as the marble Ancients are:
5   'Tis he whose life, though a vapor's wreath,
      Was charged with the lightning's burning breath—
      Stonewall, stormer of the war.

But who shall hymn the Roman heart?
  A stoic he, but even more;
10 The iron will and lion thew
  Were strong to inflict as to endure:
      Who like him could stand, or pursue?
      His fate the fatalist followed through;
      In all his great soul found to do
15   Stonewall followed his star.

He followed his star on the Romney march
  Through the sleet to the wintry war;
And he followed it on when he bowed the grain—
  The Wind of the Shenandoah;
20   At Gaines's Mill in the giants' strain—
      On the fierce forced stride to Manassas-plain,
      Where his sword with thunder was clothed again,
      Stonewall followed his star.

His star he followed athwart the flood
25   To Potomac's Northern shore,
When midway wading, his host of braves
  "My Maryland!" loud did roar—
      To red Antietam's field of graves,
      Through mountain-passes, woods and waves,
30   They followed their pagod with hymns and glaives,
      For Stonewall followed a star.

Back it led him to Marye's slope,
  Where the shock and the fame he bore;
And to green Moss-Neck it guided him—
35   Brief respite from throes of war:

To the laurel glade by the Wilderness grim,
Through climaxed victory naught shall dim,
Even unto death it piloted him—
Stonewall followed his star.

40   Its lead he followed in gentle ways
         Which never the valiant mar;
A cap we sent him, bestarred, to replace
    The sun-scorched helm of war:
         A fillet he made of the shining lace
45   Childhood's laughing brow to grace—
             Not his was a goldsmith's star.

O, much of doubt in after days
    Shall cling, as now, to the war;
Of the right and the wrong they'll still debate,
50   Puzzled by Stonewall's star:
         "Fortune went with the North elate,"
         "Ay, but the South had Stonewall's weight,
             And he fell in the South's vain war."

Confederate advance at Gaines Mill. By Alfred R. Waud.

Gettysburg.
The Check.

(JULY, 1863.)

O PRIDE of the days in prime of the months
   Now trebled in great renown,
When before the ark of our holy cause
    Fell Dagon down—
5   Dagon foredoomed, who, armed and targed,
Never his impious heart enlarged
Beyond that hour; God walled his power,
And there the last invader charged.

He charged, and in that charge condensed
10   His all of hate and all of fire;
He sought to blast us in his scorn,
    And wither us in his ire.
Before him went the shriek of shells—
Aerial screamings, taunts and yells;
15   Then the three waves in flashed advance
    Surged, but were met, and back they set:
Pride was repelled by sterner pride,
    And Right is a strong-hold yet.

Before our lines it seemed a beach
20   Which wild September gales have strown
With havoc on wreck, and dashed therewith
    Pale crews unknown—
Men, arms, and steeds. The evening sun
Died on the face of each lifeless one,
25   And died along the winding marge of fight
    And searching-parties lone.

Sloped on the hill the mounds were green,
    Our centre held that place of graves,
And some still hold it in their swoon,
30   And over these a glory waves.
The warrior-monument, crashed in fight,
Shall soar transfigured in loftier light,
    A meaning ampler bear;
Soldier and priest with hymn and prayer
35   Have laid the stone, and every bone
    Shall rest in honor there.

"9th Mass. batt.—[Capt. John W.] Bigelow's—going into position at
Gettysburg." By Alfred R. Waud after Charles W. Reed.

The House-top.
A Night Piece.

(July, 1863.)

No sleep. The sultriness pervades the air
And binds the brain—a dense oppression, such
As tawny tigers feel in matted shades,
Vexing their blood and making apt for ravage.
5   Beneath the stars the roofy desert spreads
Vacant as Libya. All is hushed near by.
Yet fitfully from far breaks a mixed surf
Of muffled sound, the Atheist roar of riot.
Yonder, where parching Sirius set in drought,
10   Balefully glares red Arson—there—and there.
The Town is taken by its rats—ship-rats
And rats of the wharves. All civil charms
And priestly spells which late held hearts in awe—
Fear-bound, subjected to a better sway
15   Than sway of self; these like a dream dissolve,
And man rebounds whole æons back in nature.
Hail to the low dull rumble, dull and dead,
And ponderous drag that shakes the wall.

Wise Draco comes, deep in the midnight roll
20   Of black artillery; he comes, though late;
In code corroborating Calvin's creed
And cynic tyrannies of honest kings;
He comes, nor parlies; and the Town, redeemed,
Gives thanks devout; nor, being thankful, heeds
25   The grimy slur on the Republic's faith implied,
Which holds that Man is naturally good,
And—more—is Nature's Roman, never to be scourged.

Stampede of Army horses. By Alfred R. Waud. *Harper's Weekly,*
February 6, 1864.

Look-out Mountain.
The Night Fight.

(NOVEMBER, 1863.)

WHO inhabiteth the Mountain
That it shines in lurid light,
And is rolled about with thunders,
And terrors, and a blight,

5   Like Kaf the peak of Eblis—
                  Kaf, the evil height?
              Who has gone up with a shouting
                  And a trumpet in the night?

              There is battle in the Mountain—
10   Might assaulteth Might;
              'Tis the fastness of the Anarch,
                  Torrent-torn, an ancient height;
              The crags resound the clangor
                  Of the war of Wrong and Right;
15   And the armies in the valley
                  Watch and pray for dawning light.

              Joy, joy, the day is breaking,
                  And the cloud is rolled from sight;
              There is triumph in the Morning
20   For the Anarch's plunging flight;
              God has glorified the Mountain
                  Where a Banner burneth bright,
              And the armies in the valley
                  They are fortified in right.

Chattanooga.

(NOVEMBER, 1863.)

              A KINDLING impulse seized the host
                  Inspired by heaven's elastic air,
              Their hearts outran their General's plan,
                  Though Grant commanded there—
5   Grant, who without reserve can dare;
              And, "Well, go on and do your will,"
                  He said, and measured the mountain then:
              So master-riders fling the rein—
                  But you must know your men.

10   On yester-morn in grayish mist,
                  Armies like ghosts on hills had fought,
              And rolled from the cloud their thunders loud
                  The Cumberlands far had caught:

"Signalling by night." By William Waud. *Harper's Weekly,* November 12, 1864.

To-day the sunlit steeps are sought.
15   Grant stood on cliffs whence all was plain,
       And smoked as one who feels no cares;
But mastered nervousness intense
       Alone such calmness wears.

The summit-cannon plunge their flame

20   Sheer down the primal wall,
        But up and up each linking troop
          In stretching festoons crawl—
          Nor fire a shot. Such men appall
        The foe, though brave. He, from the brink,
25   Looks far along the breadth of slope,
        And sees two miles of dark dots creep,
          And knows they mean the cope.

        He sees them creep. Yet here and there
          Half hid 'mid leafless groves they go;
30   As men who ply through traceries high
          Of turreted marbles show—
          So dwindle these to eyes below.
        But fronting shot and flanking shell
          Sliver and rive the inwoven ways;
35   High tops of oaks and high hearts fall,
          But never the climbing stays.

        From right to left, from left to right
          They roll the rallying cheer—
        Vie with each other, brother with brother,
40   Who shall the first appear—
          What color-bearer with colors clear
        In sharp relief, like sky-drawn Grant,
          Whose cigar must now be near the stump—
        While in solicitude his back
45   Heaps slowly to a hump.

        Near and more near; till now the flags
          Run like a catching flame;
        And one flares highest, to peril nighest—
          He means to make a name:
50   Salvos! they give him his fame.
        The staff is caught, and next the rush,
          And then the leap where death has led;
        Flag answered flag along the crest,
          And swarms of rebels fled.

55   But some who gained the envied Alp,
          And—eager, ardent, earnest there—
        Dropped into Death's wide-open arms,

Quelled on the wing like eagles struck in air—
Forever they slumber young and fair,
60   The smile upon them as they died;
Their end attained, that end a height:
Life was to these a dream fulfilled,
And death a starry night.

Skirmish in a forest.

The Armies of the Wilderness.
(1863–4.)

I.

LIKE snows the camps on Southern hills
 Lay all the winter long,
Our levies there in patience stood—
 They stood in patience strong.
5On fronting slopes gleamed other camps
 Where faith as firmly clung:
Ah, froward kin! so brave amiss—
 The zealots of the Wrong.

   In this strife of brothers
10   *(God, hear their country call),*
   However it be, whatever betide,
    Let not the just one fall.

Through the pointed glass our soldiers saw
 The base-ball bounding sent;
15They could have joined them in their sport
 But for the vale's deep rent.
And others turned the reddish soil,
 Like diggers of graves they bent:
The reddish soil and trenching toil
20   Begat presentiment.

   Did the Fathers feel mistrust?
    Can no final good be wrought?
   Over and over, again and again
    Must the fight for the Right be fought?

25They lead a Gray-back to the crag:
 "Your earth-works yonder—tell us, man!"
"A prisoner—no deserter, I,
 Nor one of the tell-tale clan."
His rags they mark: "True-blue like you
30 Should wear the color—your Country's, man!"
He grinds his teeth: "However that be,
 Yon earth-works have their plan."

Such brave ones, foully snared
By Belial's wily plea,
35   *Were faithful unto the evil end—*
Feudal fidelity.

"Well, then, your camps—come, tell the names!"
Freely he leveled his finger then:
"Yonder—see—are our Georgians; on the crest,
40   The Carolinians; lower, past the glen,
Virginians—Alabamians—Mississippians—Kentuckians
(Follow my finger)—Tennesseeans; and the ten
Camps *there*—ask your grave-pits; they'll tell.
Halloa! I see the picket-hut, the den
45 Where I last night lay." "Where's Lee?"
"In the hearts and bayonets of all yon men!"

The tribes swarm up to war
As in ages long ago,
Ere the palm of promise leaved
50   *And the lily of Christ did blow.*

Their mounted pickets for miles are spied
Dotting the lowland plain,
The nearer ones in their veteran-rags—
Loutish they loll in lazy disdain.
55 But ours in perilous places bide
With rifles ready and eyes that strain
Deep through the dim suspected wood
Where the Rapidan rolls amain.

The Indian has passed away,
60   *But creeping comes another—*
Deadlier far. Picket,
Take heed—take heed of thy brother!

From a wood-hung height, an outpost lone,
Crowned with a woodman's fort,
65 The sentinel looks on a land of dole,
Like Paran, all amort.

Black chimneys, gigantic in moor-like wastes,
    The scowl of the clouded sky retort;
The hearth is a houseless stone again—
70   Ah! where shall the people be sought?

    Since the venom such blastment deals,
        The South should have paused, and thrice,
    Ere with heat of her hate she hatched
        The egg with the cockatrice.

75   A path down the mountain winds to the glade
    Where the dead of the Moonlight Fight lie low;
A hand reaches out of the thin-laid mould
    As begging help which none can bestow.
But the field mouse small and busy ant
80   Heap their hillocks, to hide if they may the woe:
By the bubbling spring lies the rusted canteen,
    And the drum which the drummer-boy dying let go.

    Dust to dust, and blood for blood—
        Passion and pangs! Has Time
85   *Gone back? or is this the Age*
        Of the world's great Prime?

The wagon mired and cannon dragged
    Have trenched their scar; the plain
Tramped like the cindery beach of the damned—
90   A site for the city of Cain.
And stumps of forests for dreary leagues
    Like a massacre show. The armies have lain
By fires where gums and balms did burn,
    And the seeds of Summer's reign.

95   *Where are the birds and boys?*
        Who shall go chestnutting when
    October returns? The nuts—
        O, long ere they grow again.

They snug their huts with the chapel-pews,

100   In court-houses stable their steeds—
Kindle their fires with indentures and bonds,
    And old Lord Fairfax's parchment deeds;
And Virginian gentlemen's libraries old—
    Books which only the scholar heeds—
105   Are flung to his kennel. It is ravage and range,
    And gardens are left to weeds.

Turned adrift into war
*   Man runs wild on the plain,*
Like the jennets let loose
110 *   On the Pampas—zebras again.*

Like the Pleiads dim, see the tents through the storm—
    Aloft by the hill-side hamlet's graves,
On a head-stone used for a hearth-stone there
    The water is bubbling for punch for our braves.
115 What if the night be drear, and the blast
    Ghostly shrieks? their rollicking staves
Make frolic the heart; beating time with their swords,
    What care they if Winter raves?

Is life but a dream? and so,
120 *   In the dream do men laugh aloud?*
So strange seems mirth in a camp,
*   So like a white tent to a shroud.*

II.

The May-weed springs; and comes a Man
    And mounts our Signal Hill;
125 A quiet Man, and plain in garb—
    Briefly he looks his fill,
Then drops his gray eye on the ground,
    Like a loaded mortar he is still:
Meekness and grimness meet in him—
130   The silent General.

Were men but strong and wise,
*   Honest as Grant, and calm,*

War would be left to the red and black ants,
And the happy world disarm.

135   That eve a stir was in the camps,
          Forerunning quiet soon to come
      Among the streets of beechen huts
          No more to know the drum.
      The weed shall choke the lowly door,
140   And foxes peer within the gloom,
      Till scared perchance by Mosby's prowling men,
          Who ride in the rear of doom.

              Far West, and farther South,
                  Wherever the sword has been,
145   *Deserted camps are met,*
                  And desert graves are seen.

      The livelong night they ford the flood;
          With guns held high they silent press,
      Till shimmers the grass in their bayonets' sheen—
150   On Morning's banks their ranks they dress;
      Then by the forests lightly wind,
          Whose waving boughs the pennons seem to bless,
      Borne by the cavalry scouting on—
          Sounding the Wilderness.

155   *Like shoals of fish in spring*
                      That visit Crusoe's isle,
                  The host in the lonesome place—
                      The hundred thousand file.

      The foe that held his guarded hills
160   Must speed to woods afar;
      For the scheme that was nursed by the Culpepper hearth
          With the slowly-smoked cigar—
      The scheme that smouldered through winter long
          Now bursts into act—into war—
165   The resolute scheme of a heart as calm
          As the Cyclone's core.

The fight for the city is fought
In Nature's old domain;
Man goes out to the wilds,
170   *And Orpheus' charm is vain.*

In glades they meet skull after skull
  Where pine-cones lay—the rusted gun,
Green shoes full of bones, the mouldering coat
  And cuddled-up skeleton;
175   And scores of such. Some start as in dreams,
  And comrades lost bemoan:
By the edge of those wilds Stonewall had charged—
  But the Year and the Man were gone.

At the height of their madness
180   *The night winds pause,*
Recollecting themselves;
But no lull in these wars.

A gleam!—a volley! And who shall go
  Storming the swarmers in jungles dread?
185   No cannon-ball answers, no proxies are sent—
  They rush in the shrapnel's stead.
Plume and sash are vanities now—
  Let them deck the pall of the dead;
They go where the shade is, perhaps into Hades,
190   Where the brave of all times have led.

There's a dust of hurrying feet,
  Bitten lips and bated breath,
And drums that challenge to the grave,
  And faces fixed, forefeeling death.

195   What husky huzzahs in the hazy groves—
  What flying encounters fell;
Pursuer and pursued like ghosts disappear
  In gloomed shade—their end who shall tell?

The crippled, a ragged-barked stick for a crutch,
    Limp to some elfin dell—
Hobble from the sight of dead faces—white
    As pebbles in a well.

Few burial rites shall be;
    No priest with book and band
Shall come to the secret place
    Of the corpse in the foeman's land.

Watch and fast, march and fight—clutch your gun!
    Day-fights and night-fights; sore is the stress;
Look, through the pines what line comes on?
    Longstreet slants through the hauntedness!
'Tis charge for charge, and shout for yell:
    Such battles on battles oppress—
But Heaven lent strength, the Right strove well,
    And emerged from the Wilderness.

Emerged, for the way was won;
    But the Pillar of Smoke that led
Was brand-like with ghosts that went up
    Ashy and red.

None can narrate that strife in the pines,
    A seal is on it—Sabæan lore!
Obscure as the wood, the entangled rhyme
    But hints at the maze of war—
Vivid glimpses or livid through peopled gloom,
    And fires which creep and char—
A riddle of death, of which the slain
    Sole solvers are.

Long they withhold the roll
    Of the shroudless dead. It is right;
Not yet can we bear the flare
    Of the funeral light.

"Engineer officer examining roads outside the lines—1863." By Alfred R. Waud.

On the Photograph of a Corps Commander.

Ay, man is manly. Here you see
　　The warrior-carriage of the head,
And brave dilation of the frame;
　　And lighting all, the soul that led
5　In Spottsylvania's charge to victory,
　　Which justifies his fame.

A cheering picture. It is good
　　To look upon a Chief like this,
In whom the spirit moulds the form.
10　　Here favoring Nature, oft remiss,
With eagle mien expressive has endued
　　A man to kindle strains that warm.

"Ely's ford." By Alfred R. Waud. *Harper's Weekly,* May 28, 1864.

Trace back his lineage, and his sires,
  Yeoman or noble, you shall find
15 Enrolled with men of Agincourt,
  Heroes who shared great Harry's mind.
Down to us come the knightly Norman fires,
  And front the Templars bore.

Nothing can lift the heart of man
20   Like manhood in a fellow-man.
The thought of heaven's great King afar
  But humbles us—too weak to scan;
But manly greatness men can span,
  And feel the bonds that draw.

The Swamp Angel.

THERE is a coal-black Angel
  With a thick Afric lip,
And he dwells (like the hunted and harried)
  In a swamp where the green frogs dip.
5 But his face is against a City
  Which is over a bay of the sea,
And he breathes with a breath that is blastment,
  And dooms by a far decree.

By night there is fear in the City,
10   Through the darkness a star soareth on;
There's a scream that screams up to the zenith,
  Then the poise of a meteor lone—
Lighting far the pale fright of the faces,
  And downward the coming is seen;
15 Then the rush, and the burst, and the havoc,
  And wails and shrieks between.

It comes like the thief in the gloaming;
  It comes, and none may foretell
The place of the coming—the glaring;
20   They live in a sleepless spell

That wizens, and withers, and whitens;
   It ages the young, and the bloom
Of the maiden is ashes of roses—
   The Swamp Angel broods in his gloom.

25   Swift is his messengers' going,
            But slowly he saps their halls,
         As if by delay deluding.
            They move from their crumbling walls
         Farther and farther away;
30   But the Angel sends after and after,
         By night with the flame of his ray—
            By night with the voice of his screaming—
         Sends after them, stone by stone,
            And farther walls fall, farther portals,
35   And weed follows weed through the Town.

"Smoking bacon. Army Teamsters at Hdqters, Brandy Station, Va."

Is this the proud City? the scorner
  Which never would yield the ground?
Which mocked at the coal-black Angel?
  The cup of despair goes round.
40 Vainly she calls upon Michael
  (The white man's seraph was he),
For Michael has fled from his tower
  To the Angel over the sea.

Who weeps for the woeful City
45   Let him weep for our guilty kind;
Who joys at her wild despairing—
  Christ, the Forgiver, convert his mind.

The Battle for the Bay.

(AUGUST, 1864.)

O MYSTERY of noble hearts,
  To whom mysterious seas have been
In midnight watches, lonely calm and storm,
  A stern, sad discipline,
5 And rooted out the false and vain,
  And chastened them to aptness for
  Devotion and the deeds of war,
And death which smiles and cheers in spite of pain.

Beyond the bar the land-wind dies,
10   The prows becharmed at anchor swim:
A summer night; the stars withdrawn look down—
  Fair eve of battle grim.
The sentries pace, bonetas glide;
  Below, the sleeping sailors swing,
15   And in their dreams to quarters spring,
Or cheer their flag, or breast a stormy tide.

But drums are beat: *Up anchor all!*
  The triple lines steam slowly on;
Day breaks, and through the sweep of decks each man
20   Stands coldly by his gun—
As cold as it. But he shall warm—

Warm with the solemn metal there,
And all its ordered fury share,
In attitude a gladiatorial form.

25 The Admiral—yielding to the love
        Which held his life and ship so dear—
    Sailed second in the long fleet's midmost line;
            Yet thwarted all their care:
    He lashed himself aloft, and shone
30   Star of the fight, with influence sent
            Throughout the dusk embattlement;
    And so they neared the strait and walls of stone.

    No sprightly fife as in the field,
        The decks were hushed like fanes in prayer;
35 Behind each man a holy angel stood—
            He stood, though none was 'ware.
    Out spake the forts on either hand,
        Back speak the ships when spoken to,
        And set their flags in concert true,
40 And *On and in!* is Farragut's command.

    But what delays? 'mid wounds above
        Dim buoys give hint of death below—
    Sea-ambuscades, where evil art had aped
            Hecla that hides in snow.
45 The centre-van, entangled, trips;
        The starboard leader holds straight on:
        A cheer for the Tecumseh!—nay,
    Before their eyes the turreted ship goes down!

    The fire redoubles. While the fleet
50   Hang dubious—ere the horror ran—
    The Admiral rushes to his rightful place—
            Well met! apt hour and man!—
    Closes with peril, takes the lead,
        His action is a stirring call;
55   He strikes his great heart through them all,
    And is the genius of their daring deed.

    The forts are daunted, slack their fire,
        Confounded by the deadlier aim

And rapid broadsides of the speeding fleet,
60   And fierce denouncing flame.
Yet shots from four dark hulls embayed
     Come raking through the loyal crews,
     Whom now each dying mate endues
With his last look, anguished yet undismayed.

65   A flowering time to guilt is given,
     And traitors have their glorying hour;
O late, but sure, the righteous Paramount comes—
     Palsy is on their power!
So proved it with the rebel keels,
70   The strong-holds past: assailed, they run;
     The Selma strikes, and the work is done:
The dropping anchor the achievement seals.

But no, she turns—the Tennessee!
     The solid Ram of iron and oak,
75   Strong as Evil, and bold as Wrong, though lone—
     A pestilence in her smoke.
The flag-ship is her singled mark,
     The wooden Hartford. Let her come;
     She challenges the planet of Doom,
80   And naught shall save her—not her iron bark.

Slip anchor, all! and at her, all!
     Bear down with rushing beaks—and now!
First the Monongahela struck—and reeled;
     The Lackawana's prow
85   Next crashed—crashed, but not crashing; then
     The Admiral rammed, and rasping nigh
     Sloped in a broadside, which glanced by:
The Monitors battered at her adamant den.

The Chickasaw plunged beneath the stern
90   And pounded there; a huge wrought orb
From the Manhattan pierced one wall, but dropped;
     Others the seas absorb.
Yet stormed on all sides, narrowed in,
     Hampered and cramped, the bad one fought—
95   Spat ribald curses from the port
Whose shutters, jammed, locked up this Man-of-Sin.

No pause or stay. They made a din
   Like hammers round a boiler forged;
Now straining strength tangled itself with strength,
100   Till Hate her will disgorged.
The white flag showed, the fight was won—
   Mad shouts went up that shook the Bay;
   But pale on the scarred fleet's decks there lay
A silent man for every silenced gun.

105 And quiet far below the wave,
   Where never cheers shall move their sleep,
Some who did boldly, nobly earn them, lie—
    Charmed children of the deep.
But decks that now are in the seed,
110   And cannon yet within the mine,
   Shall thrill the deeper, gun and pine,
Because of the Tecumseh's glorious deed.

"U.S. Transport 'Oriental.'"

Sheridan at Cedar Creek.

(OCTOBER, 1864.)

SHOE the steed with silver
  That bore him to the fray,
When he heard the guns at dawning—
  Miles away;
5 When he heard them calling, calling—
    Mount! nor stay:
      Quick, or all is lost;
      They've surprised and stormed the post,
      They push your routed host—
10   Gallop! retrieve the day.

House the horse in ermine—
  For the foam-flake blew
White through the red October;
  He thundered into view;
15 They cheered him in the looming,
  Horseman and horse they knew.
      The turn of the tide began,
      The rally of bugles ran,
      He swung his hat in the van;
20   The electric hoof-spark flew.

Wreathe the steed and lead him—
  For the charge he led
Touched and turned the cypress
  Into amaranths for the head
25 Of Philip, king of riders,
  Who raised them from the dead.
      The camp (at dawning lost),
      By eve, recovered—forced,
      Rang with laughter of the host
30   At belated Early fled.

Shroud the horse in sable—
  For the mounds they heap!
There is firing in the Valley,
  And yet no strife they keep;
35 It is the parting volley,

"Sheridan's Ride."

It is the pathos deep.
　　There is glory for the brave
　　Who lead, and nobly save,
　　But no knowledge in the grave
40　Where the nameless followers sleep.

In the Prison Pen.

(1864.)

LISTLESS he eyes the palisades
　　And sentries in the glare;
'Tis barren as a pelican-beach—
　　But his world is ended there.

5　Nothing to do; and vacant hands
　　Bring on the idiot-pain;
He tries to think—to recollect,
　　But the blur is on his brain.

Around him swarm the plaining ghosts
10　Like those on Virgil's shore—
A wilderness of faces dim,
　　And pale ones gashed and hoar.

A smiting sun. No shed, no tree;
　　He totters to his lair—
15　A den that sick hands dug in earth
　　Ere famine wasted there,

Or, dropping in his place, he swoons,
　　Walled in by throngs that press,
Till forth from the throngs they bear him dead—
20　Dead in his meagreness.

The College Colonel.

HE rides at their head;
　　A crutch by his saddle just slants in view,
One slung arm is in splints, you see,

Serving rations to exchanged Union prisioners on board the *New York*.
By William Waud. *Harper's Weekly*, December 10, 1864.

        Yet he guides his strong steed—how coldly too.

5   He brings his regiment home—
             Not as they filed two years before,
           But a remnant half-tattered, and battered, and worn,
           Like castaway sailors, who—stunned
             By the surf's loud roar,
10   Their mates dragged back and seen no more—
           Again and again breast the surge,
             And at last crawl, spent, to shore.

           A still rigidity and pale—
             An Indian aloofness lones his brow;
15   He has lived a thousand years
           Compressed in battle's pains and prayers,
             Marches and watches slow.

There are welcoming shouts, and flags;
　　Old men off hat to the Boy,
20　Wreaths from gay balconies fall at his feet,
　　But to *him*—there comes alloy.

It is not that a leg is lost,
　　It is not that an arm is maimed,
It is not that the fever has racked—
25　　Self he has long disclaimed.

But all through the Seven Days' Fight,
　　And deep in the Wilderness grim,
And in the field-hospital tent,
　　And Petersburg crater, and dim
30　Lean brooding in Libby, there came—
　　Ah heaven!—what *truth* to him.

The Eagle of the Blue.

ALOFT he guards the starry folds
　　Who is the brother of the star;
The bird whose joy is in the wind
　　Exulteth in the war.

5　No painted plume—a sober hue,
　　His beauty is his power;
That eager calm of gaze intent
　　Foresees the Sibyl's hour.

Austere, he crowns the swaying perch,
10　　Flapped by the angry flag;
The hurricane from the battery sings,
　　But his claw has known the crag.

Amid the scream of shells, his scream
　　Runs shrilling; and the glare
15　Of eyes that brave the blinding sun
　　The vollied flame can bear.

The pride of quenchless strength is his—
　　Strength which, though chained, avails;

"Capt. Davis, Capt. Hernard, Lieut. Wharton."

20   The very rebel looks and thrills—
         The anchored Emblem hails.

Though scarred in many a furious fray,
    No deadly hurt he knew;
Well may we think his years are charmed—
    The Eagle of the Blue.

A Dirge for McPherson,
Killed in front of Atlanta.

(JULY, 1864.)

ARMS reversed and banners craped—
    Muffled drums;
Snowy horses sable-draped—
    McPherson comes.

5   *But, tell us, shall we know him more,*
              Lost-Mountain and lone Kenesaw?

Brave the sword upon the pall—
    A gleam in gloom;
So a bright name lighteth all
10   McPherson's doom.

Bear him through the chapel-door—
    Let priest in stole
Pace before the warrior
    Who led. Bell—toll!

15   Lay him down within the nave,
    The Lesson read—
Man is noble, man is brave,
    But man's—a weed.

Take him up again and wend
20   Graveward, nor weep:
There's a trumpet that shall rend
    This Soldier's sleep.

"Signal Station Pony Mt. Culpepper, Va." By Alfred R. Waud. *Harper's Weekly*,
October 3, 1863.

"[Gen. Thomas L.] Rosser attacking the rear Oct. 8th, 1864—Harrisonburg,
Shenandoah Valley." By Alfred R. Waud.

Pass the ropes the coffin round,
    And let descend;
25   Prayer and volley—let it sound
    McPherson's end.

True fame is his, for life is o'er—
Sarpedon of the mighty war.

At the Cannon's Mouth.
Destruction of the Ram Albemarle by the Torpedo-launch.

(OCTOBER, 1864.)

PALELY intent, he urged his keel
    Full on the guns, and touched the spring;
Himself involved in the bolt he drove
Timed with the armed hull's shot that stove
5   His shallop—die or do!
Into the flood his life he threw,
    Yet lives—unscathed—a breathing thing
To marvel at.

            He has his fame;
10   But that mad dash at death, how name?

Had Earth no charm to stay the Boy
    From the martyr-passion? Could he dare
Disdain the Paradise of opening joy
    Which beckons the fresh heart every where?
15   Life has more lures than any girl
    For youth and strength; puts forth a share
Of beauty, hinting of yet rarer store;
And ever with unfathomable eyes,
        Which bafflingly entice,
20   Still strangely does Adonis draw.
And life once over, who shall tell the rest?
Life is, of all we know, God's best.
What imps these eagles then, that they
Fling disrespect on life by that proud way
25   In which they soar above our lower clay.

Pretense of wonderment and doubt unblest:
　　In Cushing's eager deed was shown
　　A spirit which brave poets own—
That scorn of life which earns life's crown;
　　Earns, but not always wins; but *he*—
　　The star ascended in his nativity.

30

Infantryman. By Alfred R. Waud.

The March to the Sea.

(December, 1864)

Not Kenesaw high-arching,
　　Nor Allatoona's glen—
Though there the graves lie parching—
　　Stayed Sherman's miles of men;
5　From charred Atlanta marching
　　They launched the sword again.
　　　　　The columns streamed like rivers
　　　　　　Which in their course agree,
　　　　　And they streamed until their flashing
10　　　　　Met the flashing of the sea:
　　　　　　　It was glorious glad marching,
　　　　　　　That marching to the sea.

They brushed the foe before them
　　(Shall gnats impede the bull?);
15　Their own good bridges bore them
　　Over swamps or torrents full,
And the grand pines waving o'er them
　　Bowed to axes keen and cool.
　　　　　The columns grooved their channels,
20　　　　　Enforced their own decree,
　　　　　And their power met nothing larger
　　　　　Until it met the sea:
　　　　　　　It was glorious glad marching,
　　　　　　　A marching glad and free.

25　Kilpatrick's snare of riders
　　In zigzags mazed the land,
Perplexed the pale Southsiders
　　With feints on every hand;
Vague menace awed the hiders
30　　In forts beyond command.
　　　　　To Sherman's shifting problem
　　　　　　No foeman knew the key;
　　　　　But onward went the marching
　　　　　　Unpausing to the sea:
35　　　　　　It was glorious glad marching,
　　　　　　　The swinging step was free.

The flankers ranged like pigeons
   In clouds through field or wood;
The flocks of all those regions,
40   The herds and horses good,
Poured in and swelled the legions,
   For they caught the marching mood.
         A volley ahead! They hear it;
         And they hear the repartee:
45   Fighting was but frolic
         In that marching to the sea:
            It was glorious glad marching,
            A marching bold and free.

All nature felt their coming,
50   The birds like couriers flew,
And the banners brightly blooming
   The slaves by thousands drew,
And they marched beside the drumming,
   And they joined the armies blue.
55   The cocks crowed from the cannon
           (Pets named from Grant and Lee),
         Plumed fighters and campaigners
         In that marching to the sea:
            It was glorious glad marching,
60   For every man was free.

The foragers through calm lands
   Swept in tempest gay,
And they breathed the air of balm-lands
   Where rolled savannas lay,
65 And they helped themselves from farm-lands—
   As who should say them nay?
         The regiments uproarious
           Laughed in Plenty's glee;
         And they marched till their broad laughter
70   Met the laughter of the sea:
            It was glorious glad marching,
            That marching to the sea.

The grain of endless acres
   Was threshed (as in the East)
75 By the trampling of the Takers,

Soldier with dagger.

Strong march of man and beast;
The flails of those earth-shakers
Left a famine where they ceased.
  The arsenals were yielded;
80   The sword (that was to be),
  Arrested in the forging,
   Rued that marching to the sea:
    It was glorious glad marching,
    But ah, the stern decree!

85 For behind they left a wailing,
  A terror and a ban,
And blazing cinders sailing,
 And houseless households wan,
Wide zones of counties paling,
90 And towns where maniacs ran.
   Was it Treason's retribution—
   Necessity the plea?
  They will long remember Sherman
  And his streaming columns free—
95   They will long remember Sherman
   Marching to the sea.

The Frenzy in the Wake.
Sherman's advance through the Carolinas.

(FEBRUARY, 1865.)

So strong to suffer, shall we be
 Weak to contend, and break
The sinews of the Oppressor's knee
 That grinds upon the neck?
5   O, the garments rolled in blood
   Scorch in cities wrapped in flame,
  And the African—the imp!
   He gibbers, imputing shame.

Shall Time, avenging every woe,
10 To us that joy allot
Which Israel thrilled when Sisera's brow
 Showed gaunt and showed the clot?

Curse on their foreheads, cheeks, and eyes—
The Northern faces—true
15   To the flag we hate, the flag whose stars
Like planets strike us through.

From frozen Maine they come,
Far Minnesota too;
They come to a sun whose rays disown—
20   May it wither them as the dew!
The ghosts of our slain appeal:
"Vain shall our victories be?"
But back from its ebb the flood recoils—
Back in a whelming sea.

25   With burning woods our skies are brass,
The pillars of dust are seen;
The live-long day their cavalry pass—
No crossing the road between.
We were sore deceived—an awful host!
30   They move like a roaring wind.
Have we gamed and lost? but even despair
Shall never our hate rescind.

"[Alfred] Pleasanton's Cavalry deployed as Skirmishers." By Alfred R. Waud.
Harper's Weekly, November 22, 1862.

The Fall of Richmond.
The tidings received in the Northern Metropolis.

(APRIL, 1865.)

WHAT mean these peals from every tower,
  And crowds like seas that sway?
The cannon reply; they speak the heart
  Of the People impassioned, and say—
5   A city in flags for a city in flames,
  Richmond goes Babylon's way—
      Sing and pray.

O weary years and woeful wars,
  And armies in the grave;
10   But hearts unquelled at last deter
The helmed dilated Lucifer—
  Honor to Grant the brave,
Whose three stars now like Orion's rise
  When wreck is on the wave—
15   *Bless his glaive.*

Well that the faith we firmly kept,
  And never our aim forswore
For the Terrors that trooped from each recess,
When fainting we fought in the Wilderness,
20 And Hell made loud hurrah;
But God is in Heaven, and Grant in the Town,
  And Right through might is Law—
    God's way adore.

The Surrender at Appomattox.

(APRIL, 1865.)

As billows upon billows roll,
  On victory victory breaks;
Ere yet seven days from Richmond's fall
  And crowning triumph wakes
5   The loud joy-gun, whose thunders run

Ruins of a flour mill at Richmond, April, 1865. By Alfred R. Waud.

By sea-shore, streams, and lakes.
    The hope and great event agree
    In the sword that Grant received from Lee.

    The warring eagles fold the wing,
10   But not in Cæsar's sway;
Not Rome o'ercome by Roman arms we sing,
    As on Pharsalia's day,
But Treason thrown, though a giant grown,
    And Freedom's larger play.
15   All human tribes glad token see
    In the close of the wars of Grant and Lee.

"Rebel officers coming into Richmond by the Pontoon bridge to give themselves
up." By Alfred R. Waud.

A Canticle:
Significant of the national exaltation of enthusiasm at the close of the War.

O THE precipice Titanic
　　Of the congregated Fall,
And the angle oceanic
　　Where the deepening thunders call—
5　　　　And the Gorge so grim,
　　　　And the firmamental rim!
Multitudinously thronging
　　The waters all converge,
Then they sweep adown in sloping
10　　Solidity of surge.

　　　The Nation, in her impulse
　　　　Mysterious as the Tide,
　　In emotion like an ocean
　　　　Moves in power, not in pride;
15　　And is deep in her devotion
　　　　As Humanity is wide.
　　Thou Lord of hosts victorious,
　　　　The confluence Thou hast twined;
　　By a wondrous way and glorious
20　　　A passage Thou dost find—
　　　　A passage Thou dost find:
　　Hosanna to the Lord of hosts,
　　　　The hosts of human kind.

　　Stable in its baselessness
25　　　When calm is in the air,
　　The Iris half in tracelessness
　　　　Hovers faintly fair.
　　Fitfully assailing it
　　　　A wind from heaven blows,
30　　Shivering and paling it
　　　　To blankness of the snows;
　　While, incessant in renewal,
　　　　The Arch rekindled grows,
　　Till again the gem and jewel
35　　　Whirl in blinding overthrows—
　　Till, prevailing and transcending,

Lo, the Glory perfect there,
And the contest finds an ending,
For repose is in the air.

40   But the foamy Deep unsounded,
And the dim and dizzy ledge,
And the booming roar rebounded,
And the gull that skims the edge!
The Giant of the Pool
45   Heaves his forehead white as wool—
Toward the Iris ever climbing
From the Cataracts that call—
Irremovable vast arras
Draping all the Wall.

50   The Generations pouring
From times of endless date,
In their going, in their flowing
Ever form the steadfast State;
And Humanity is growing
55   Toward the fullness of her fate.

Thou Lord of hosts victorious,
Fulfill the end designed;
By a wondrous way and glorious
A passage Thou dost find—
60   A passage Thou dost find:
Hosanna to the Lord of hosts,
The hosts of human kind.

"General [D. M.] Gregg's troops going into action, Culpepper Va."
By Alfred R. Waud. *Harper's Weekly*, October 3, 1863.

The Martyr.
Indicative of the passion of the people on the 15th of April, 1865.

**Negro soldier at ease.
By Alfred R. Waud.**

GOOD Friday was the day
  Of the prodigy and crime,
When they killed him in his pity,
  When they killed him in his prime
5 Of clemency and calm—
    When with yearning he was filled
    To redeem the evil-willed,
And, though conqueror, be kind;
  But they killed him in his kindness,
10 In their madness and their blindness,
And they killed him from behind.

      There is sobbing of the strong,
        And a pall upon the land;
      But the People in their weeping
15   Bare the iron hand:
      Beware the People weeping
        When they bare the iron hand.

He lieth in his blood—
  The father in his face;
20 They have killed him, the Forgiver—
  The Avenger takes his place,
The Avenger wisely stern,
    Who in righteousness shall do
    What the heavens call him to,
25 And the parricides remand;
    For they killed him in his kindness,
    In their madness and their blindness,
And his blood is on their hand.

      There is sobbing of the strong,
30   And a pall upon the land;
      But the People in their weeping
          Bare the iron hand:
      Beware the People weeping
        When they bare the iron hand.

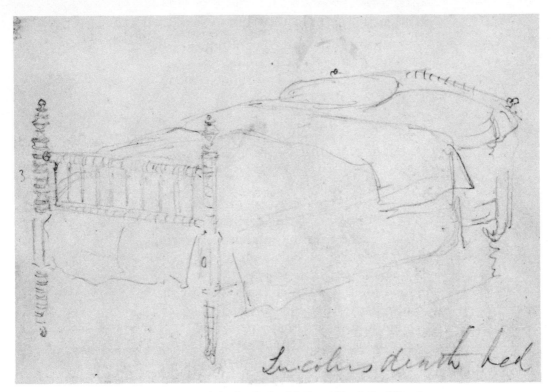

"Lincoln's death bed." By Alfred R. Waud.

"The Coming Storm":
A Picture by S. R. Gifford, and owned by E. B. Included
in the N. A. Exhibition, April, 1865.

ALL feeling hearts must feel for him
   Who felt this picture. Presage dim—
Dim inklings from the shadowy sphere
   Fixed him and fascinated here.

5   A demon-cloud like the mountain one
   Burst on a spirit as mild
As this urned lake, the home of shades.
   But Shakespeare's pensive child

Never the lines had lightly scanned,
10   Steeped in fable, steeped in fate;
The Hamlet in his heart was 'ware,
   Such hearts can antedate.

No utter surprise can come to him
Who reaches Shakespeare's core;
15 That which we seek and shun is there—
Man's final lore.

Rebel Color-bearers at Shiloh:
*A plea against the vindictive cry raised by civilians shortly
after the surrender at Appomattox.*

THE color-bearers facing death
White in the whirling sulphurous wreath,
  Stand boldly out before the line;
Right and left their glances go,
5   Proud of each other, glorying in their show;
Their battle-flags about them blow,
  And fold them as in flame divine:
Such living robes are only seen
Round martyrs burning on the green—
10   And martyrs for the Wrong have been.

Perish their Cause! but mark the men—
Mark the planted statues, then
Draw trigger on them if you can.

The leader of a patriot-band
15   Even so could view rebels who so could stand;
  And this when peril pressed him sore,
Left aidless in the shivered front of war—
  Skulkers behind, defiant foes before,
And fighting with a broken brand.
20   The challenge in that courage rare—
Courage defenseless, proudly bare—
Never could tempt him; he could dare
Strike up the leveled rifle there.

Sunday at Shiloh, and the day
25   When Stonewall charged—McClellan's crimson May,
And Chickamauga's wave of death,
And of the Wilderness the cypress wreath—
    All these have passed away.
The life in the veins of Treason lags,

30   Her daring color-bearers drop their flags,
              And yield. *Now* shall we fire?
                    Can poor spite be?
              Shall nobleness in victory less aspire
              Than in reverse? Spare Spleen her ire,
35   And think how Grant met Lee.

Horseman with flag. By Alfred R. Waud.

The Muster.
Suggested by the Two Days' Review at Washington.

(MAY, 1865.)

THE Abrahamic river—
  Patriarch of floods,
Calls the roll of all his streams
  And watery multitudes:
5   Torrent cries to torrent,
        The rapids hail the fall;
      With shouts the inland freshets
        Gather to the call.

  The quotas of the Nation,
10   Like the water-shed of waves,
  Muster into union—
    Eastern warriors, Western braves.

  Martial strains are mingling,
    Though distant far the bands,
15   And the wheeling of the squadrons
    Is like surf upon the sands.

  The bladed guns are gleaming—
    Drift in lengthened trim,
  Files on files for hazy miles—
20   Nebulously dim.

  O Milky Way of armies—
    Star rising after star,
  New banners of the Commonwealths,
    And eagles of the War.

25   The Abrahamic river
    To sea-wide fullness fed,
  Pouring from the thaw-lands
    By the God of floods is led:
      His deep enforcing current
30   The streams of ocean own,
      And Europe's marge is evened
        By rills from Kansas lone.

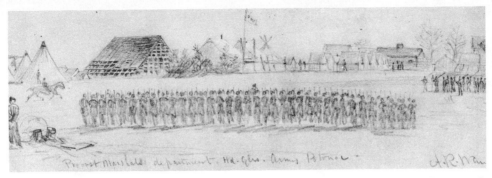

"Provost Marshals' department. Hd. Qtrs. Army Potomac." By Alfred R. Waud.
Harper's Weekly, April 18, 1863.

Aurora-Borealis.
Commemorative of the Dissolution of Armies at the Peace.

(MAY, 1865.)

WHAT power disbands the Northern Lights
   After their steely play?
The lonely watcher feels an awe
   Of Nature's sway,
      As when appearing,
      He marked their flashed uprearing
In the cold gloom—
   Retreatings and advancings,
(Like dallyings of doom),
      Transitions and enhancings,
      And bloody ray.

The phantom-host has faded quite,
   Splendor and Terror gone—
Portent or promise—and gives way
      To pale, meek Dawn;
      The coming, going,
      Alike in wonder showing—

Alike the God,
   Decreeing and commanding
The million blades that glowed,
   The muster and disbanding—
   Midnight and Morn.

5

10

15

20

The Released Rebel Prisoner.

(June, 1865.)

Armies he's seen—the herds of war,
   But never such swarms of men
As now in the Nineveh of the North—
   How mad the Rebellion then!

5   And yet but dimly he divines
   The depth of that deceit,
And superstition of vast pride
   Humbled to such defeat.

Seductive shone the Chiefs in arms—
10   His steel the nearest magnet drew;
Wreathed with its kind, the Gulf-weed drives—
   'Tis Nature's wrong they rue.

His face is hidden in his beard,
   But his heart peers out at eye—
15 And such a heart! like a mountain-pool
   Where no man passes by.

He thinks of Hill—a brave soul gone;
   And Ashby dead in pale disdain;
And Stuart with the Rupert-plume,
20   Whose blue eye never shall laugh again.

He hears the drum; he sees our boys
   From his wasted fields return;
Ladies feast them on strawberries,
   And even to kiss them yearn.

25 He marks them bronzed, in soldier-trim,
   The rifle proudly borne;
They bear it for an heir-loom home,
   And he—disarmed—jail-worn.

Home, home—his heart is full of it;
30   But home he never shall see,
Even should he stand upon the spot:
   'Tis gone!—where his brothers be.

The cypress-moss from tree to tree
   Hangs in his Southern land;
35   As weird, from thought to thought of his
   Run memories hand in hand.

And so he lingers—lingers on
   In the City of the Foe—
His cousins and his countrymen
40   Who see him listless go.

"Post Office. Army Potomac." [Detail.] By Alfred R. Waud. *Harper's Weekly,*
April 18, 1863.

A Grave near Petersburg, Virginia.

HEAD-BOARD and foot-board duly placed—
   Grassed is the mound between;
Daniel Drouth is the slumberer's name—
   Long may his grave be green!

5   Quick was his way—a flash and a blow,
   Full of his fire was he—
A fire of hell—'tis burnt out now—
   Green may his grave long be!

"Rebs." By Alfred R. Waud.

May his grave be green, though he
10   Was a rebel of iron mould;
Many a true heart—true to the Cause,
    Through the blaze of his wrath lies cold.

May his grave be green—still green
    While happy years shall run;
15 May none come nigh to disinter
    The—*Buried Gun.*

"Capt. Steven's battery on the 6th Corps Skirmish line [Cold Harbor, Va.]."
By Alfred R. Waud. *Harper's Weekly,* June 25, 1864.

"Formerly a Slave."
An idealized Portrait, by E. Vedder, in the Spring Exhibition of the National Academy, 1865.

THE sufferance of her race is shown,
    And retrospect of life,
Which now too late deliverance dawns upon;
    Yet is she not at strife.

5   Her children's children they shall know
            The good withheld from her;
        And so her reverie takes prophetic cheer—
            In spirit she sees the stir

        Far down the depth of thousand years,
10   And marks the revel shine;
        Her dusky face is lit with sober light,
            Sibylline, yet benign.

"View of Fort Clifton showing the Water Battery and obstruction in the Appomattox River sketched from Battery B 2nd U. S. regulars (colored)." By William Waud. *Harper's Weekly,* July 23, 1864.

The Apparition.
(A Retrospect.)

CONVULSIONS came; and, where the field
    Long slept in pastoral green,
A goblin-mountain was upheaved
(Sure the scared sense was all deceived),
5   Marl-glen and slag-ravine.

The unreserve of Ill was there,
    The clinkers in her last retreat;

But, ere the eye could take it in,
Or mind could comprehension win,
10   It sunk!—and at our feet.

So, then, Solidity's a crust—
    The core of fire below;
All may go well for many a year,
But who can think without a fear
15   Of horrors that happen so?

Soldier with folded arms. By Alfred R. Waud.

Magnanimity Baffled.

"SHARP words we had before the fight;
  But—now the fight is done—
Look, here's my hand," said the Victor bold,
  "Take it—an honest one!
5 What, holding back? I mean you well;
  Though worsted, you strove stoutly, man;
The odds were great; I honor you;
  Man honors man.

"Pickets fraternizing over coffee and exchanging newspapers," detail from a panel of "Scenes near Richmond." By Alfred R. Waud. *Harper's Weekly,* July 26, 1862.

"Still silent, friend? can grudges be?
10   Yet am I held a foe?—
Turned to the wall, on his cot he lies—
   Never I'll leave him so!
Brave one! I here implore your hand;
  Dumb still? all fellowship fled?
15 Nay, then, I'll have this stubborn hand!"
   He snatched it—it was dead.

On the Slain Collegians.

Youth is the time when hearts are large,
   And stirring wars
Appeal to the spirit which appeals in turn
   To the blade it draws.
5 If woman incite, and duty show
  (Though made the mask of Cain),
Or weather it be Truth's sacred cause,
  Who can aloof remain
That shares youth's ardor, uncooled by the snow
10   Of wisdom or sordid gain?

The liberal arts and nurture sweet
Which give his gentleness to man—
  Train him to honor, lend him grace
Through bright examples meet—
15 That culture which makes never wan
With underminings deep, but holds
  The surface still, its fitting place,
  And so gives sunniness to the face
And bravery to the heart; what troops
20 Of generous boys in happiness thus bred—
  Saturnians through life's Tempe led,
Went from the North and came from the South,
With golden mottoes in the mouth,
  To lie down midway on a bloody bed.

25 Woe for the homes of the North,
And woe for the seats of the South:
All who felt life's spring in prime,
And were swept by the wind of their place and time—

All lavish hearts, on whichever side,
30   Of birth urbane or courage high,
Armed them for the stirring wars—
Armed them—some to die.
    Apollo-like in pride,
Each would slay his Python—caught
35 The maxims in his temple taught—
  Aflame with sympathies whose blaze
Perforce enwrapped him—social laws,
  Friendship and kin, and by-gone days—
Vows, kisses—every heart unmoors,
40 And launches into the seas of wars.
What could they else—North or South?
Each went forth with blessings given
By priests and mothers in the name of Heaven;
    And honor in both was chief.
45 Warred one for Right, and one for Wrong?
So be it; but they both were young—
Each grape to his cluster clung,
All their elegies are sung.

The anguish of maternal hearts
50   Must search for balm divine;
But well the striplings bore their fated parts
  (The heavens all parts assign)—
Never felt life's care or cloy.
Each bloomed and died an unabated Boy;
55 Nor dreamed what death was—thought it mere
Sliding into some vernal sphere.
They knew the joy, but leaped the grief,
Like plants that flower ere comes the leaf—
Which storms lay low in kindly doom,
60 And kill them in their flush of bloom.

America.

I.

WHERE the wings of a sunny Dome expand
I saw a Banner in gladsome air—
Starry, like Berenice's Hair—
Afloat in broadened bravery there;

"Funeral 1st Mass. arty. Harrison's landing."

5   With undulating long-drawn flow,
     As rolled Brazilian billows go
     Voluminously o'er the Line.
     The Land reposed in peace below;
       The children in their glee
10   Were folded to the exulting heart
       Of young Maternity.

II.

Later, and it streamed in fight
   When tempest mingled with the fray,
And over the spear-point of the shaft
15   I saw the ambiguous lightning play.
Valor with Valor strove, and died:
Fierce was Despair, and cruel was Pride;
And the lorn Mother speechless stood,
Pale at the fury of her brood.

III.

20 Yet later, and the silk did wind
      Her fair cold form;
Little availed the shining shroud,
   Though ruddy in hue, to cheer or warm.
A watcher looked upon her low, and said—
25   She sleeps, but sleeps, she is not dead.

Ford near Shepherdston on the Potomac with pickets firing across the river. By Alfred R. Waud. *Harper's Weekly,* October 11, 1862.

But in that sleep contortion showed
The terror of the vision there—
A silent vision unavowed,
Revealing earth's foundation bare,
30   And Gorgon in her hidden place.
It was a thing of fear to see
So foul a dream upon fair a face,
And the dreamer lying in that starry shroud.

IV.

But from the trance she sudden broke—
25   The trance, or death into promoted life;
At her feet a shivered yoke,
And in her aspect turned to heaven
No trace of passion or of strife—
A clear calm look. It spake of pain,
40   But such as purifies from stain—
Sharp pangs that never come again—
And triumph repressed by knowledge meet,
Power dedicate, and hope grown wise,

And youth matured for age's seat—
45   Law on her brow and empire in her eyes.
        So she, with graver air and lifted flag;
While the shadow, chased by light,
Fled along the far-drawn height,
        And left her on the crag.

"5th excelsior."   By Alfred R. Waud.

On the Home Guards
who perished in the Defense of Lexington, Missouri.

THE men who here in harness died
    Fell not in vain, though in defeat.
They by their end well fortified
    The Cause, and built retreat
(With memory of their valor tried)
For emulous hearts in many an after fray—
Hearts sore beset, which died at bay.

5

"Funeral of Col. Vosburgh. The Hearse approaching the R. R. Depot." [Detail.]
By Alfred R. Waud. *New York Illustrated News*, June 8, 1861.

Inscription
for Graves at Pea Ridge, Arkansas.

LET none misgive we died amiss
  When here we strove in furious fight:
Furious it was; nathless was this
  Better than tranquil plight,
5   And tame surrender of the Cause
Hallowed by hearts and by the laws.
    We here who warred for Man and Right,
The choice of warring never laid with us.
    There we were ruled by the traitor's choice.
10   Nor long we stood to trim and poise,
But marched, and fell—victorious!

"Group of Rhode Island Soldiers. Company C. Full Dress with Blanket, Fatigue. Officer. Full Marching order. Burnside rifles." By Alfred R. Waud. "This uniform is dark blue shirt belted round waist—black felt hat and gray pants. The blanket is Scarlet with black bar near edge. Try and Keep the likeness of the Captain his beard is very gray." {Note on back of sketch.}

"Arms at port." By Alfred R. Waud.

The Fortitude of the North
under the Disaster of the Second Manassas.

THEY take no shame for dark defeat
    While prizing yet each victory won,
Who fight for the Right through all retreat,
    Nor pause until their work is done.
5   The Cape-of-Storms is proof to every throe;
    Vainly against that foreland beat
Wild winds aloft and wilder waves below:
    The black cliffs gleam through rents in sleet
When the livid Antarctic storm-clouds glow.

On the Men of Maine
killed in the Victory of Baton Rouge, Louisiana.

AFAR they fell. It was the zone
    Of fig and orange, cane and lime
(A land how all unlike their own,
    With the cold pine-grove overgrown),
5   But still their Country's clime.
And there in youth they died for her—
        The Volunteers,
For her went up their dying prayers:
    So vast the Nation, yet so strong the tie.
10 What doubt shall come, then, to deter
    The Republic's earnest faith and courage high.

An Epitaph.

WHEN Sunday tidings from the front
    Made pale the priest and people,
And heavily the blessing went,
    And bells were dumb in the steeple;
5   The Soldier's widow (summering sweetly here,
    In shade by waving beeches lent)
    Felt deep at heart her faith content,
And priest and people borrowed of her cheer.

"Battle near Upperville {Va.}. Ashby Gap in Distance." By Alfred R. Waud.
Harper's Magazine, July 11, 1863.

Inscription
for Marye's Heights, Fredericksburg.

To them who crossed the flood
And climbed the hill, with eyes
  Upon the heavenly flag intent,
  And through the deathful tumult went
Even unto death: to them this Stone—
Erect, where they were overthrown—
  Of more than victory the monument.

5

"Discovering the bodies of the slain in the Potomac river." By Alfred R. Waud.

The Mound by the Lake.

THE grass shall never forget this grave.
When homeward footing it in the sun
   After the weary ride by rail,
The stripling soldiers passed her door,
5   Wounded perchance, or wan and pale,
She left her household work undone—
Duly the wayside table spread,
   With evergreens shaded, to regale
Each travel-spent and grateful one.
10   So warm her heart—childless—unwed,
Who like a mother comforted.

"Yorktown."

On the Slain at Chickamauga.

HAPPY are they and charmed in life
   Who through long wars arrive unscarred
At peace. To such the wreath be given,
If they unfalteringly have striven—
5   In honor, as in limb, unmarred.
Let cheerful praise be rife,
   And let them live their years at ease,
Musing on brothers who victorious died—
   Loved mates whose memory shall ever please.

10   And yet mischance is honorable too—
   Seeming defeat in conflict justified
Whose end to closing eyes is hid from view.
The will, that never can relent—
The aim, survivor of the bafflement,
15   Make this memorial due.

"Hospital attendants collecting the wounded after the engagement. Within our lines near Hatchers run." By William Waud. *Harper's Weekly*, October 29, 1864.

"Gen. Butler's Canal At Dutch Gap [James River east of Petersburg]."
By William Waud. *Harper's Weekly,* November 5, 1864.

An uninscribed Monument
on one of the Battle-fields of the Wilderness.

SILENCE and Solitude may hint
   (Whose home is in yon piny wood)
What I, though tableted, could never tell—
The din which here befell,
5   And striving of the multitude.
The iron cones and spheres of death
   Set round me in their rust,
      These, too, if just,
Shall speak with more than animated breath.
10   Thou who beholdest, if thy thought,
Not narrowed down to personal cheer,
Take in the import of the quiet here—
   The after-quiet—the calm full fraught;
Thou too wilt silent stand—
15   Silent as I, and lonesome as the land.

On Sherman's Men
who fell in the Assault of Kenesaw Mountain, Georgia.

THEY said that Fame her clarion dropped
  Because great deeds were done no more—
That even Duty knew no shining ends,
And Glory—'twas a fallen star!

5   But battle can heroes and bards restore.
      Nay, look at Kenesaw:
Perils the mailed ones never knew
Are lightly braved by the ragged coats of blue,
And gentler hearts are bared to deadlier war.

"A Regiment waiting for the order to march."

On the Grave
of a young Cavalry Officer killed in the Valley of Virginia.

BEAUTY and youth, with manners sweet, and friends—
  Gold, yet a mind not unenriched had he
Whom here low violets veil from eyes.
  But all these gifts transcended be:
5   His happier fortune in this mound you see.

"The Last Resting Place," detail from a panel of "Scenes near Richmond."
By Alfred R. Waud. *Harper's Weekly*, July 26, 1862.

A Requiem
for Soldiers lost in Ocean Transports.

WHEN, after storms that woodlands rue,
    To valleys comes atoning dawn,
The robins blithe their orchard-sports renew;
    And meadow-larks, no more withdrawn,
Caroling fly in the languid blue;
The while, from many a hid recess,
Alert to partake the blessedness,
The pouring mites their airy dance pursue.

So, after ocean's ghastly gales,
10   When laughing light of hoyden morning breaks,
Every finny hider wakes—
From vaults profound swims up with glittering scales;
Through the delightsome sea he sails,
With shoals of shining tiny things
15   Frolic on every wave that flings
Against the prow its showery spray;
All creatures joying in the morn,
Save them forever from joyance torn,
Whose bark was lost where now the dolphins play;
20   Save them that by the fabled shore,
Down the pale stream are washed away,
Far to the reef of bones are borne;
And never revisits them the light,
Nor sight of long-sought land and pilot more;
25   Nor heed they now the lone bird's flight
Round the lone spar where mid-sea surges pour.

"U.S. Transport 'Matanzas,' "

"R. R. bridge over the Chickahominy," detail from a panel of "Scenes near Richmond." By Alfred R. Waud. *Harper's Weekly,* July 26, 1862.

On a natural Monument
in a field of Georgia.

No trophy this—a Stone unhewn,
   And stands where here the field immures
The nameless brave whose palms are won.
Outcast they sleep; yet fame is nigh—
   Pure fame of deeds, not doers;
Nor deeds of men who bleeding die
   In cheer of hymns that round them float:
In happy dreams such close the eye.
But withering famine slowly wore,
   And slowly fell disease did gloat.
Even Nature's self did aid deny;
They choked in horror the pensive sigh.
   Yea, off from home sad Memory bore
(Though anguished Yearning heaved that way),
Lest wreck of reason might befall.
   As men in gales shun the lee shore,
Though there the homestead be, and call,
And thitherward winds and waters sway—
As such lorn mariners, so fared they.
But naught shall now their peace molest.
   Their fame is this: they did endure—
Endure, when fortitude was vain
To kindle any approving strain
Which they might hear. To these who rest,
   This healing sleep alone was sure.

Commemorative of a Naval Victory.

SAILORS there are of gentlest breed,
   Yet strong, like every goodly thing;
The discipline of arms refines,
   And the wave gives tempering.
5   The damasked blade its beam can fling;
It lends the last grave grace:
The hawk, the hound, and sworded nobleman
   In Titian's picture for a king,
Are of hunter or warrior race.

10   In social halls a favored guest
   In years that follow victory won,
How sweet to feel your festal fame

   In woman's glance instinctive thrown:
   Repose is yours—your deed is known,
15   It musks the amber wine;
It lives, and sheds a light from storied days
   Rich as October sunsets brown,
Which make the barren place to shine.

But seldom the laurel wreath is seen
20   Unmixed with pensive pansies dark;
There's a light and a shadow on every man
   Who at last attains his lifted mark—
   Nursing through night the ethereal spark.
Elate he never can be;
25   He feels that spirits which glad had hailed his worth,
   Sleep in oblivion.—The shark
Glides white through the phosphorus sea.

"Patapsco engaging Sullivan's Isl. {S.C.} Batteries."

"14th Brooklyn."

Presentation to the Authorities,
by Privates, of Colors captured in Battles ending in the
Surrender of Lee.

THESE flags of armies overthrown—
Flags fallen beneath the sovereign one
In end foredoomed which closes war;
We here, the captors, lay before
5   The altar which of right claims all—
Our Country. And as freely we,
   Revering ever her sacred call,
Could lay our lives down—though life be
Thrice loved and precious to the sense
10 Of such as reap the recompense
   Of life imperiled for just cause—
Imperiled, and yet preserved;
While comrades, whom Duty as strongly nerved,
Whose wives were all as dear, lie low.
15 But these flags given, glad we go
   To waiting homes with vindicated laws.

The Returned Volunteer to his Rifle.

OVER this hearth—my father's seat—
   Repose, to patriot-memory dear,
Thou tried companion, whom at last I greet
   By steepy banks of Hudson here.
5 How oft I told thee of this scene—
The Highlands blue—the river's narrowing sheen.
Little at Gettysburg we thought
To find such haven; but God kept it green.
Long rest! with belt, and bayonet, and canteen.

The Scout toward Aldie.

THE cavalry-camp lies on the slope
  Of what was late a vernal hill,
But now like a pavement bare—
An outpost in the perilous wilds
    Which ever are lone and still;
      But Mosby's men are there—
      Of Mosby best beware.

Great trees the troopers felled, and leaned
  In antlered walls about their tents;
Strict watch they kept; 'twas *Hark!* and *Mark!*
Unarmed none cared to stir abroad
  For berries beyond their forest-fence:
      As glides in seas the shark,
      Rides Mosby through green dark.

"Officer, Private, Rhode Island Reg. Blue shirt. Grey pants." By Alfred R. Waud.

15   All spake of him, but few had seen
          Except the maimed ones or the low;
      Yet rumor made him every thing—
      A farmer—woodman—refugee—
          The man who crossed the field but now;
20   A spell about his life did cling—
              Who to the ground shall Mosby bring?

      The morning-bugles lonely play,
          Lonely the evening-bugle calls—
      Unanswered voices in the wild;
25   The settled hush of birds in nest
          Becharms, and all the wood enthralls:
              Memory's self is so beguiled
              That Mosby seems a satyr's child.

      They lived as in the Eerie Land—
30   The fire-flies showed with fairy gleam;
      And yet from pine-tops one might ken
      The Capitol Dome—hazy—sublime—
          A vision breaking on a dream:
              So strange it was that Mosby's men
35   Should dare to prowl where the Dome was seen.

      A scout toward Aldie broke the spell.—
          The Leader lies before his tent
      Gazing at heaven's all-cheering lamp
      Through blandness of a morning rare;
40   His thoughts on bitter-sweets are bent:
              His sunny bride is in the camp—
              But Mosby—graves are beds of damp!

      The trumpet calls; he goes within;
          But none the prayer and sob may know:
45   Her hero he, but bridegroom too.
      Ah, love in a tent is a queenly thing,
          And fame, be sure, refines the vow;
              But fame fond wives have lived to rue,
              And Mosby's men fell deeds can do.

50   *Tan-tara! tan-tara! tan-tara!*
          Mounted and armed he sits a king;

For pride she smiles if now she peep—
Elate he rides at the head of his men;
He is young, and command is a boyish thing:
55   They file out into the forest deep—
Do Mosby and his rangers sleep?

The sun is gold, and the world is green,
Opal the vapors of morning roll;
The champing horses lightly prance—
60 Full of caprice, and the riders too
Curving in many a caricole.
But marshaled soon, by fours advance—
Mosby had checked that airy dance.

By the hospital-tent the cripples stand—
65   Bandage, and crutch, and cane, and sling,
And palely eye the brave array;
The froth of the cup is gone for them
(Caw! caw! the crows through the blueness wing):
Yet these were late as bold, as gay;
70   But Mosby—a clip, and grass is hay.

How strong they feel on their horses free,
Tingles the tendoned thigh with life;
Their cavalry-jackets make boys of all—
With golden breasts like the oriole;
75   The chat, the jest, and laugh are rife.
But word is passed from the front—a call
For order; the wood is Mosby's hall.

To which behest one rider sly
(Spurred, but unarmed) gave little heed—
80 Of dexterous fun not slow or spare,
He teased his neighbors of touchy mood,
Into plungings he pricked his steed:
A black-eyed man on a coal-black mare,
Alive as Mosby in mountain air.

85   His limbs were long, and large, and round;
He whispered, winked—did all but shout:
A healthy man for the sick to view;
The taste in his mouth was sweet at morn;

Little of care he cared about.
90   And yet of pains and pangs he knew—
In others maimed by Mosby's crew.

The Hospital Steward—even he
(Sacred in person as a priest),
And on his coat-sleeve broidered nice
95   Wore the caduceus, black and green.
No wonder he sat so light on his beast;
This cheery man in suit of price
Not even Mosby dared to slice.

They pass the picket by the pine
100   And hollow log—a lonesome place;
His horse adroop, and pistol clean;
'Tis cocked—kept leveled toward the wood;
Strained vigilance ages his childish face.
Since midnight has that stripling been
105   Peering for Mosby through the green.

Splashing they cross the freshet-flood,
And up the muddy bank they strain;
A horse at a spectral white-ash shies—
One of the span of the ambulance,
110   Black as a hearse. They give the rein:
Silent speed on a scout were wise,
Could cunning baffle Mosby's spies.

Rumor had come that a band was lodged
In green retreats of hills that peer
115   By Aldie (famed for the swordless charge).
Much store they'd heaped of captured arms
And, peradventure, pilfered cheer;
For Mosby's lads oft hearts enlarge
In revelry by some gorge's marge.

120   "Don't let your sabres rattle and ring;
To his oat-bag let each man give heed—
There now, that fellow's bag's untied,
Sowing the road with the precious grain.
Your carbines swing at hand—you need!

125   Look to yourselves, and your nags beside,
          Men who after Mosby ride."

       Picked lads and keen went sharp before—
          A guard, though scarce against surprise;
       And rearmost rode an answering troop,
130   But flankers none to right or left
          No bugle peals, no pennon flies:
             Silent they sweep, and fain would swoop
             On Mosby with an Indian whoop.

       On, right on through the forest land,
135   Nor man, nor maid, nor child was seen—
       Not even a dog. The air was still;
       The blackened hut they turned to see,
          And spied charred benches on the green;
             A squirrel sprang from the rotting mill
140   Whence Mosby sallied late, brave blood to spill.

       By worn-out fields they cantered on—
          Drear fields amid the woodlands wide;
       By cross-roads of some olden time,
       In which grew groves; by gate-stones down—
145   Grassed ruins of secluded pride:
             A strange lone land, long past the prime,
             Fit land for Mosby or for crime.

       The brook in the dell they pass. One peers
          Between the leaves: "Ay, there's the place—
150   There, on the oozy ledge—'twas there
       We found the body (Blake's, you know);
          Such whirlings, gurglings round the face—
             Shot drinking! Well, in war all's fair—
             So Mosby says. The bough—take care!"

155   Hard by, a chapel. Flower-pot mould
          Danked and decayed the shaded roof;
       The porch was punk; the clapboards spanned
       With ruffled lichens gray or green;
          Red coral-moss was not aloof;
160   And mid dry leaves green dead-man's-hand
             Groped toward that chapel in Mosby-land.

They leave the road and take the wood,
   And mark the trace of ridges there—
A wood where once had slept the farm—
165   A wood where once tobacco grew
     Drowsily in the hazy air,
       And wrought in all kind things a calm—
       Such influence, Mosby! bids disarm.

To ease even yet the place did woo—
170   To ease which pines unstirring share,
For ease the weary horses sighed:
Halting, and slackening girths, they feed,
   Their pipes they light, they loiter there;
      Then up, and urging still the Guide,
175   On, and after Mosby ride.

This Guide in frowzy coat of brown,
   And beard of ancient growth and mould,
Bestrode a bony steed and strong,
As suited well with bulk he bore—
180   A wheezy man with depth of hold
      Who jouncing went. A staff he swung—
      A wight whom Mosby's wasp had stung.

Burnt out and homeless—hunted long!
   That wheeze he caught in autumn-wood
185 Crouching (a fat man) for his life,
And spied his lean son 'mong the crew
   That probed the covert. Ah! black blood
      Was his 'gainst even child and wife—
      Fast friends to Mosby. Such the strife.

190 A lad, unhorsed by sliding girths,
   Strains hard to readjust his seat
Ere the main body show the gap
'Twixt them and the rear-guard; scrub-oaks near
   He sidelong eyes, while hands move fleet;
195   Then mounts and spurs. One drops his cap—
      "Let Mosby find!" nor heeds mishap.

A gable time-stained peeps through trees:
   "You mind the fight in the haunted house?

That's it; we clenched them in the room—
200   An ambuscade of ghosts, we thought,
      But proved sly rebels on a bouse!
         Luke lies in the yard." The chimneys loom:
         Some muse on Mosby—some on doom.

Less nimbly now through brakes they wind,
205   And ford wild creeks where men have drowned;
They skirt the pool, avoid the fen,
And so till night, when down they lie,
    Their steeds still saddled, in wooded ground:
      Rein in hand they slumber then,
210   Dreaming of Mosby's cedarn den.

But Colonel and Major friendly sat
    Where boughs deformed low made a seat.
The Young Man talked (all sworded and spurred)
Of the partisan's blade he longed to win,
215   And frays in which he meant to beat.
      The grizzled Major smoked, and heard:
      "But what's that—Mosby?" "No, a bird."

A contrast here like sire and son,
    Hope and Experience sage did meet;
220   The Youth was brave, the Senior too;
But through the Seven Days one had served,
    And gasped with the rear-guard in retreat:
      So he smoked and smoked, and the wreath he blew—
      "Any *sure* news of Mosby's crew?"

225   He smoked and smoked, eying the while
    A huge tree hydra-like in growth—
Moon-tinged—with crook'd boughs rent or lopped—
Itself a haggard forest. "Come!"
    The Colonel cried, "to talk you're loath;
230   D'ye hear? I say he must be stopped,
      This Mosby—caged, and hair close cropped."

"Of course; but what's that dangling there?"
    "Where?" "From the tree—that gallows-bough;"
    "A bit of frayed bark, is it not?"
235   "Ay—or a rope; did *we* hang last?—

Don't like my neckerchief any how;"
He loosened it: "O ay, we'll stop
This Mosby—but that vile jerk and drop!"

By peep of light they feed and ride,
240 Gaining a grove's green edge at morn,
And mark the Aldie hills uprear
And five gigantic horsemen carved
  Clear-cut against the sky withdrawn;
    Are more behind? an open snare?
245   Or Mosby's men but watchmen there?

The ravaged land was miles behind,
  And Loudon spread her landscape rare;
Orchards in pleasant lowlands stood,
Cows were feeding, a cock loud crew,
250 But not a friend at need was there;
    The valley-folk were only good
    To Mosby and his wandering brood.

What best to do? what mean yon men?
  Colonel and Guide their minds compare;
255 Be sure some looked their Leader through;
Dismounted, on his sword he leaned
  As one who feigns an easy air;
    And yet perplexed he was they knew—
    Perplexed by Mosby's mountain-crew.

260 The Major hemmed as he would speak,
  But checked himself, and left the ring
Of cavalrymen about their Chief—
Young courtiers mute who paid their court
  By looking with confidence on their king;
265   They knew him brave, foresaw no grief—
    But Mosby—the time to think is brief.

The Surgeon (sashed in sacred green)
  Was glad 'twas not for *him* to say
What next should be; if a trooper bleeds,
270 Why he will do his best, as wont,
  And his partner in black will aid and pray;

But judgment bides with him who leads,
And Mosby many a problem breeds.

275
This Surgeon was the kindliest man
    That ever a callous trade professed;
He felt for him, that Leader young,
And offered medicine from his flask:
    The Colonel took it with marvelous zest.
        For such fine medicine good and strong,
280
        Oft Mosby and his foresters long.

A charm of proof. "Ho, Major, come—
    Pounce on you men! Take half your troop,
Through the thickets wind—pray speedy be—
And gain their rear. And, Captain Morn,
285
    Picket these roads—all travelers stop;
        The rest to the edge of this crest with me,
        That Mosby and his scouts may see."

Commanded and done. Ere the sun stood steep,
    Back came the Blues, with a troop of Grays,
290
Ten riding double—luckless ten!—
Five horses gone, and looped hats lost,
    And love-locks dancing in a maze—
        Certes, but sophomores from the glen
        Of Mosby—not his veteran men.

295
"Colonel," said the Major, touching his cap,
    "We've had our ride, and here they are."
"Well done! how many found you there?"
"As many as I bring you here."
    "And no one hurt?" "There'll be no scar—
300
        One fool was battered." "Find their lair?"
        "Why, Mosby's brood camp every where."

He sighed, and slid down from his horse,
    And limping went to a spring-head nigh.
"Why, bless me, Major, not hurt, I hope?"
305
"Battered my knee against a bar
    When the rush was made; all right by-and-by.—
        Halloa! they gave you too much rope—
        Go back to Mosby, eh? elope?"

Just by the low-hanging skirt of wood
310   The guard, remiss, had given a chance
For a sudden sally into the cover—
But foiled the intent, nor fired a shot,
    Though the issue was a deadly trance;
        For, hurled 'gainst an oak that humped low over,
315   Mosby's man fell, pale as a lover.

They pulled some grass his head to ease
    (Lined with blue shreds a ground-nest stirred).
The Surgeon came—"Here's a to-do!"
"Ah!" cried the Major, darting a glance,
320   This fellow's the one that fired and spurred
        Down hill, but met reserves below—
        My boys, not Mosby's—so we go!"

The Surgeon—bluff, red, goodly man—
    Kneeled by the hurt one; like a bee
325 He toiled. The pale young Chaplain too—
(Who went to the wars for cure of souls,
    And his own student-ailments)—he
        Bent over likewise; spite the two,
        Mosby's poor man more pallid grew.

330 Meanwhile the mounted captives near
    Jested; and yet they anxious showed;
Virginians; some of family-pride,
And young, and full of fire, and fine
    In open feature and cheek that glowed;
335   And here thralled vagabonds now they ride—
        But list! one speaks for Mosby's side.

"Why, three to one—your horses strong—
    Revolvers, rifles, and a surprise—
Surrender we account no shame!
340 We live, are gay, and life is hope;
    We'll fight again when fight is wise.
        There are plenty more from where we came;
        But go find Mosby—start the game!"

Yet one there was who looked but glum;
345   In middle-age, a father he,

And this his first experience too:
"They shot at my heart when my hands were up—
   This fighting's crazy work, I see!"
      But noon is high; what next to do?
350   The woods are mute, and Mosby is the foe.

"Save what we've got," the Major said;
   "Bad plan to make a scout too long;
The tide may turn, and drag them back,
And more beside. These rides I've been,
355   And every time a mine was sprung.
      To rescue, mind, they won't be slack—
      Look out for Mosby's rifle-crack."

"We'll welcome it! give crack for crack!
   Peril, old lad, is what I seek."
360 "O then, there's plenty to be had—
By all means on, and have our fill!"
    With that, grotesque, the writhed his neck,
      Showing a scar by buck-shot made—
      "Kind Mosby's Christmas gift," he said.

365 "But, Colonel, my prisoners—let a guard
   Make sure of them, and lead to camp.
That done, we're free for a dark-room fight
If so you say." The other laughed;
   "Trust me, Major, nor throw a damp.
370   But first to try a little sleight—
      Sure news of Mosby would suit me quite."

Herewith he turned—"Reb, have a dram?"
   Holding the Surgeon's flask with a smile
To a young scapegrace from the glen.
375 "O yes!" he eagerly replied,
   "And thank you, Colonel, but—any guile?
      For if you think we'll blab—why, then
      You don't know Mosby or his men."

The Leader's genial air relaxed.
380   "Best give it up," a whisperer said.
"By heaven, I'll range their rebel den!"
"They'll treat you well," the captive cried;

"They're all like us—handsome—well bred:
In wood or town, with sword or pen,
385   Polite is Mosby, bland his men."

"Where were you, lads, last night?—come, tell!"
"We?—at a wedding in the Vale—
The bridegroom our comrade; by his side
Belisent, my cousin—O, so proud
390   Of her young love with old wounds pale—
A Virginian girl! God bless her pride—
Of a crippled Mosby-man the bride!"

"Four walls shall mend that saucy mood,
And moping prisons tame him down,"
395   Said Captain Cloud. "God help that day,"
Cried Captain Morn, "and he so young.
But hark, he sings—a madcap one!"
*"O we multiply merrily in the May,
The birds and Mosby's men, they say!"*

400   While echoes ran, a wagon old,
Under stout guard of Corporal Chew
Came up; a lame horse, dingy white,
With clouted harness; ropes in hand,
Cringed the humped driver, black in hue;
405   By him (for Mosby's band a sight)
A sister-rebel sat, her veil held tight.

"I picked them up," the Corporal said,
"Crunching their way over stick and root,
Through yonder wood. The man here—Cuff—
410   Says they are going to Leesburg town."
The Colonel's eye took in the group;
The veiled one's hand he spied—enough!
Not Mosby's. Spite the gown's poor stuff,

Off went his hat: "Lady, fear not;
415   We soldiers do what we deplore—
I must detain you till we march."
The stranger nodded. Nettled now,
He grew politer than before:—
" 'Tis Mosby's fault, this halt and search."
420   The lady stiffened in her starch.

"My duty, madam, bids me now
   Ask what may seem a little rude.
Pardon—that veil—withdraw it, please
(Corporal! make every man fall back);
425   Pray, now, I do but what I should;
         Bethink you, 'tis in masks like these
        That Mosby haunts the villages."

Slowly the stranger drew her veil,
   And looked the Soldier in the eye—
430 A glance of mingled foul and fair;
Sad patience in a proud disdain,
   And more than quietude. A sigh
      She heaved, as if all unaware,
       And far seemed Mosby from her care.

435 She came from Yewton Place, her home,
   So ravaged by the war's wild play—
Campings, and foragings, and fires—
That now she sought an aunt's abode.
   Her kinsmen? In Lee's army, they.
440   The black? A servant, late her sire's.
     And Mosby? Vainly he inquires.

He gazed, and sad she met his eye;
   "In the wood yonder were you lost?"
No; at the forks they left the road
445 Because of hoof-prints (thick they were—
     Thick as the words in notes thrice crossed),
      And fearful, made that episode.
      In fear of Mosby? None she showed.

Her poor attire again he scanned:
450   "Lady, once more; I grieve to jar
On all sweet usage, but must plead
To have what peeps there from your dress;
     That letter—'tis justly prize of war."
      She started—gave it—she must need.
455   " 'Tis not from Mosby? May I read?"

And straight such matter he perused
   That with the Guide he went apart.

The Hospital Steward's turn began:
"Must squeeze this darkey; every tap
460   Of knowledge we are bound to start."
            "Garry," she said, "tell all you can
            Of Colonel Mosby—that brave man."

"Dun know much, sare; and missis here
            Know less dan me. But dis I know—"
465   "Well, what?" "I dun know what I know."
"A knowing answer!" The hump-back coughed,
            Rubbing his yellowish wool like tow.
                "Come—Mosby—tell!" "O dun look so!
                My gal nursed missis—let we go."

470   "Go where?" demanded Captain Cloud;
            "Back into bondage? Man, you're free!"
"Well, *let* we free!" The Captain's brow
Lowered; the Colonel came—had heard:
            "Pooh! pooh! his simple heart I see—
475   A faithful servant.—Lady" (a bow),
            "Mosby's abroad—with us you'll go.

"Guard! look to your prisoners; back to camp!
            The man in the grass—can he mount and away?
Why, how he groans!" "Bad inward bruise—
480   Might lug him along in the ambulance."
            "Coals to Newcastle! let him stay.
                Boots and saddles!—our pains we lose,
                Nor care I if Mosby hear the news!"

But word was sent to a house at hand,
485   And a flask was left by the hurt one's side.
They seized in that same house a man,
Neutral by day, by night a foe—
            So charged his neighbor late, the Guide.
                A grudge? Hate will do what it can;
490   Along he went for a Mosby-man.

No secrets now; the bugle calls;
            The open road they take, nor shun
The hill; retrace the weary way.
But one there was who whispered low,

495   "This is a feint—we'll back anon;
    Young Hair-Brains don't retreat, they say;
    A brush with Mosby is the play!"

  They rode till eve. Then on a farm
  That lay along a hill-side green,
500 Bivouacked. Fires were made, and then
  Coffee was boiled; a cow was coaxed
   And killed, and savory roasts were seen;
   And under the lee of a cattle-pen
   The guard supped freely with Mosby's men.

505 The ball was bandied to and fro;
   Hits were given and hits were met:
  "Chickamauga, Feds—take off your hat!"
  "But the Fight in the Clouds repaid you, Rebs!"
   "Forgotten about Manassas yet?"
510   Chatting and chaffing, and tit for tat,
  Mosby's clan with the troopers sat.

  "Here comes the moon!" a captive cried;
   "A song! what say? Archy, my lad!"
  Hailing the still one of the clan
515 (A boyish face with girlish hair),
   "Give us that thing poor Pansy made
    Last year." He brightened, and began;
   And this was the song of Mosby's man:

    Spring is come; she shows her pass—
520   *Wild violets cool!*
    South of woods a small close grass—
     A vernal wood!
    Leaves are a'bud on the sassafras—
     They'll soon be full:
525   *Blessings on the friendly screen—*
    I'm for the South! says the leafage green.

    Robins! fly, and take your fill
     Of out-of-doors—
    Garden, orchard, meadow, hill,
530   *Barns and bowers;*
    Take your fill, and have your will—

178 THE BATTLE-PIECES OF HERMAN MELVILLE

> *Virginia's yours!*
> *But, bluebirds! keep away, and fear*
> *The ambuscade in bushes here.*

535 "A green song that," a sergeant said;
  "But where's poor Pansy? gone, I fear."
"Ay, mustered out at Ashby's Gap."
"I see; now for a live man's song;
  Ditty for ditty—prepare to cheer.
540   My bluebirds, you can fling a cap!
    You barehead Mosby-boys—why—clap!"

> *Nine Blue-coats want a-nutting*
>   *Slyly in Tennessee—*
> *Not for chestnuts—better than that—*
545   *Hush, you bumble-bee!*
>   *Nutting, nutting—*
>   *All through the year there's nutting!*

> *A tree they spied so yellow,*
>   *Rustling in motion queer;*
550 *In they fired, and down they dropped—*
>   *Butternuts, my dear!*
>   *Nutting, nutting—*
>   *Who'll 'list to go a-nutting?*

Ah! why should good fellows foemen be?
555   And who would dream that foes they were—
Larking and singing so friendly then—
A family likeness in every face.
  But Captain Cloud made sour demur:
    "Guard! keep your prisoners *in* the pen,
560   And let none talk with Mosby's men."

That captain was a valorous one
  (No irony, but honest truth),
Yet down from his brain cold drops distilled,
Making stalactites in his heart—
565   A conscientious soul, forsooth;
    And with a formal hate was filled
    Of Mosby's band; and some he'd killed.

Meantime the lady rueful sat,
　Watching the flicker of a fire
570　Where the Colonel played the outdoor host
In brave old hall of ancient Night.
　But ever the dame grew shyer and shyer,
　　Seeming with private grief engrossed—
　　Grief far from Mosby, housed or lost.

575　The ruddy embers showed her pale.
　The Soldier did his best devoir:
"Some coffee?—no?—a cracker?—one?"
Cared for her servant—sought to cheer:
　"I know, I know—a cruel war!
580　　But wait—even Mosby 'll eat his bun;
　　The Old Hearth—back to it anon!"

But cordial words no balm could bring;
　She sighed, and kept her inward chafe,
And seemed to hate the voice of glee—
585　Joyless and tearless. Soon he called
　An escort: "See this lady safe
　　In yonder house.—Madam, you're free.
　　And now for Mosby.—Guide! with me."

("A night-ride, eh?") "Tighten your girths!
590　　But, buglers! not a note from you.
Fling more rails on the fires—a blaze!"
("Sergeant, a feint—I told you so—
　Toward Aldie again. Bivouac, adieu!")
　　After the cheery flames they gaze,
595　　Then back for Mosby through the maze.

The moon looked through the trees, and tipped
　The scabbards with her elfin beam;
The Leader backward cast his glance,
Proud of the cavalcade that came—
600　A hundred horses, bay and cream:
　　"Major! look how the lads advance—
　　Mosby we'll have in the ambulance!"

"No doubt, no doubt:—was that a hare?—
　First catch, then cook; and cook him brown."

605   Trust me to catch," the other cried—
          "The lady's letter!—a dance, man, dance
          This night is given in Leesburg town!"
              "He'll be there too!" wheezed out the Guide;
              "That Mosby loves a dance and ride!"

610   "The lady, ah!—the lady's letter—
          A *lady,* then, is in the case,"
          Muttered the Major. "Ay, her aunt
          Writes her to come by Friday eve
          (To-night), for people of the place,
615   At Mosby's last fight jubilant,
              A party give, though table-cheer be scant."

          The Major hemmed. "Then this night-ride
          We owe to her?—One lighted house
          In a town else dark.—The moths, begar!
620   Are not quite yet all dead!" "How? how?"
          "A mute, meek, mournful little mouse!—
              Mosby has wiles which subtle are—
              But woman's wiles in wiles of war!"

          "Tut, Major! by what craft or guile—"
625   "Can't tell! but he'll be found in wait.
          Softly we enter, say, the town—
          Good! pickets post, and all so sure—
              When—crack! the rifles from every gate,
                  The Gray-backs fire—dash up and down—
630   Each alley unto Mosby known!"

          "Now, Major, now—you take dark views
              Of a moonlight night." "Well, well, we'll see,"
          And smoked as if each whiff were gain.
          The other mused; then sudden asked,
635   "What would you do in grand decree?"
                  "I'd beat, if I could, Lee's armies—then
                  Send constables after Mosby's men."

          "Ay! ay!—you're odd." The moon sailed up;
              On through the shadowy land they went.
640   *"Names must be made and printed be!"*
          Hummed the blithe Colonel. "Doc, your flask!

Major, I drink to your good content.
My pipe is out—enough for me!
One's buttons shine—does Mosby see?

645   "But what comes here?" A man from the front
Reported a tree athwart the road.
"Go round it, then; no time to bide;
All right—go on! Were one to stay
For each distrust of a nervous mood,
650   Long miles we'd make in this our ride
Through Mosby-land.—On! with the Guide!"

Then sportful to the Surgeon turned:
"Green sashes hardly serve by night!"
"Nor bullets nor bottles," the Major sighed,
655   "Against these moccasin-snakes—such foes
As seldom come to solid fight:
They kill and vanish; through grass they glide;
Devil take Mosby!"—his horse here shied.

"Hold! look—the tree, like a dragged balloon;
660   A globe of leaves—some trickery here;
My nag is right—best now be shy."
A movement was made, a hubbub and snarl;
Little was plain—they blindly steer.
The Pleiads, as from ambush sly,
665   Peep out—Mosby's men in the sky!

As restive they turn, how sore they feel,
And cross, and sleepy, and full of spleen,
And curse the war. "Fools, North and South!"
Said one right out. "O for a bed!
670   O now to drop in this woodland green!"
He drops as the syllables leave his mouth—
Mosby speaks from the undergrowth—

Speaks in a volley! out jets the flame!
Men fall from their saddles like plums from trees;
675   Horses take fright, reins tangle and bind;
"Steady—dismount—form—and into the wood!"
They go, but find what scarce can please:

Their steeds have been tied in the field behind,
And Mosby's men are off like the wind.

680   Sound the recall! vain to pursue—
The enemy scatters in wilds he knows,
To reunite in his own good time;
And, to follow, they need divide—
To come lone and lost on crouching foes:
685   Maple and hemlock, beech and lime,
Are Mosby's confederates, share the crime.

"Major," burst in a bugler small,
"The fellow we left in Loudon grass—
Sir Slyboots with the inward bruise,
690   His voice I heard—the very same—
Some watchword in the ambush pass;
Ay, sir, we had him in his shoes—
We caught him—Mosby—but to lose!"

"Go, go!—these saddle-dreamers! Well,
695   And here's another.—Cool, sir, cool!"
"Major, I saw them mount and sweep,
And one was humped, or I mistake,
And in the skurry dropped his wool."
"A wig! go fetch it:—the lads need sleep;
700   They'll next see Mosby in a sheep!

"Come, come, fall back! reform your ranks—
All's jackstraws here! Where's Captain Morn?—
We've parted like boats in a raging tide!
But stay—the Colonel—did he charge?
705   And comes he there? 'Tis streak of dawn;
Mosby is off, the woods are wide—
Hist! there's a groan—this crazy ride!"

As they searched for the fallen, the dawn grew chill;
They lay in the dew: "Ah! hurt much, Mink?
710   And—yes—the Colonel!" Dead! but so calm
That death seemed nothing—even death,
The thing we deem every thing heart can think;
Amid wilding roses that shed their balm,
Careless of Mosby he lay—in a charm!

715 The Major took him by the hand—
  Into the friendly clasp it bled
(A ball through heart and hand he rued):
"Good-by!" and gazed with humid glance;
  Then in a hollow revery said,
720   "The weakest thing is lustihood;
   But Mosby"—and he checked his mood.

"Where's the advance?—cut off, by heaven!
  Come, Surgeon, how with your wounded there?"
"The ambulance will carry all."
725 "Well, get them in; we go to camp.
  Seven prisoners gone? for the rest have care."
   Then to himself, "This grief is gall;
   That Mosby!—I'll cast a silver ball!"

"Ho!" turning—"Captain Cloud, you mind
730 The place where the escort went—so shady?
Go, search every closet low and high,
And barn, and bin, and hidden bower
  Every covert—find that lady!
   And yet I may misjudge her—ay,
735   Women (like Mosby) mystify.

"We'll see. Ay, Captain, go—with speed!
  Surround and search; each living thing
Secure; that done, await us where
We last turned off. Stay! fire the cage
740 If the birds be flown." By the cross-road spring
   The bands rejoined; no words; the glare
   Told all. Had Mosby plotted there?

The weary troop that wended now—
  Hardly it seemed the same that pricked
745 Forth to the forest from the camp:
Foot-sore horses, jaded men;
  Every backbone felt as nicked,
   Each eye dim as a sick-room lamp,
   All faces stamped with Mosby's stamp.

750 In order due the Major rode—
  Chaplain and Surgeon on either hand;

A riderless horse a negro led;
In a wagon the blanketed sleeper went;
  Then the ambulance with the bleeding band;
755   And, an emptied oat-bag on each head,
          Went Mosby's men, and marked the dead.

What gloomed them? what so cast them down,
  And changed the cheer that late they took,
As double-guarded now they rode
760 Between the files of moody men?
    Some sudden consciousness they brook,
        Or dread the sequel. That night's blood
        Disturbed even Mosby's brotherhood.

The flagging horses stumbled at roots,
765   Floundered in mires, or clinked the stones;
No rider spake except aside;
But the wounded cramped in the ambulance,
    It was horror to hear their groans—
        Jerked along in the woodland ride,
770   While Mosby's clan their revery hide.

The Hospital Steward—even he—
  Who on the sleeper kept his glance,
Was changed; late bright-black beard and eye
Looked now hearse-black; his heavy heart,
775   Like his fagged mare, no more could dance;
        His grape was now a raisin dry:
        'Tis Mosby's homily—*Man must die.*

The amber sunset flushed the camp
  As on the hill their eyes they fed;
780 The pickets dumb looks at the wagon dart;
A handkerchief waves from the bannered tent—
    As white, alas! the face of the dead:
        Who shall the withering news impart?
        The bullet of Mosby goes through heart to heart!

785 They buried him where the lone ones lie
  (Lone sentries shot on midnight post)—
A green-wood grave-yard hid from ken,
Where sweet-fern flings an odor nigh—

Yet held in fear for the gleaming ghost!
790   Though the bride should see threescore and ten,
She will dream of Mosby and his men.

Now halt the verse, and turn aside—
The cypress falls athwart the way;
No joy remains for bard to sing;
795   And heaviest dole of all is this,
That other hearts shall be as gay
As hers that now no more shall spring:
To Mosby-land the dirges cling.

"Guerrilla." By Alfred R. Waud.

"Lost Horsemen in search of a road." By Alfred R. Waud. *Harper's Weekly,*
December 13, 1862.

"Mill at Stannardsville {Va.} containing grain for the C. S. Government."
By Alfred R. Waud. *Harper's Weekly*, March 26, 1864.

Lee in the Capitol.

(April, 1866.)

HARD pressed by numbers in his strait,
   Rebellion's soldier-chief no more contends—
Feels that the hour is come of Fate,
   Lays down one sword, and widened warfare ends.
5   The captain who fierce armies led
Becomes a quiet seminary's head—
Poor as his privates, earns his bread.
In studious cares and aims engrossed,
   Strives to forget Stuart and Stonewall dead—
10 Comrades and cause, station and riches lost,
   And all the ills that flock when fortune's fled.
No word he breathes of vain lament,
   Mute to reproach, nor hears applause—
His doom accepts, perforce content,
15   And acquiesces in asserted laws;
Secluded now would pass his life,
And leave to time the sequel of the strife.
   But missives from the Senators ran;
Not that they now would gaze upon a swordless foe,
20 And power made powerless and brought low:
   Reasons of state, 'tis claimed, require the man.
Demurring not, promptly he comes
By ways which show the blackened homes,
   And—last—the seat no more his own,
25 But Honor's; patriot grave-yards fill
The forfeit slopes of that patrician hill,
   And fling a shroud on Arlington.
The oaks ancestral all are low;
No more from the porch his glance shall go
30 Ranging the varied landscape o'er,
Far as the looming Dome—no more.
One look he gives, then turns aside,
Solace he summons from his pride:
"So be it! They await me now
35 Who wrought this stinging overthrow;
They wait me; not as on the day
Of Pope's impelled retreat in disarray—
By me impelled—when toward yon Dome

The clouds of war came rolling home."
40   The burst, the bitterness was spent,
The heart-burst bitterly turbulent,
And on he fared.

                    In nearness now
He marks the Capitol—a show
45   Lifted in amplitude, and set
With standards flushed with the glow of Richmond yet;
     Trees and green terraces sleep below.
Through the clear air, in sunny light,
The marble dazes—a temple white.

50   Intrepid soldier! had his blade been drawn
For yon starred flag, never as now
Bid to the Senate-house had he gone,
But freely, and in pageant borne,
As when brave numbers without number, massed,
55   Plumed the broad way, and pouring passed—
Bannered, beflowered between the shores
Of faces, and the dinn'd huzzas,
And balconies kindling at the sabre-flash,
'Mid roar of drums and guns, and cymbal-crash,
60   While Grant and Sherman shone in blue—
Close of the war and victory's long review.

Yet pride at hand still aidful swelled,
And up the hard ascent he held.
The meeting follows. In his mien
65   The victor and the vanquished both are seen—
All that he is, and what he late had been.
Awhile, with curious eyes they scan
The Chief who led invasion's van—
Allied by family to one,
70   Founder of the Arch the Invader warred upon:
Who looks at Lee must think of Washington;
In pain must think, and hide the thought,
So deep with grievous meaning it is fraught.

Secession in her soldier shows
75   Silent and patient; and they feel
     (Developed even in just success)

Dim inklings of a hazy future steal;
  Their thoughts their questions well express:
"Does the sad South still cherish hate?
80   Freely will Southern men with Northern mate?
The blacks—should we our arm withdraw,
Would that betray them? some distrust your law.
And how if foreign fleets should come—
Would the South then drive her wedges home?"
85   And more hereof. The Virginian sees—
Replies to such anxieties.
Discreet his answers run—appear
Briefly straightforward, coldly clear.

"If now," the Senators, closing, say,
90   "Aught else remain, speak out, we pray."

Hereat he paused; his better heart
Strove strongly then; prompted a worthier part
Than coldly to endure his doom.
Speak out? Ay, speak, and for the brave,
95   Who else no voice or proxy have;
Frankly their spokesman here become,
And the flushed North from her own victory save.
That inspiration overrode—
Hardly it quelled the galling load
100   Of pesonal ill. The inner feud
He, self-contained, a while withstood;
They waiting. In his troubled eye
Shadows from clouds unseen they spy;
They could not mark within his breast
105   The pang which pleading thought oppressed:
He spoke, nor felt the bitterness die.

"My word is given—it ties my sword;
Even were banners still abroad,
Never could I strive in arms again
110   While you, as fit, that pledge retain.
Our cause I followed, stood in field and gate—
All's over now, and now I follow Fate.
But this is naught. A People call—
A desolated land, and all
115   The brood of ills that press so sore,

The natural offspring of this civil war,
Which ending not in fame, such as might rear
Fitly its sculptured trophy here,
Yields harvest large of doubt and dread
120   To all who have the heart and head
To feel and know. How shall I speak?
Thoughts knot with thoughts, and utterance check.
Before my eyes there swims a haze,
Through mists departed comrades. gaze—
125   First to encourage, last that shall upbraid!
How shall I speak? The South would fain
Feel peace, have quiet law again—
Replant the trees for homestead-shade.
       You ask if she recants: she yields.
130   Nay, and would more; would blend anew,
As the bones of the slain in her forests do,
Bewailed alike by us and you.
       A voice comes out from these charnel-fields,
A plaintive yet unheeded one:
135   *'Died all in vain? both sides undone?'*
Push not your triumph; do not urge
Submissiveness beyond the verge.
Intestine rancor would you bide,
Nursing eleven sliding daggers in your side?
140   Far from my thought to school or threat;
I speak the things which hard beset.
Where various hazards meet the eyes,
To elect in magnanimity is wise.
Reap victory's fruit while sound the core;
145   What sounder fruit than re-established law?
I know your partial thoughts do press
Solely on us for war's unhappy stress;
But weigh—consider—look at all,
And broad anathema you'll recall.
150   The censor's charge I'll not repeat,
That meddlers kindled the war's white heat—
Vain intermeddlers and malign,
Both of the palm and of the pine;
I waive the thought—which never can be rife—
155   Common's the crime in every civil strife:
But this I feel, that North and South were driven
By Fate to arms. For *our* unshriven,

What thousands, truest souls, were tried—
    As never may any be again—
160 All those who stemmed Secession's pride,
But at last were swept by the urgent tide
    Into the chasm. I know their pain.
A story here may be applied:
'In Moorish lands there lived a maid
165   Brought to confess by vow the creed
    Of Christians. Fain would priests persuade
That now she must approve by deed
    The faith she kept. "What deed?" she asked.
"Your old sire leave, nor deem it sin,
170   And come with us." Still more they tasked
The sad one: "If heaven you'd win—
    Far from the burning pit withdraw,
Then must you learn to hate your kin,
    Yea, side against them—such the law,
175 For Moor and Christian are at war."
"Then will I never quit my sire,
But here with him through every trial go,
Nor leave him though in flames below—
God help me in his fire!" '
180 So in the South; vain every plea
'Gainst Nature's strong fidelity;
    True to the home and to the heart,
Throngs cast their lot with kith and kin,
    Foreboding, cleaved to the natural part—
185 Was this the unforgivable sin?
These noble spirits are yet yours to win.
Shall the great North go Sylla's way?
Proscribe? prolong the evil day?
Confirm the curse? infix the hate?
190 In Union's name forever alienate?
From reason who can urge the plea—
Freemen conquerors of the free?
When blood returns to the shrunken vein,
Shall the wound of the Nation bleed again?
195 Well may the wars wan thought supply,
And kill the kindling of the hopeful eye,
Unless you do what even kings have done
In leniency—unless you shun
To copy Europe in her worst estate—
200 Avoid the tyranny you reprobate."

He ceased. His earnestness unforeseen
Moved, but not swayed their former mien;
 And they dismissed him. Forth he went
Through vaulted walks in lengthened line
205 Like porches erst upon the Palatine:
  Historic reveries their lesson lent,
  The Past her shadow through the Future sent.

But no. Brave though the Soldier, grave his plea—
 Catching the light in the future's skies,
210 Instinct disowns each darkening prophecy:
  Faith in America never dies;
Heaven shall the end ordained fulfill,
We march with Providence cheery still.

A Meditation.
I

How often in the years that close,
 When truce had stilled the sieging gun,
The soldiers, mounting on their works,
 With mutual curious glance have run
5 From face to face along the fronting show,
And kinsman spied, or friend—even in a foe.

What thoughts conflicting than were shared,
 While sacred tenderness perforce
Welled from the heart and wet the eye;
10 And something of a strange remorse
Rebelled against the sanctioned sin of blood,
And Christian wars of natural brotherhood.

Then stirred the god within the breast—
 The witness that is man's at birth;
15 A deep misgiving undermined
  Each plea and subterfuge of earth;
They felt in that rapt pause, with warning rife,
Horror and anguish for the civil strife.

Of North or South they recked not then,
20 Warm passion cursed the cause of war:
Can Africa pay back this blood
 Spilt on Potomac's shore?
Yet doubts, as pangs, were vain the strife to stay,

"Hill where Genl. [S. H.] Weed was killed and ravine from which Rebels were driven by the 3rd Corps called by the soldiers the Slaughter Pen." By Alfred R. Waud.

And hands that fain had clasped again could slay.

25   How frequent in the camp was seen
     The herald from the hostile one,
   A guest and frank companion there
     When the proud formal talk was done;
   The pipe of peace was smoked even 'mid the war,
30   And fields in Mexico again fought o'er.
   In Western battle long they lay
     So near opposed in trench or pit,
   That foeman unto foeman called
     As men who screened in tavern sit:
35   "You bravely fight" each to the other said—
   "Toss us a biscuit!" o'er the wall it sped.

   And pale on those same slopes, a boy—
     A stormer, bled in noon-day glare;
   No aid the Blue-coats then could bring,

40   He cried to them who nearest were,
        And out there came 'mid howling shot and shell
        A daring foe who him befriended well.

        Mark the great Captains on both sides,
            The soldiers with the broad renown—
45   They all were messmates on the Hudson's marge,
            Beneath one roof they laid them down;
        And, free from hate in many an after pass,
        Strove as in school-boy rivalry of the class.

        A darker side there is; but doubt
50   In Nature's charity hovers there:
        If men for new agreement yearn,
            Then old upbraiding best forbear:
        "The South's the sinner!" Well, so let it be;
        But shall the North sin worse, and stand the Pharisee?

55   O, now that brave men yield the sword,
            Mine be the manful soldier view;
        By how much more they boldly warred,
            By so much more is mercy due:
        When Vicksburg fell, and the moody files marched out,
60   Silent the victors stood, scorning to raise a shout.

"Harper's Ferry by Moonlight—Maryland heights—Potomac river—Loudon
heights—Bolivar heights—Dec. 1863." By Alfred R. Waud.

SUPPLEMENT

WERE I fastidiously anxious for the symmetry of this book, it would close with the notes. But the times are such that patriotism—not free from solicitude—urges a claim overriding all literary scruples.

It is more than a year since the memorable surrender, but events have not yet rounded themselves into completion. Not justly can we complain of this. There has been an upheaval affecting the basis of things; to altered circumstances complicated adaptations are to be made; there are difficulties great and novel. But is Reason still waiting for Passion to spend itself? We have sung of the soldiers and sailors, but who shall hymn the politicians?

In view of the infinite desirableness of Re-establishment, and considering that, so far as feeling is concerned, it depends not mainly on the temper in which the South regards the North, but rather conversely; one who never was a blind adherent feels constrained to submit some thoughts, counting on the indulgence of his countrymen.

And, first, it may be said that, if among the feelings and opinions growing immediately out of a great civil convulsion, there are any which time shall modify or do away, they are presumably those of a less temperate and charitable cast.

There seems no reason why patriotism and narrowness should go together, or why intellectual impartiality[1] should be confounded with political trimming, or why serviceable truth should keep cloistered because not partisan. Yet the work of Reconstruction, if admitted to be feasible at all, demands little but common sense and Christian charity. Little but these? These are much.

Some of us are concerned because as yet the South shows no penitence. But what exactly do we mean by this? Since down to the close of the war she never confessed any for braving it, the only penitence now left her is that which springs solely from the sense of discomfiture; and since this evidently would be a contrition hypocritical, it would be unworthy in us to demand it. Certain it is that penitence, in the sense of voluntary humiliation, will never be displayed. Nor does this afford just ground for unreserved condemnation. It is enough, for all practical purposes, if the South have been taught by the terrors of civil war to feel that Secession, like Slavery, is against Destiny; that both now lie buried in one grave; that her fate is linked with ours; and that together we comprise the Nation.

The clouds of heroes who battled for the Union it is needless to eulogize here. But how of the soldiers on the other side? And when of a free community we name the soldiers, we thereby name the people. It was in subserviency to the slave-interest that Secession was plotted; but it was under the plea, plausibly urged, that certain inestimable rights guaranteed by the Constitution was directly menaced, that the people of the South were cajoled into revolution. Through the arts of the conspirators and the perversity of fortune, the most sensitive love of liberty was entrapped into the support of a war whose implied end was the erecting in our advanced century of an Anglo-American empire based upon the systematic degradation of man.

Spite this clinging reproach, however, signal military virtues and achievements have conferred upon the Confederate arms historioc fame, and upon certain of the commanders a renown extending beyond the sea—a renown which we of the North could not suppress, even if we would. In personal character, also, not a few of the military leaders of the South enforce forbearance; the memory of others the North refrains from disparaging; and some, with more or less of reluctance, she can respect. Posterity, sympathizing with our convictions, but removed from our passions, may perhaps go farther here. If George IV. could, out of the graceful instinct of a gentleman,[2] raise an honorable monument in the great fane of Christendom over the remains of the enemy of his dynasty, Charles Edward, the invader of England and victor in the rout at Preston Pans—upon whose head the king's ancestor but one reign removed had set a price— is it probable that the grandchildren of General Grant will pursue with rancor, or slur by sour neglect, the memory of Stonewall Jackson?[3]

But the South herself is not wanting in recent histories and biographies which record the deeds of her chieftains—writings freely published at the North by loyal houses, widely read here, and with a deep though saddened interest. By students of the war such works are hailed as welcome accessories, and tending to the completeness of the record.

Supposing a happy issue out of present perplexities, then, in the generation next to come, Southerners there will be wielding allegiance to the Union, feeling all their interests bound up in it, and yet cherishing unrebuked that kind of feeling for the memory of the soldiers of the fallen Confederacy that Burns, Scott, and the Ettrick Shepherd[4] felt for the memory of the gallant clansmen ruined through their fidelity to the Stuarts —a feeling whose passion was tempered by the poetry imbuing it, and which in no wise affected their loyalty to the Georges, and which, it may be added, indirectly contributed excellent things to literature. But, setting this view aside, dishonorable would it be in the South were she willing to abandon to shame the memory of brave men who with signal personal disinterestedness warred in her behalf, though from motives, as we believe, so deplorably astray.

Patriotism is not baseness, neither is it inhumanity. The mourners who this summer bear flowers to the mounds of the Virginian and Georgian dead are, in their domestic bereavement and proud affection, as sacred in the eye of Heaven as are those who go with similar offerings of tender grief and love into the cemeteries of our Northern martyrs. And yet, in one aspect, how needless to point the contrast.

Cherishing such sentiments, it will hardly occasion surprise that, in looking over the battle-pieces in he foregoing collection, I have been tempted to withdraw or modify some of them, fearful lest in presenting, though but dramatically and by way of a poetic record, the passions and epithets of civil war, I might be contributing to a bitterness which every sensible American must wish at an end. So, too, with the emotion of victory as reproduced on some pages, and particularly toward the close. It should not be construed into an exultation misapplied—an exultation as ungenerous as unwise, and made to minister, however indirectly, to that kind of censoriousness too apt to be produced in certain natures by success after trying reverses. Zeal is not of necessity religion, neither is it always of the same essence with poetry or patriotism.

There were excesses which marked the conflict, most of which are perhaps inseparable from a civil strife so intense and prolonged, and involving warfare in some border countries new and imperfectly civilized. Barbarities also there were, for which the Southern people collectively can hardly be held responsible, though perpetrated by ruffians in their name. But surely other qualities—exalted ones—courage and fortitude matchless,[5] were likewise displayed, and largely; and justly may these be held the characteristic traits, and not the former.

In this view, what Northern writer, however patriotic, but must revolt from acting on paper a part any way akin to that of the live dog to the dead·lion; and yet it is right to rejoice for our triumph, so far as it may justly imply an advance for our whole country and for humanity.

Let it be held no reproach to any one that he pleads for reasonable consideration for our late enemies, now stricken down and unavoidably debarred, for the time, from speaking through authorized agencies for themselves. Nothing has been urged here in the foolish hope of conciliating those men—few in number, we trust—who have resolved never to be reconciled to the Union. On such hearts every thing is thrown away except it be religious commiseration, and the sincerest. Yet let them call to mind that unhappy Secessionist, not a military man, who with impious alacrity fired the first shot of the Civil War at Sumter, and a little more than four years afterward fired the last one into his own heart at Richmond.[6]

Noble was the gesture into which patriotic passion surprised the people in a utilitarian time and country; yet the glory of the war falls short of its pathos—a pathos which now at last ought to disarm all animosity.

How many and earnest thoughts still rise, and how hard to repress them. We feel what past years have been, and years, unretarded years, shall come.

May we all have moderation; may we all show candor. Though, perhaps, nothing could ultimately have averted the strife, and though to treat of human actions is to deal wholly with second causes, nevertheless, let us not cover up or try to extenuate what, humanly speaking, is the truth—namely, that those unfraternal denunciations, continued through years, and which at last inflamed to deeds that ended in bloodshed, were reciprocal; and that, had the preponderating strength and the prospect of its unlimited increase lain on the other side, on ours might have lain those actions which now in our late opponents we stigmatize under the name of Rebellion. As frankly let us own—what it would be unbecoming to parade were foreigners concerned—that our triumph was won not more by skill and bravery than by superior resources and crushing numbers; that it was a triumph, too, over a people for years politically misled by designing men, and also by some honestly-erring men, who from their position could not have been otherwise than broadly influential; a people who, though, indeed, they sought to perpetuate the curse of slavery, and even extend it, were not the authors of it, but (less fortune, not less righteous than we) were the fated inheritors; a people who, having a like origin with ourselves, share essentially in whatever worthy qualities we may possess. No one can add to the lasting reproach which hopeless defeat has now cast upon Secession by withholding the recognition of these verities.

Surely we ought to take it to heart that that kind of pacification, based upon principles operating equally all over the land, which lovers of their country yearn for, and which our arms, though signally triumphant, did not bring about, and which law-making, however anxious, or energetic, or repressive, never by itself can achieve, may yet be largely aided by generosity of sentiment public and private. Some revisionary legislation and adaptive is indispensable; but with this should harmoniously work another kind of prudence, not unallied with entire magnanimity. Benevolence and policy—Christianity and Machiavelli—dissuade from penal severities toward the subdued. Abstinence here is as obligatory as considerate care for our unfortunate fellowmen late in bonds, and, if observed, would equally prove to be wise forecast. The great qualities of the South, those attested in the War, we can perilously alienate, or we may make them nationally available at need.

The blacks, in their infant pupilage to freedom, appeal to the sympathies of every humane mind. The paternal guardianship which for the interval government exercises over them was prompted equally by duty and benevolence. Yet such kindliness should not be allowed to exclude kindliness to communities who stand nearer to us in nature. For the future of the freed slaves we may well be concerned; but the future of the whole country, involving the future of the blacks, urges a paramount claim upon our anxiety. Effective benignity, like the Nile, is not narrow in its bounty, and true policy is always broad. To be sure, it is vain to seek to glide, with moulded words, over the difficulties of the situation. And for them who are neither partisans, nor enthusiasts, nor theorists, nor cynics, there are some doubts not readily to be solved. And there are fears. Why is not the cessation of war now at length attended with the settled calm of peace? Wherefore in a clear sky do we still turn our eyes toward the South, as the Neapolitan, months after the eruption, turns his toward Vesuvius? Do we dread lest the repose may be deceptive? In the recent convulsion has the crater but shifted? Let us revere that sacred uncertainty which forever impends over men and nations. Those of us who always abhorred slavery as an atheistical iniquity, gladly we join in the exulting chorus of humanity over its downfall. But we should remember that emancipation was accomplished not by deliberate legislation; only through agonized violence could so mighty a result be effected. In our natural solicitude to confirm the benefit of liberty to the blacks, let us forbear from measures of dubious constitutional rightfulness toward our white countrymen—measures of a nature to provoke, among other of the last evils, exterminating hatred of race toward race. In imagination let us place ourselves in the unprecedented position of the Southerners—their position as regards the millions of ignorant manumitted slaves in their midst, for whom some of us now claim the suffrage. Let us be Christians toward our fellow-whites, as well as philanthropists toward the blacks, our fellow-men. In all things, and toward all, we are enjoined to do as we would be done by. Nor should we forget that benevolent desires, after passing a certain point, can not undertake their own fulfillment without incurring the risk of evils beyond those sought to be remedied. Something may well be left to the graduated care of future legislation, and to heaven. In one point of view the coexistence of the two races in the South—whether the negro be bond or free—seems (even as it did to Abraham Lincoln) a grave evil. Emancipation has ridded the country of the reproach, but not wholly of the calamity. Especially in the present transition period for both races in the South, more or less of trouble may not unreasonably be anticipated; but let us not hereafter be too swift to charge the blame exclusively in any one quarter. With certain evils men must be more or less patient. Our institutions have a potent digestion, and may in time convert and assimilate to good all elements thrown in, however originally alien.

But, so far as immediate measures looking toward permanent Re-establishment are concerned, no consideration should tempt us to pervert the national victory into oppression for the vanquished. Should plausible promise of eventual good, or a deceptive or spurious sense of duty, lead us to essay this, count we must on serious consequences, not the least of which would be divisions among the Northern adherents of the Union. Assuredly, if any honest Catos there be who thus far have gone with us, no longer will they do so, but oppose us, and as resolutely as hitherto they have supported. But this path of thought leads toward those waters of bitterness from which one can only turn aside and be silent.

But supposing Re-establishment so far advanced that the Southern seats in Congress are occupied, and by men qualified in accordance with those cardinal principles of representative government which hitherto have prevailed in the land—what then? Why, the Congressmen elected by the people of the South will—represent the people of the South. This may seem a flat conclusion; but, in view of the last five years, may there not be latent significance in it? What will be the temper of those Southern members? and, confronted by them, what will be the mood of our own representatives? In private life true reconciliation seldom follows a violent quarrel; but, if subsequent intercourse be unavoidable, nice observances and mutual are indispensable to the prevention of a new rupture. Amity itself can only be maintained by reciprocal respect, and true friends are punctilious equals. On the floor of Congress North and South are to come together after a passionate duel, in which the South, though proving her valor, has been made to bite the dust. Upon differences in debate shall acrimonious recriminations be exchanged? shall censorious superiority assumed by one section provoke defiant self-assertion on the other? shall Manassas and Chickamauga be retorted for Chattanooga and Richmond?[7] Under the supposition that the full Congress will be composed of gentlemen, all this is impossible. Yet, if otherwise, it needs no prophet of Israel to foretell the end. The maintenance of Congressional decency in the future will rest mainly with the North. Rightly will more forbearance be required from the North than the South, for the North is victor.

But some there are who may deem these latter thoughts inapplicable, and for this reason: Since the test-oath operatively excludes from Congress all who in any way participated in Secession, therefore none but Southerners wholly in harmony with the North are eligible to seats.[8] This is true for the time being. But the oath is alterable; and in the wonted fluctuations of parties not improbably it will undergo alteration, assuming such a form, perhaps, as not to bar the admission into the National Legislature of men who represent the populations lately in revolt. Such a result would involve no violation of the principles of democratic government. Not readily can one perceive how the political existence of the millions of late Secessionists can permanently be ignored by this Republic: The years of the war tried our devotion to the Union; the time of peace may test the sincerity of our faith in democracy.

In no spirit of opposition, not by way of challenge, is any thing here thrown out. These thoughts are sincere ones; they seem natural—inevitable. Here and there they must have suggested themselves to many thoughtful patriots. And, if they be just thoughts, ere long they must have that weight with the public which already they have had with individuals.

For that heroic band—those children of the furnace[9] who, in regions like Texas and Tennessee, maintained their fidelity through terrible trials— we of the North felt for them, and profoundly we honor them. Yet passionate sympathy, with resentments so close as to be almost domestic in their bitterness, would hardly in the present juncture tend to discreet legislation. Were the Unionists and Secessionists but as Guelphs and Ghibellines? If not, then far be it from a great nation now to act in the spirit that animated a triumphant town-faction in the Middle Ages. But crowding thoughts must at last be checked; and, in times like the present, one who desires to be impartially just in the expression of his views, moves as among sword-points presented on every side.

Let us pray that the terrible[10] historic tragedy of our time may not have been enacted without instructing our whole beloved country through terror and pity;[11] and may fulfillment verify in the end those expectations which kindle the bards of Progress and Humanity.

THE END.

Notes

The capitalization of the original edition has been followed for the poem titles in the text. It has been modernized for the table of contents and, as here, the notes.

The Portent

John Brown with 21 followers captured the arsenal at Harpers Ferry, Virginia on October 16, 1859 in an abortive attempt to foment slave insurrection. He was tried on charges of "treason to the Commonwealth" and "conspiring with slaves to commit treason and murder," found guilty, and executed by hanging on December 2.

The imagery of the poem is predominantly visual and much of it derives from the human body, usually Brown's. Kinetic images such as that of the body swaying pendulum-like from the gallows (lines 1–2) help to establish the stress pattern and to justify the nearly identical syllable count in corresponding lines of the two stanzas. Opposing this regularity is the substitution of assonantal, consonantal, identical, and eye rhymes for those of a more usual sort. The avoidance of conventional rhyme creates intensity by playing regularity against irregularity. It also seems to be part of a deliberate attempt at understatement, as though under-rhyming might prevent the "horrors of war" theme from getting out of control and interfering with the reconciliation theme which is to come. Furthermore, it emphasizes by subtle contrast the regularity of the double refrain which is vital to the structure and meaning of the poem (see note on line 4). Finally, it makes possible the use of rhyme as a means of unifying the two stanzas (cf. lines 2 and 9), as do the alliteration (cf. lines 1 and 8) and the double refrain.

In the original edition "The Portent" is not listed in the table of contents but follows immediately after it, in format serving as a preface to the other poems. The only poem set in italic type, it is further distinguished by an intervening blank verso.

Line 2. *such the law*: the laws of physics and the laws of man. References to the law occur often in *Battle-Pieces* and in Melville's other writings—most memorably in his last work, *Billy Budd,* where society requires the hanging of a man who, like John Brown, is not clearly and unequivocally guilty. This phrase is also used ironically in "Lee in the Capitol" (line 174).

Line 3. *Gaunt*: as a description of the shadow this is suitable because Brown is haggard from his experience and is forbidding both in his personal appearance and in what he symbolizes. The dark shadow represents the intrusion of death into the green valley. Cf. "Misgivings" (lines 2–3) where "autumn brown" sweeps into a "valley."

Lines 3–4. Major military operations in the Shenandoah Valley include General T. J. (Stonewall) Jackson's brilliant diversionary campaign of May–June 1862, which slowed General George B. McClellan's advance on Richmond, and General Philip Sheridan's activities as commander of the Middle Military Division from August 1864 to March 1865, as a result of which, according to Sheridan himself, "A crow would have had to carry its rations if it had flown across the valley." Therefore, "the shadow on your green" is not only literally John Brown's with all accompanying symbolic significance, but also a reference to the devastation brought to the Shenandoah by war.

Line 4. Because the Shenandoah Valley was noted for its fertility and beauty and had already accumulated a romantic aura, and because of the euphony of the word itself, it is an apt choice for the refrain. It gains importance from its central position in both stanzas, thus serving to separate lines with iambic emphasis from those with trochaic emphasis; from its brevity in contrast to lines which precede and follow; and from the considerable number of words with which it alliterates. With "John Brown," it forms a double refrain which enhances the meaning as well as the formal unity of the poem. The "Shenandoah" refrain suggests fertility, life, and peace; the "John Brown" refrain suggests devastation, death, and war. The modulated accents of "Shenandoah" contrast with the three heavy and ominous stresses of the second refrain. The color contrast is mentioned above (notes on lines 3, 3–4). Symbolically, the image of the Shenandoah Valley represents the outcome of the sins of the South and an extension of the sins of the nation and of mankind.

Line 5. John Brown's letter of October 22, 1859 to Judge Daniel R. Tilden of Cleveland, Ohio, requesting legal aid, begins: "I am here [Charlestown, Virginia] a prisoner, with several cuts in my head, and bayonet stabs in my body." Cf. Shakespeare, *Henry V*, IV, i, 245: ". . . but it is no English treason to cut French crowns," and *Richard III*, III, ii, 43–44: "I'll have this crown of mine cut from my shoulders/Before I see the crown so foul misplac'd." In *White-Jacket* (Chap. 56, "A Shore Emperor on Board a Man-of-war") Melville puns on *crown* in the senses of head and coronet. He uses *crown* in the sense of head in *Mardi* (Chap. 138, "Of the Isle of Diranda"). The crown is a traditional emblem of the state, which has been hurt by the "cut." It may also signify the sensibility or conscience which has been aroused.

Line 6. *Lo*: behold, also prostrate since line 5 suggests that Brown has been struck down, and dead since *low* meaning death is used in "Shiloh" (line 17), in "Stonewall Jackson" (line 14), and elsewhere. A similar pun on *lo* is in "Shelley's Vision" (line 8) in *Timoleon*. Although Brown lies low in death he hangs high enough on the scaffold to cast a retributive shadow. Ultimately he becomes a symbolic meteor, a heavenly body which influences the destiny of the earth below.

Lines 8–10. As the cap placed by the executioner over the head of the condemned man conceals his face, so the future is also veiled. Brown's personal suffering seems all the more intense because it is thus private and spatially confined.

Line 9. *draw*: remove so as to disclose, as with a veil; portray, delineate.

Line 10. The association of prophecies, prophets, and veils may have been suggested to Melville by Schiller's poem, "The Veiled Image at Sais." He owned a set of Schiller (Sealts nos. 347, 349) and in *Moby-Dick* (Chap. 76, "The Battering-Ram") refers to "the dread goddess's veil at Sais." Melville in 1862 acquired Thomas Moore's *Lalla Rookh,* consisting of four Eastern stories in verse, the first of which is "The Veiled Prophet of Khorassan" (Sealts no. 370). The phrase, "I am the Veiled Persian Prophet," appears in *Mardi* (Chap. 97, "Faith and Knowledge").

Line 12. The cap cannot completely conceal Brown's beard any more than the significance and result of Brown's death can be suppressed. Attention is further drawn to this striking image because of the length of the line and its position between two of the shortest in the poem.

Lines 12–14. In English literature meteors have been associated with wars and disasters from the time of the Anglo-Saxon Chronicle. Thus the entry for the fateful year 1066 begins with a record of a "hairy star" regarded as an omen, and the tradition continues in Shakespeare, e.g. *King John*, III, iv, 157–58: "And call them meteors, prodigies, and signs,/ Abortives, presages, and tongues of heaven." Milton associated *streaming* with *meteor* in *Paradise Lost,* I, 536–37: "Th'Imperial Ensign, which full high advanc't/ Shone like a Meteor streaming to the Wind"; and Edmund Waller uses similar language in connection with the banner of James, Duke of York, in "Instructions to a Painter" (lines 269–70): "His dreadful streamer (like a comet's hair,/ Threat'ning destruction) hasten their despair." Samuel Butler in *Hudibras* (Pt. 1, Canto 1, lines 239–48), a book Melville knew well (Sealts nos. 104 and 105), describes the "tawny beard" of Sir Hudibras as a "hairy meteor" which foretells disaster. Thomas Gray's

"The Bard: A Pindaric Ode" (lines 19-21) describes a Welsh bard: (Loose his beard and hoary hair/ Streamed, like a meteor, to the troubled air) ." Gray's note states that "the image was taken from a well-known picture of Raphael, representing the Supreme Being in the vision of Ezekiel." Henry A. Murray, editor of *Pierre,* argues convincingly that "The Bard" was the source of the name Plinlimmon (p. 475) .

Grammatically *streaming beard* is in apposition with *meteor of war* but so is the refrain, "Weird John Brown." This is in keeping with the synecdochic quality of the phrase and emphasizes Brown's function as portent by relating him even more closely to the meteor.

Line 13. *Weird* in the sense of odd, eccentric, is appropriate because of Brown's character and physical appearance. Even in death there is a lack of propriety, a shamelessness, in the exposure of his beard. The word also identifies Brown with the Weirds, making him an instrument of fate and prophecy, and paradoxically because of the cap he is a blind seer. The refrain is incremental. Brown is no longer merely someone to whom attention is called. His significance is now stated.

Line 14. Melville's brother Thomas was captain of a clipper ship, "The Meteor." Melville sailed with him from Boston on May 30, 1860, landing at San Francisco on October 12. The poem "To the Master of the *Meteor*," in *John Marr,* recalls this voyage.

Misgivings

In his note to "The Conflict of Convictions," Melville writes of "doubts and misgivings" rife in 1860–61.

Lines 2–3. The language here recalls the image in "The Portent" of the body of John Brown casting a dark shadow across the Shenandoah Valley.

Line 5. The image of the crashing spire suggests that the restraining and purifying power of the church has declined. Cf. "The House-top" (lines 13–15) : "And priestly spells which late held hearts in awe—/ . . . these like a dream dissolve."

Line 7. For other instances of the pairing of "fair" and "foul" see "The Scout toward Aldie," note on line 430.

Line 8. Fogle ("Melville and the Civil War," p. 64) points out that whereas the logical progress of the first stanza is "from the particular to the general, the second stanza reverses the process, as a generalization about nature is exemplified concretely."

Lines 11–13. The Journal of Melville's Voyage in a Clipper Ship" (p. 123) contains this entry for August 7, 1860: "Entered the Strait of Le Maire, & through the short day had a fine view of the land on both sides—

Horrible snowy mountains—black, thunder-cloud woods—gorges—hell-land-scape." The next day he continued: "Just before sunset, in a squall, the mist lifted & showed, within 12 or fifteen miles the horrid sight of Cape Horn—(the Cape proper)—a black, bare steep cliff, the face of it facing the South Pole; with[in] some miles were other awful islands and rocks—an infernal group." For Melville Cape Horn is often a symbol of anguish and trial. Cf. "The Fortitude of the North" (line 5).

Line 13. The image of the violent storm serves a double purpose: it forces recognition of the dark side of nature and it portends yet other storms to come.

Line 14. The rafters, which as the upper part of a building are sugges-tive of man's effort to control the land, and the keel, which as the bottom and longitudinal axis of a ship represent man's attempts to use the sea for his own purposes, are imagined in their primal form as hemlock and oak (Berlind, "Notes," p. 33). Cf. "The House-top" (line 16): "And man rebounds whole aeons back in nature."

The Conflict of Convictions

The gloomy lull of the early part of the winter of 1860-1, seeming big with final disaster to our institutions, affected some minds that believed them to constitute one of the great hopes of mankind, much as the eclipse which came over the promise of the first French Revolution affected kindred natures, throwing them for the time into doubts and misgivings universal. [Melville's Note]

The "Preface" to *Billy Budd* establishes the context of the French Revolution with its initial promise of "rectification of the Old World's hereditary wrongs," the disappointment when "the Revolution itself became a wrongdoer," and the final result, "what to some thinkers apparently it since turned out to be—a political advance along nearly the whole line for Europeans."

Melville drew upon Milton for theme and setting. *Paradise Lost* has as its subject "Man's First Disobedience"; "The Conflict of Convictions" is concerned with "man's latter fall." Miltonic imagery and allusions pervade Melville's poem. The result is to enlarge the significance of the Civil War, itself a puny affair beside the War in Heaven, when it is shown to be a metaphor for the basic and unending struggle of the forces of Yea and Nay.

The title has a double meaning. In a general way it refers to the clash of issues in the impending war. More specifically, it directs attention to the thematic conflicts of this particular poem and to its formal structure. These conflicts, as Warren points out ("Melville the Poet," p. 214), "relate to

Melville's concern with the fundamental ironical dualities of existence: will against necessity, action against idea, youth against age, the changelessness of man's heart against the concept of moral progress, the bad doer against the good deed, the bad result against the good act, ignorance against fate, etc."

The poem is cast as a dialogue, reminiscent of a medieval debate, and in form is similar to "The Armies of the Wilderness" and "Donelson." It consists of seven stanzas of irregular length and varied meter, to each of which is attached a coarse, relentless, metrically irregular, and deliberately unpoetic chorus. The first six stanzas alternate between nay-saying pessimism and a restrained optimism, with the choruses functioning as summary and comment. The seventh stanza provides a qualified resolution. However, it should be noted that in the first stanza, where Satan's host seems triumphant, "Heaven's ominous silence" prevails over the derision from the abyss, and in the last stanza, despite its tone, the possibility of a stronger "Iron Dome" is held forth (see note on line 79).

Line 6. The latter fall was man's loss of the second Eden, America, as a result of a new manifestation of original sin—a general manifestation, by no means identified simply with slavery or rebellion. In "Misgivings" (line 7) Melville sees America as "the world's fairest hope linked with man's foulest crime." Cf. *Clarel* (IV, xxi, 130–34):

> Whatever happens in the end,
> Be sure 'twill yield to one and all
> New confirmation of the fall
> Of Adam.

Here Ungar is discussing the future of America.

Line 8. Cf. *Aeneid,* VI, 304: "Old, but a god's old age is fresh and green."

Line 10. The apocryphal Book of Tobit tells how Raphael saved Tobias, bridegroom of Sara, from the devil Asmodeus. In *Paradise Lost* Raphael is "the sociable Spirit" sent by God "to render Man inexcusable." Pleasant but relatively ineffectual, he stands in contrast to "Michael the warrior one" (line 48). A "white enthusiast" is an epithet for an ineffectual idealist.

Line 11. *aims, whereat Christ's* (revision in Melville's copy).

Line 12. Cf. Matthew 6:24 and *Paradise Lost,* I, 679–82.

Lines 22–23. Cf. Milton's sonnet, "When I consider" (line 14): "They also serve who only stand and wait."

Line 37. Cf. Matthew 27:50: "Jesus, when he had cried again with a loud voice, yielded up the ghost."

Lines 38–39. Cf. Mark 15:29–30: "And they that passed by railed on him, wagging their heads, and saying, Ah, thou that destroyest the temple, and buildest it in three days, Save thyself, and come down from the cross."

Line 44. Melville visited Washington in March 1861. He would have seen the construction of an iron dome for the Capitol to replace one of wood and brick demolished in 1855. For other examples of the dome as a symbol of the state, see "The Victor of Antietam" (line 29), "The Scout toward Aldie" (lines 32–35), and "Lee in the Capitol" (lines 33, 38).

Line 52. *bears a taper dim* (revision in Melville's copy).

Line 53. *braves* (revision in Melville's copy).

Line 54. *Which foldeth him* (revision in Melville's copy).

16   *The Conflict of Convictions.*

> *(Tide-mark*
> *And top of the ages' strife,*
> *Verge where they called the world to come,*
> *The last advance of life—*
> *Ha ha, the rust on the Iron Dome!)*

Nay, but revere the hid event;
  In the cloud a sword is girded on,
I mark a twinkling in the tent
  Of Michael the warrior one.
Senior wisdom suits not now,
The light is on the youthful brow.

> *(Ay, in caves the miner see:* a taper dim
> *His forehead bears a blinking light;*
> *Darkness so he feebly braves* Which foldeth him
> *A meagre wight!)*

But He who rules is old—is old;
Ah! faith is warm, but heaven with age is cold.

> *(Ho ho, ho ho,*
> *The cloistered doubt*
> *Of olden times*
> *Is blurted out!)*

Line 61. Cf. Daniel 7:9. See "A Canticle," note on lines 44–45. In "The New Ancient of Days," a posthumously published poem, Melville sets up a similar verbal opposition to the biblical epithet.

Line 65. Cf. "America" (lines 29–30), where the "earth's foundations bare" reveal the "Gorgon in her hidden place" and "Timoleon" (lines 128–31):

> Within perturbed Timoleon here
> Such deeps were bared as when the sea,
> Convulsed, vacates its shoreward bed,
> And Nature's last reserves show nakedly.

In *Clarel* (II, xxiii, 34–35) the rain-soaked Siddim Plain is said to look "As 'twere the quaking sea-bed bared/ By the Caracas." Caracas suffered severely from an earthquake in 1812. Perhaps more pertinent to the origin of this striking trope was Melville's stay of more than two months, during the period in 1843–44 when he served aboard the "United States," at Callao near Lima, which had been destroyed by an earthquake in 1746. The original city sank beneath the waters of the bay, where it remained visible. Melville mentions the Lima earthquake in *Mardi* (Chap. 165, "They Round the Stormy Cape of Capes"), and in *Moby-Dick* (Chap. 42, "The Whiteness of the Whale") refers to Lima's "cathedral-toppling earthquakes" and "stampedoes of her frantic seas." Other metaphors for the revelation of the hidden power that is the source of both terror and enlightenment are "the core of fire" of "The Apparition" (line 12), "Shakespeare's core" of "The Coming Storm" (line 14), and the shark of "Commemorative of a Naval Victory" (line 26 and note on lines 26–27).

Line 75. Particular attention is drawn to the crucial image of the "Iron Dome" through similarity of sound, and proximity to the word "Dominion" and the use of eye rhyme. Also note the material from which it is made and the size of the shadow it casts.

Line 79. Richard Chase states that the "tragedy of the war seemed to Melville to be its mindless destruction of the past, which he feared might make it impossible for America to fulfill 'the Founders' dream' " (*Melville: A Critical Study,* p. 231). Warren suggests that the strengthening of the "Iron Dome" may be "at the expense of the 'Founders' dream' " (Melville the Poet," p. 216), the implication being that victory may corrupt unless it is accompanied by compassion and understanding. This is in keeping with Melville's point of view in many poems, for example "Lee in the Capitol" (line 97), where he writes of saving the "North from her own victory." However, it could be argued that Melville saw the "Founders' dream" as limited because it did not sufficiently take into consideration the evil ingredient in man's nature. Cf. "The House-top," note on line 25.

If this is true, then the loss of the "Founders' dream" is not to be regretted.

Lines 85–88. In *Pierre* (Bk. V, Chap. 3) where Lucy and Isabel first appear in opposition, Melville writes: "Eye for eye, and tooth for tooth. Eternally inexorable and unconcerned is Fate, a mere heartless trader in men's joys and woes." Fate takes on the character of Jehovah as a result of the biblical phrase. Through the allegory of *Mardi* (Chap. 162, "They Visit the Extreme South of Vivenza") Melville had considered the possibility of war arising from the slavery issue. The poet Yoomy assumed that divine support would be forthcoming for the cause of the slaves, that "Oro," the Mardian god, would "van to the right." Babbalanja the philosopher thought otherwise, advising that "Oftimes, the right fights single-handed against the world; and Oro champions none."

Line 90. *prophesy* is Melville's spelling.

Apathy and Enthusiasm

The opposition indicated in the title governs the formal structure of the poem. The contrast is further elaborated by juxtaposing winter and spring, age and youth, doubt and faith, death and resurrection. Both stanzas end on a note of foreboding, and the opposition is unresolved. Emphasizing the heavy cost of achievement, Melville implies that enthusiasm, even for a just cause, is a callow trait and that there is a certain melancholy grandeur in the apathy which comes with clear-sighted acceptance of doom.

For another pairing of apathy and enthusiasm see Melville's "The Fiddler," a short story published in 1854: ". . . Hautboy seemed intuitively to hit the exact line between enthusiasm and apathy. It was plain that while Hautboy saw the world pretty much as it was, yet he did not theoretically espouse its bright side nor its dark side. . . . his extraordinary cheerfulness did not arise either from deficiency of thought or feeling."

Lines 14–18. The "strife of brothers" theme, based upon a number of actual instances and almost inevitable metaphorically, appears often in Civil War literature. Melville used it in "The Armies of the Wilderness" (lines 9–12, in "A Meditation" (lines 10–12) , and elsewhere.

Lines 24–35. An editorial entitled "The Resurrection of Patriotism" from the New York *Times* of April 16, 1861 (*Rebellion Record,* I, 62) , seems to have been a major source for this poem and may have suggested the Easter imagery. Cf. lines 28–35 with these extracts from the editorial:
". . . the hearts of our own people had begun to sink within them, at the apparent insensibility of the public to the dangers that menaced the Government. The public mind seemed to have been demoralized.—the public heart seemed insensible. . . . But all this is changed. The cannon which bombarded Sumter awoke strange echoes, and touched forgotten chords in the American heart. American loyalty leaped instantly to life,

and stood radiant and ready for the fierce encounter." The editorial concludes: "We have reason to exalt in the noble demonstration of American loyalty, which events of the last few days have called forth from every quarter of the country. . . . Whatever may be the character of the contest, we have no fear or misgiving as to the final issue."

Line 27. Cf. Matthew 27:51–53.

Line 28. *the rising of the people* parallels the Resurrection imagery above.

Line 29. Connotatively *springing* suggests the season in contrast to *winter* (line 24) .

Line 31. Because of reference to the Resurrection, Lent, and Easter, *pass* suggests *Pasch*. The phrase *came to pass* is biblical.

Line 38. Erebus, son of Chaos and brother of Night, personifies darkness, but is also the name of the cavern through which the souls of the dead pass on their journey to Hades. In *Billy Budd* (Chap. 24) , Melville glosses the name of a French ship, "Erebus," as "Hell."

Line 43. In spite of having no etymological connection with the verb *to see, old saw* as used here hints of something seen before, foreseen. The way is prepared for this suggestion by the use of *foreboding* (line 40) and *forever* (line 41) , and the role of the elders as prophets without honor.

Lines 44–45. Whatever the source of "the forest proverb," it does not derive from the beardless Iroquois.

The March into Virginia

The first major engagement of the Civil War took place on July 21, 1861, along Bull Run near Manassas Junction, a railroad depot between Richmond and the Shenandoah Valley. Here General Irvin McDowell and 30,000 men were routed by 24,000 Confederates under General P. G. T. Beauregard. On August 29–30, 1862 Lee defeated General John Pope on the same battlefield.

Lines 1–11. This poem continues the discourse between youth and age begun in "Apathy and Enthusiasm." Initial emphasis is on positive possibilities implicit in "trust and cheer." Although the ardors of youth are "turbid" and its joys "vain," they can be stepping-stones to maturity and are part of an ordered if inscrutable plan. But youth is heedless of any surmises but its own.

Line 12. *forecasteth*: predicts; but also, shapes beforehand, predetermines.

Line 15. *foreclosures*: prior discoveries; but also, preventions. As a legal term compare with "precedent" (line 13) and with "lets and bars" (line 1) , which suggests the need for legal controls but also their limitations. Cf. "such the law" (line 2, "The Portent") .

Lines 16–30. Melville may have obtained details about the weather and the elation of the inexperienced Union soldiers from a news account in the New York *World* of July 23, 1861 (*Rebellion Record*, II, 81–89). Cf., for example: ". . . what excitement was added to the occasion by the salutations and last assurances of the many comrades dearer than the rest! The spirit of the soldiery was magnificent."

Line 17. The word *prodigal*, i.e. wasteful or extravagant, recalls the parable of the prodigal son (Luke 15:11–32) who receives enlightenment through experience.

Line 21. The foliage of the "leafy neighborhood" conceals one-time good neighbors who are now enemies (Barrett, "Differences in Melville's Poetry," p. 613). Cf. "The Scout Toward Aldie" lines 525–26): "Blessings on the friendly screen—/ I'm for the South! says the leafage green."

Line 22. The "Bacchic glee" of the young soldiers relates them to the excited devotees of the god of wine. But the comparison also suggests intoxication and frenzy, and implies a limitation upon their valor, which is made to seem spurious and irresponsible.

Line 23. The worship of Moloch required the sacrifice of children. Cf. Milton's roll call of demons in *Paradise Lost* (I, 392–98), which begins: "First *Moloch*, horrid King besmear'd with blood/ Of human sacrifice, and parents' tears."

Lines 26–28. The jogging meter and feminine rhyme give these lines a frivolous quality which is in keeping with the behavior and emotions of the young soldiers. A like tone prevails in the couplet which follows, but there is a drastic shift, suitable to the content, in the last stanza. Here the lines are longer, the rhyme pattern more subtle, and the pace more stately.

Line 33. *days be spent* – (*Harper's*).

Line 34. Gunfire literally and figuratively produces light. The word *lightsome* (line 32) is played against *enlightened* (line 34). The "vollied glare" may be related to the region of Tophet (II Kings 23:10) where children "pass through the fire to Molech." Cf. note on line 23 above.

Lines 34–36. Some will find enlightenment through death in battle. Survivors will carry with them the burden of self-understanding which will enable them to endure the further agony of another defeat on the same field. For the depth of understanding which war can bring, see also "Shiloh" (line 16) and "The College Colonel" (line 31). The "Shock of Enlightenment" is "a ceremony used in all degrees of Symbolic Masonry" to signify "the change . . . in the intellectual condition of the candidate." (*Encyclopedia of Freemasonry*, ed. by Albert G. Mackey, rev. 1924.) See note on line 36 for use of *shock* in Melville's revisions.

Line 35. *Or some survive* (revision in Elizabeth Melville's copy).

Line 36. *Thy after shock, Manassas, share.* Manassas's second throe *and deadlier share. Thy second shock, Manassas, share.* (Revisions in Melville's copy).

Lyon

General Nathaniel Lyon was killed at Wilson Creek on August 10, 1861, in a minor but hard-fought action during the Confederate attempt to gain military control of Missouri. He became the first major Northern hero, and as such the subject of much verse. In this battle Federal troops numbering 5,400 were opposed by 11,600 Confederates, and they suffered 1,235 casualties to the Confederate 1,184.

Melville used newspaper accounts reprinted in *The Rebellion Record* (II, 511–19) from the *Missouri Democrat* and the New York *Tribune* as his source for such details as the size of the forces engaged (p. 511), the discussion of possible retreat (p. 515), the night march and enemy campfires (p. 512), the fight in the cornfield (Diary, 62; *passim*, newspaper accounts), Lyon's courage despite wounds (p. 516), and the inexperience of the soldiers (p. 513).

Line 1. Because of his name and his conduct, Melville associates Lyon with the animal traditionally emblematic of courage and with Richard I, the Lion-Hearted, of legendary fame. This is accomplished by the stark title of the poem (for source, see note on line 24), the refrain, and the repetition of the word "heart" (lines 1, 5, 25, 42). Cf. *Israel Potter* (Chap. 22, "Something Further of Ethan Allen . . ."), where Melville writes that Ethan Allen had "a heart plump as Coeur de Lion's."

Line 19. Orion, a giant famed as a hunter, was accidentally killed by Diana, who transformed him into the most brilliant constellation in the northern winter sky. Lyon's horse is here so named for the sake of the rhyme. The New York *Tribune* of August 11, 1861 (*Rebellion Record*, II, 516) states: "Up to this time Gen. Lyon had received two wounds and had his fine dapple gray shot from under him." See also references to "star-browed Orion" (line 29) and the death of "black Orion" (lines 33–34).

Line 23. *trooping clouds*: refers to the weather but probably also to the massed enemy troops. A Missouri *Record* article dated August 11, 1861 (*Rebellion Record*, II, 512) says of Confederate forces that "their clouds of cavalry were visible."

Line 24. In the poetry section of *The Rebellion Record* (III, 20) is a poem by "H. P." entitled "Lyon" and containing these lines:

> They feared not death—men bless the field
> That patriot soldiers die on—

Fair Freedom's cause was sword and shield,
And at their head was Lyon.

This stanza may have given Melville the phrase *a field to die on* (lines 24, 39) as well as his unfortunate refrain and the title itself. Cf. line 16, "The Conflict of Convictions."

Line 52. Like the name of the horse, that of Corporal Tryon is un-historical, the product of the demands of rhyme. The Missouri *Democrat* states (*Rebellion Record,* II, 513) that Lyon responded to the call of a group of Iowa soldiers, not otherwise identified.

Lines 61–65. The last stanza returns to the prophecy theme which was introduced at the beginning of the poem and which has been important in all of the preceding poems. Because he can read in his heart his own fate and does not shrink from it, Lyon is worthy of being translated, and fit company for the prophets and armies of Zion who greet him.

Line 63. *flight:* the act both of flying and of fleeing.

Line 65. *greet pale Lyon* (revision in copies of Melville and Mrs. Melville).

Ball's Bluff

Colonel Edward D. Baker, friend of Lincoln and former senator, received permission to make "a slight demonstration" against Confederate positions on the fords of the Potomac near Ball's Bluff, Virginia. He attacked on October 21, 1861, but was ambushed and killed. This fiasco led to bitter charges, including those of political favoritism and treason in high places. Baker himself fought valiantly.

Line 16. Cf. Keats, "Isabella, or the Pot of Basil," 323: "As when of healthful midnight sleep bereft" (Sealts no. 305).

Dupont's Round Fight

Samuel Francis DuPont commanded the Union fleet which reduced Forts Walker and Beauregard on Port Royal Sound, South Carolina, November 7, 1861. His successful naval maneuver (see "Plan") secured a base for subsequent operations along the South Atlantic coast. This poem is the first celebration of a Northern victory. It is written in ballad stanza, and Melville adheres to a degree of regularity in form remarkable for him. This regularity is appropriate in a poem which has as its theme the necessity for "rules."

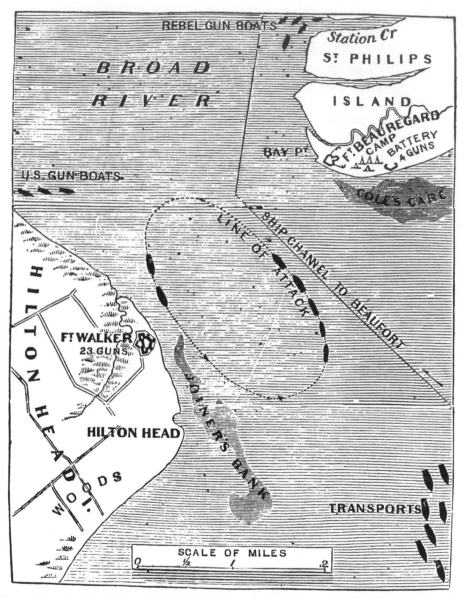

"Plan of the Battle of Port Royal, S. C.," by G. C. Plicque, as reproduced from the New York *Tribune* in *The Rebellion Record*.

The "Plan of the Battle of Port Royal, S.C." is from *The Rebellion Record* (III, 106). The caption states: "The plan of attack was simple and effective, being for the ships to steam in a circle, or ellipse, running close to one shore as they came *down* the river, drifting or steaming as slowly as possible past the batteries there, and paying their fiery respects, then making the turn to go back, and as they went *up* the river, favoring the other batteries with a similar compliment." The "Plan" makes clear Melville's source and the appropriateness of his mathematical and astronomical imagery.

Lines 1–4. The poem is one of several which concern Melville's literary theory and the philosophical assumptions on which it is based. Others include "Art" and "Greek Architecture" in *Timoleon*. Melville sees a fundamental unity of esthetics ("Art whose aim is sure") and nature ("stars divine"), both subject to a like discipline.

Line 3. The phrase "evolving rhyme" suggests an organic theory of poetry and Darwinian influence; but note that "rhyme" remains subordinate to "rules."

Lines 3–4. The antecedent of *they* is uncertain, perhaps deliberately so, but the sense is clear. The "rules" are lasting and permanent, and the "evolving rhyme and stars divine" will endure if they observe them.

Lines 5–8. Like art and nature, human actions are subject to rules. Cf. *Mardi* (Chap. 143, "Wherein Babbalanja Discourses of Himself"): "In his roundabout chapter on 'Cycles and Epicycles, with Notes on the Ecliptic,' he thus discourseth:—'All things revolve upon some center, to them fixed; . . .'" For other examples of the revolving-circle metaphor and its function, see "A Canticle," note on line 24.

Lines 9–12. The rules of "time and measure" (line 1) which govern art and nature are institutionalized by man in the law. "The rebel," like Milton's rebel angels, is in revolt against law and will inevitably be defeated.

Line 12. In form and meaning the poem reaches its conclusion with the word *Law*. Its terminal position, its use as a rhyme word preceded by internal rhyme ("Unity" and "victory"), its position in the stress pattern, the use of capitalization, and its situation in the only run-on line in the poem all give it unusual emphasis.

The Stone Fleet

"The terrible Stone Fleet, on a mission as pitiless as the granite that freights it, sailed this morning from Port Royal, and before two days are past will have made Charleston an inland city. The ships are all old whalers, and cost the government from $2500 to $5000 each. Some of them were once famous ships."—(From Newspaper Correspondence of the day.)

Sixteen vessels were accordingly sunk on the bar at the river entrance. Their names were as follows:

Amazon,	Leonidas,
America,	Maria Theresa,
American,	Potomac,
Archer,	Rebecca Simms,
Courier,	L. C. Richmond,
Fortune,	Robin Hood,
Herald,	Tenedos,
Kensington,	William Lee.

All accounts seem to agree that the object proposed was not accomplished. The channel is even said to have become ultimately benefited by the means employed to obstruct it. [Melville's note]

The attempt to block the main entrance to Charleston harbor took place on December 20, 1861. Another effort, against a secondary channel, was made on January 26, 1862. The newspaper quotation in Melville's note is from the beginning of a dispatch to the New York *Tribune* dated December 17, 1861, "off Port Royal Entrance" (*Rebellion Record*, III, 503–4). Melville seems to have had at least a slight association with several of the vessels listed. Thomas W. Melville (1806–44) of Pittsfield, Massachusetts, his older cousin, "the true Ishmael of the family" as Leon Howard calls him (*Melville*, p. 91), served on the "Amazon," out of Fairhaven, in 1838 and again in 1841. The "Acushnet" during the time Melville was aboard spoke the "Herald," New Bedford, and the "William Lee," Newport (Leyda, *Log*, pp. 121, 128). The "Rebecca Sims" in 1854 had the distinction of taking the whale which had stove in the "Ann Alexander" three years before, an event which very much excited Melville (Leyda, *Log*, p. 487; *Letters*, pp. 139–40). The name "Tenedos" would have interested him. It is the Aegean island near the Dardanelles to which the Greeks withdrew temporarily when they built the Trojan Horse, and which was a naval station of Xerxes in the Persian Wars. Melville saw Tenedos from shipboard when he visited Constantinople (*Journal . . . to Europe and the Levant*, pp. 104–5). He owned a copy of Marlowe's plays (Sealts no. 348) and may have recalled from *Tamburlaine* (II, iv, 87–88) the less well-known quotation about Helen's beauty which "drew a thousand ships into Tenedos."

Line 1. Although there is no evidence that Melville is the spokesman here, the rare instance of the personal pronoun suggests his rather sentimental identification with the sea, whaling, and the obsolete, and nostalgia for his lost youth. The puns, colloquialisms, trite expressions, ellipses, and sometimes jocular tone may be an attempt to prevent an appearance of excessive sentimentality.

Line 3. Cf. New York *Tribune,* December 17, 1861 (*Rebellion Record,* III, 504) : ". . . and her bluff bows nod to us rather gracefully."

Line 5. Thus the obsolete are served; and/or, thus the obsolete serve.

Line 9. The New York *Tribune* article took note of the departed glories of the "Tenedos." Melville himself did not round the Horn in her.

Lines 13–14. On January 11, 1862, *Harper's Weekly,* bound volumes of which Melville owned, reprinted newspaper accounts which described the "Robin Hood"—but not the "Tenedos"—as an East Indiaman.

Line 17. *escheat*: in the legal sense, reversion to the rightful owner, in this instance the sea; also, cheated in her old age of proper respect and decent burial.

Line 23. *seat*: place, situation; estate of the patrician families.

Line 27. "Some stanch old ships died very hard, settling very slowly, and still upright when they had felt the bottom." New York *Tribune* (*Rebellion Record,* III, 508) .

Lines 34–35. The New York *Tribune* (*ibid.*) stated that the "work of the expedition [was] a complete success." But marine worms later ate away the hulls of the ships and their granite cargoes sank into the mud.

Donelson

The surrender of Fort Donelson on the Cumberland River near Dover, Tennessee, on February 16, 1862, forced the Confederacy to abandon its positions in Kentucky and to lose a large part of northern Tennessee. More important, it placed Grant in a position to split the South by driving down the Mississippi River to Vicksburg. Collaborating with Commodore Andrew H. Foote, who commanded the Western Flotilla of the Navy at the beginning of the war, Grant exploited the rivers as lines of operation. Fort Donelson was a turning point in the war and brought Grant into prominence.

The poem covers the period from Wednesday, February 12, through the following Sunday. An almost cinematic technique is used, the scene alternating between the watchers around the bulletin board, with which the poem begins and ends, and the participants in the battle. Melville uses roman type for the passages devoted to the watchers and italics (with small capitals to simulate newspaper bulletins) for the participants, and he gives the watchers' passages in the past tense and the participants' passages in the present. But this playing of one against the other is his somewhat artful device for dramatizing by contrast, their essential similarity of situation. Melville shows this similarity by emphasizing the universal prevalence of suffering. The weather afflicts the soldiers, both North and South, and the watchers at the bulletin board. The tide of battle at Donelson is reflected in the storm in the city which necessitates lighting the "office-gas" (lines 317–18) and, more important, arouses within some of the watchers themselves a counterpart of the agony of the soldiers. Their lot includes suffering "as harrowing/ As Donelson" (lines 328–29), and they are given to musing "on right and wrong/ And mysteries dimly sealed" (lines 265–66). Common suffering, then, is evidence of the basic oneness of the watchers and participants. And common suffering enjoins them to be compassionate, opening the way for eventual reconciliation, a possibility enhanced by Melville's demonstrating the universal qualities of a specific event.

Imagery associated with flowing water—the slashing rains of the storm, the surging flood of Yankee and Rebel charges, the military action on the Cumberland River, the dripping of the sodden paper on the bulletin board, the tears of sorrow and of joyous relief following the news of the battle—is a further unifying device. In the end the fusion is total. The names of the soldiers killed in battle reach the watchers by means of the rain-soaked casualty list, which "like a river flows/ Down the pale sheet" to join, finally, "the whelming waters" (lines 448–50), and the prospect is held out that Fort Donelson itself, the very symbol of war, will "ebb away," submerged by the waters of the river (lines 457–58).

Rhyme is used unobtrusively as a controlling device. Slant rhyme and eye rhyme appear rather frequently. The vocabulary, especially of the battle passages, abounds in military terminology, technical words, journalese, and even slang ("vim," line 39)—none of which is surprising in view of Melville's principal source, contemporary newspaper accounts culled from *The Rebellion Record* (IV, 170–87), and of his desire to impart a sense of immediacy and realism. The Donelson newspaper articles are discussed in the introduction (pp.16-19), as an example of how Melville used *The Rebellion Record*.

Lines 1–3. The reference is probably to the "Trent" affair. John Slidell and James Mason, Confederate commissioners on their way to England, were forcibly removed from the British mail steamer "Trent" by a Union warship on November 8, 1861. They were held at Boston until January 1, 1862, when British pressure accomplished their release.

Line 80. William R. Morrison, of the Forty-ninth Illinois, was wounded leading an attack on a Confederate redoubt.

Lines 85–86. Cannon were often posted in front of infantry, exposing artillerymen to hazardous fire.

Line 112. Jarrard (*Poems . . . Critical Edition,* p. 301) doubts a double meaning of *too* and suggests the addition of a comma for clarification.

Line 115. Cf. Milton, *Comus*, 428: "By grots and caverns shagged with horrid shades."

Line 160. Northern Democrats who favored a negotiated peace were known as Copperheads.

Line 188. Commodore, afterwards Rear Admiral Andrew H. Foote. He was seriously wounded at Donelson.

Line 212. *planet*: a transliteration of a Greek word meaning "a wanderer." Note astronomical connotation of "starboard" in the same line.

Line 217. Nothing could contain or restrain the "Louisville"; but "continent" also suggests massive power such as that of an immense area of land.

Lines 225–28. This passage refers to events which took place on St. Valentine's Day. Melville's source was a news story written at Fort Donelson, February 17, 1862, for the Missouri *Democrat* (*Rebellion Record*, IV, 179–80) : The artillery "would occasionally exchange a valentine, as they were playfully called but there were no such bloody affairs as had characterized the day previous."

Line 253. "The rebels have a flag flying from the Fort which is thought to be a black one." New York *Times*, February 15, 1862 (*Rebellion Record*, IV, 173) .

Lines 349–51. Cf. Shakespeare, *Richard II*, II, i, 40–50.

Line 383. General Lewis Wallace, best remembered as the author of *Ben Hur*, commanded a division at Fort Donelson.

Line 443. *from the cross street* (revision in Melville's copy) .

Lines 450–61. In the last stanza Melville makes clear that his purpose is not primarily to salute a victory and make the name "Donelson" memorable even though he has emphasized the critical nature of the battle and attempted to raise the name to an epic level. Rather, he prays that Fort Donelson as symbol of war and as specific source of grief for the defeated and exultation for the victorious might be washed away into nothingness. In this way a kind of nihilistic reconciliation will occur. The agency, he hopes, will be "Time" (line 451) and nature in the form of the river (line 458). In thus using the river, Melville rounds out the image of flowing water (cf. lines 448–50 and see prefatory note) .

The Cumberland

The first attack by an ironclad on a wooden man-of-war took place off Newport News, Virginia, in Chesapeake Bay on March 8, 1862, when the Confederate armored ship "Merrimac" rammed and sank the "Cumberland." The "Cumberland" fought heroically, losing 117 men out of its crew of 376. By the use of the ironclad, the Confederates hoped to break the Union blockade. This poem and the three which follow show how sensitive Melville was to the significance of the event. A long passage is devoted to the "Cumberland" and ironclads in the nostalgic narrative poem, "Bridegroom Dick," in *John Marr*.

"The Cumberland" is the first of five poems to be published in *Harper's New Monthly Magazine* prior to the publication of *Battle-Pieces*. It appeared in March 1866 (XXXII, 474). Prepublication seems to have been for promotional purposes; Melville did not receive additional payment (Leyda, *Log*, p. 680).

Line 16. *Proud a name (Harper's)*.

Line 20. *sinking, flaming (Harper's)*.

Lines 21–22. Cf. Baltimore *American (Rebellion Record,* IV, 274): "This last shot was fired by an active little fellow named Matthew Tenney. . . . As his port was left open by the recoil of the gun, he jumped to scramble out but the water rushed in with so much force that he was washed back and drowned."

Line 29. *crew (Harper's)*.

Line 30. *shall live; outlive (Harper's)*.

Baltimore *American (Rebellion Record,* IV, 274): "The Cumberland sank in water nearly to her cross-trees. She went down with her *flag still flying,* and it still flies from her mast above the water. . . ." This image inevitably found its way into song and story. A folk ballad, "The Cumberland and the Merrimac," concludes: "And then they sank . . .,/ The Stars and Stripes still flying from her mainmast's highest peak." Cf. "In the Turret" (lines 18–19). The "Pequod" of *Moby-Dick* (Chap. 135, "The Chase—Third Day") sank with flag flying.

In the Turret

Lieutenant John Lorimer Worden, commander of the Union iron-clad "Monitor," arrived dramatically the day after the "Merrimac" sank the "Cumberland." In the clash of the ironclads neither was able to sink the other. The "Merrimac" did not move against the Union fleet again, but her presence at Norfolk, Virginia deprived McClellan's army of naval support in the Peninsular campaign.

Line 1. Prior to the battle Worden had impressed naval officers with his sense of resolution and duty. See "Report of Capt. G. J. Van Brunt, U.S.N., Commanding the Frigate 'Minnesota'" (*Rebellion Record,* IV, 267). The duty theme here and at the end (lines 37–40) frames the poem.

Line 4. References to diving are significant for Melville and appear often in his writings. For example, cf. "In a Church of Padua" (lines 14–

15), in *Timoleon,* where he apostrophizes a confessional booth with "Dread Diving bell! In thee inurned/ What hollows the priest must sound." On March 3, 1849, Melville, writing Evert Duyckinck, said of Emerson (*Letters,* p. 79) : "I love all men who *dive.* Any fish can swim near the surface, but it takes a great whale to go down five miles or more. . . ." When he visited the Cave of the Sibyl near Naples on February 24, 1857, Melville wrote (*Journal . . . to Europe and the Levant,* p. 186) : "What in God's name were such places made for, & why? Surely man is a strange animal. Diving into the bowels of the earth rather than building up to the sky. How clear an indication that he sought darkness rather than light." Fogle ("Melville and the Civil War," p. 73) suggests: "Worden's courage consists of his self-abnegating subordination to his vessel. He is a slave to the strength he rules, a prisoner in his own fortress. He is 'Sealed as in a diving-bell,' 'Cribbed in a craft,' 'in the Turret walled/ By adamant,' riveted in to his duty." This emphasis seems too negative. The diving bell confines but permits deep plunges; the craft restricts but in it Worden can "escape the gale"; the turret imprisons but protects, the rivets are binding but also strengthening. Cf. note on lines 25–33.

Lines 5-6. *Alcides*: patronymic of Hercules. He descended into the Underworld to recover Alcestis, wife of Admetus, who had died so that her husband might be spared.

Line 12. The "Monitor" encountered heavy weather on the voyage to Hampton Roads (*Rebellion Record,* IV, 270) .

Line 13. *cribbed*: confined to the limited space of the ship; confined by the limitations of his "craft" in both the sense of the vessel and craftsmanship or technical skill. Perhaps there is also an intended reference to a small bedstead, in view of line 15. In *White-Jacket* (Chap. 54, " 'The People' Are Given 'Liberty' ") Melville uses *cribbed* primarily in the sense of confined but in a context which suggests the nursery bed.

Lines 15–16. Cf. Deuteronomy 3:11: "For only Og king of Bashan remained of the remnant of giants; behold, his bedstead was a bedstead of iron." According to rabbinical lore, Og escaped the Flood by climbing on top of the ark. He was slain by Moses, the legend continues, when he became entangled with a mountain which he had pulled up to throw at the Israelites. In *Clarel* (III, xi, 192 and xxvii, 172) a huge Albanian soldier is referred to as Og. In "Bridegroom Dick" (line 360) , in *John Marr,* a giant sailor is called "A reeling King Ogg." See also line 36.

Line 19. Baltimore *American* (*Rebellion Record,* IV, 275) : ". . . the Congress was in a bright sheet of flame fore and aft. She continued to burn until twelve o'clock at night, her guns loaded and trained, going off as they became heated."

Line 25. *adamant*: poetically, the hardest iron or steel, or anything very hard and indestructible (*N.E.D.*).

Lines 25–33. *spirit forewarning*: this appears to serve three purposes. First, it is a gothic effect, intensifying the terror of Worden's unprecedented situation. Second, it may refer to Worden's eye injury. According to the Baltimore *American* (*Rebellion Record*, IV, 276), "Lieut. Worden, at the time he was injured, was looking out of the eye-holes of the pilot-house, which are simply horizontal slits, about half an inch wide. A round shot from the Merrimac struck against these slits . . . causing some scalings from the iron, and fragments of paint to fly with great force against his eyes." Symbolically, the eye injury is a warning against blindness to the implications of the ironclads and also against the risks of attempting to scrutinize too closely. Third, the spirit forewarns against the "goblin-snare" of the new technology, a danger which the blinded Worden is able to see.

Worden's heroism is possible because he neither misuses nor is used by technology. Worden uses the imagery of technology in his reply (lines 35 and 40), indicating his awareness of both its possibilities and demands.

Lines 42–44. That Worden survived and that the "Monitor" on December 31, 1862 went down in a storm off Cape Hatteras further suggest his understanding of the limitations of both man and machine.

Melville owned an engraving by James T. Willmore after Turner's painting, "The Fighting Téméraire."

The Temeraire

The *Temeraire,* that storied ship of the old English fleet, and the subject of the well-known painting by Turner, commends itself to the mind seeking for some one craft to stand for the poetic ideal of those great historic wooden warships, whose gradual displacement is lamented by none more than by regularly educated navy officers, and of all nations. [Melville's note]

While in London in 1857, Melville saw "The Fighting Téméraire" in the National Gallery on Trafalgar Square. His journal states (*Journal . . . to Europe and the Levant,* p. 259): "Visited the Vernon & Turner galleries. Sunset scenes of Turner. 'Burial of Wilkie.' The Shipwreck. 'The Fighting [Téméraire] taken to her last berth.' "

Melville may have taken the phrase "fighting Temeraire" (line 13) from the title of the Turner painting, while "pigmy steam-tug" (line 55) may have been suggested by the foreground, and the image in lines 9–12 by the masts of the anchored fleet. The time is sunset, hence the reference to "parting light" (line 9). But less literally, the reference to "parting light" in conjunction with reefed canvas is suggestive of the displacement of wood and sail by iron and steam.

The ship was captured from the French in 1798 and, as Melville observes of similar vessels in *White-Jacket* (Chap. 64, "Man-of-war Trophies"), served "to commemorate the heroism of the conqueror." The name means "one who dares."

Lines 7–8. The decline in the symbolic meaningfulness of heraldry is mentioned also in the "Southern Cross" passage of *Clarel* (II, xxx, 58–59): "With symbols vain once counted wise,/ And gods declined to heraldries?"

Line 11. *shrouded*: ropes supporting the masts; but also suggesting cerements.

Line 17. *brave and rare* (revision in Melville's copy).

Line 20. Some of the cannon of old times, especially the brass ones, unlike the more effective ordnance of the present day, were cast in shapes which Cellini might have designed, were gracefully enchased, generally with the arms of the country. A few of them—field-pieces—captured in our earlier wars, are preserved in arsenals and navy-yards. [Melville's note]

Armorial: pertaining to heraldic arms; but also suggesting ordnance.

Line 26. *can*: drinking vessel.

Line 33. On December 25, 1849, shortly before embarking at Portsmouth for the United States, Melville "took a short stroll into the town." There he "Passed the famous 'North Corner.' Saw the 'Victory,' Nelson's ship at anchor" (*Journal of a Visit to London*, p. 82). Cf. *Billy Budd*, (Chap. 4): "Nevertheless, to anybody who can hold the present at its worth without being inappreciative of the past, it may be forgiven, if to such an one the solitary old hulk at Portsmouth, Nelson's *Victory*, seems to float there, not alone as the decaying monument of a fame incorruptible, but also as a poetic reproach, softened by its picturesqueness, to the *Monitors* and yet mightier hulls of the European iron-clads."

Lines 33–34. In the column at Trafalgar the "Temeraire" was the second ship. The "Victory" was first.

Lines 36–37. Cf. Robert Southey, *The Life of Nelson* (Chap. 9, "The Death of Lord Nelson"): "He [Nelson] wore that day, as usual, his Admiral's frock coat, bearing on the left breast four stars of the different orders with which he was invested." In *Billy Budd* (Chap. 4), Melville says of Nelson that "a sort of priestly motive led him to dress his own person in the jewelled vouchers of his own shining deeds. . . ."

Line 38. Cf. Revelation 10:1: "And I saw another mighty angel come down from heaven . . . and his face was as it were the sun . . ." Also cf. *Paradise Lost*, III, 622–23: "Saw within ken a glorious Angel stand,/ The same whom *John* saw also in the Sun."

Lines 39–45. Cf. Southey, *Life of Nelson* (Chap. 9): ". . . the Victory ran on board the *Redoubtable*, just as her tiller ropes were shot away. . . . Captain Harvey, in the *Temeraire*, fell on board the *Redoubtable* on the other side; another enemy was in like manner on board the *Temeraire;* so that these four ships formed a compact tier as if they had been moored together, their heads all lying the same way."

Line 51. The epithet "Titan" is apt because of the size and power of the oaken warships, and it also recalls Jupiter's overthrow of the Titans.

Lines 55–56. Cf. "Apathy and Enthusiasm" (lines 36–37) and "The Bell Tower," in *Piazza Tales*: " . . . Proceed from comparatively pigmy aims to Titanic ones."

A Utilitarian View of the Monitor's Fight

The Union ironclad "Monitor," built by the marine engineer John Ericsson, engaged the "Merrimac" at 9 A.M. May 9, 1862, in Hampton Roads, Virginia. It withdrew two hours later to replenish its ammunition but returned in less than an hour. The "Merrimac" concentrated its fire on the "Monitor's" sight hole and a direct hit blinded Lieutenant Worden, the commander, forcing a second withdrawal (see "In the Turrett," esp. note on lines 25–33). The duel was inconclusive, no serious damage having been done to either vessel, but the destruction of the Federal fleet was prevented.

Melville's references in *Billy Budd* (Chap. 4) to "martial utilitarians" and "Benthamites of war" indicate his wry awareness of the decline of chivalry which accompanied more mundane preoccupations, and in the "Supplement" to *Battle-Pieces* he seems to marvel at the surge of patriotism which swept "the people in a utilitarian time and country."

As early as 1855 Melville had written of the change in the nature of war. In *Israel Potter* (Chap. 19) he described the battle between the "Bonhomme Richard" and the "Serapis" thus: "Up to their long death-dealing batteries, the trained men of the Serapis stood and toiled in mechanical magic of discipline. They tended those rows of guns, as Lowell girls the rows of looms in a cotton factory. The Parcae were not more methodical; Atropos not more fatal; the automation chessplay not more irresponsible." Melville makes clear that he deliberately sought a style which was appropriate to the new kind of warfare (lines 1–2). This style is anti-poetic. The lines grind and clank like heavy machinery, and the rhythm pounds relentlessly. There is much enjambment, giving an effect of inexorable forward movement. Rhyme is used sparingly, occurring only in the second and sixth lines of each stanza. In most of these it is feminine rhyme, whose impertinent quality is another thrust at the bedraggled dignity of war. In such rhymes as fans–artisans, heroic–caloric, plates–Fates, and weather–feather, Melville has paired words which in this context have contrary associations. For example, the "fans/ Of banners" are part of the panoply of former wars, while the "artisans" are the principals of modern war; and the metallic sound of gunshot striking the "plates" of the iron-clads opposes the words of the "Fates" who presided over Homeric battles. The main images are drawn either from mechanical devices or from cere-monies of gallantry now profaned, and they include imagery of sound and smell as well as that of sight which Melville usually favored. The vocabulary runs to monosyllables and technological terms. The details of the event, unlike those of the epic battles, are not worth the telling (line 19). And the poem is as devoid of emotion (line 16), the seedbed of traditional poetry, as are the engines which propel the ironclad. The poem concludes on a note of grim satisfaction that the outward appearance of war has changed, approximating the reality to a greater degree.

Line 1. *apt*: suitable; polished. Cf. "The Battle for the Mississippi," line 9.

Line 4. *His painted pomp* (revision in Melville's copy). Cf. line 26.

Line 5. *ply*: idiomatically, one also plies a trade. Cf. line 12.

Line 7. *gaud*: the connotation of tawdriness is intensified because of the stress pattern and the word's poised position at the end of the line. Enjambment, which is speeded up by the alliteration with "glory," forces additional attention on "gaud."

Line 15. Cf. "On Sherman's Men" (lines 7–9) :

> Perils the mailed ones never knew
> Are lightly braved . . . ,
> And gentler hearts are bared to deadlier war.

Lines 16–18. The Baltimore *American* (*Rebellion Record*, IV, 276) tells how the officers of the "Monitor" mastered the mechanical techniques needed to control the ironclad.

Lines 20–22. Cf. Emerson, "Concord Hymn" (line 4) : "And fired the shot heard round the world." The Emersonian echo and the reference to the "messages from the Fates" recall epic occasions which contrast with the "blacksmith's fray" of modern war.

Line 22. Cf. "Bridegroom Dick" (lines 512–13), in *John Marr* which describes the "Merrimac" as "A blacksmith's unicorn in armor *cap-a-pie*."

Line 27. *War shall yet be* (revision in Melville's copy).

Line 30. Melville often associated plumes with colorful military display. Cf. "The Armies of the Wilderness" (line 188), "The Released Rebel Prisoner" (line 19), "Lee in the Capitol" (line 55), and "A Battle Picture" from the posthumously published miscellaneous poems. But here the heat of the blacksmith's forge which the engineer calculates has singed the plumes.

Shiloh

Shiloh is on the Tennessee River near the Mississippi–Tennessee line. There on Sunday, April 6, 1862, Albert Sidney Johnston, commander of the Confederate Army of Mississippi, attacked Grant, who was moving south. Grant did not expect battle and had disposed his troops to take advantage of favorable camping facilities. In the two-day battle Federal losses were 13,047. Confederate casualties were 10,694 including General Johnston, who was killed. Both sides claimed victory, but the Confederates withdrew to Corinth, Mississippi, having failed to destroy the invading army which was splitting the Confederacy along the Mississippi.

Among the many documents on Shiloh available in *The Rebellion Record* (IV, 356–417), Melville drew mainly from an account in the Cincinnati *Gazette* of April 9, 1862. This is apparently the source, for example, of the passage on the rain and the reference to the church. Cf.: ". . . the ground . . . was covered with wounded. . . . The moisture . . . would cool the burning, parching thirst . . . and falling water was the best dress for the wounds" (IV, 398). Also, "Gen. Sherman camps, to the right of the little log-cabin called Shiloh church, fronted on a descending slope . . ." (IV, 387).

From his acquaintance with Renaissance painting, Melville may have known that the swallow appears as a symbol of the Incarnation in Annunciation and Nativity scenes. But more pertinent is the association with the Resurrection because of the belief that the swallow hibernated in the mud, from which it was reborn each spring.

The "wheeling" of the swallows at the beginning and end of the poem recalls the circular maneuver of the fleet in "Dupont's Round Fight," which is likewise a geometric symbol of the existence of law in nature. The image of the circling swallows also contributes to the circular structure of the poem, as do the repetition of several phrases and the feminine rhyming of the place name, "Shiloh" (cf. lines 1–4 to 17–19). Whether or not the poet intended to give the swallows a consolatory significance, such a connotation adds to the effectiveness of the circular nature of the poem's structure and imagery.

As Ronald Mason points out (*Spirit Above the Dust,* p. 217), the point of view is that of the swallows, which "we see first and last, like Hardy's Spirit of the Pities. The men are pitiable, but the men are dead . . . nothing can be done but record the final reconciliation of death. . . ."

John Bernstein ("Pacifism and Rebellion in the Writings of Melville") sees "Shiloh" as a crucial statement of Melville's attitude toward war— that it is justifiable as a clash of abstract ideas but indefensible as the strife and slaughter of individuals.

Line 1. Cf. "The Berg" (lines 16–19), in *John Marr,* where wheeling, skimming gulls are unaffected by "the foundering wreck" of a warship which strikes an iceberg:

> Nor sole the gulls in cloud that wheeled
> Circling one snow-flanked peak afar,
> But nearer fowl the floes that skimmed
> And crystal beaches, felt no jar.

Lines 8–10. The church was a focal point on the second day of the battle, a Monday, but Melville's change of the day to Sunday adds the desecration of the Sabbath to that of the church. The modifying phrase, "Around the church," also refers to the circular flight of the swallows.

Lines 14–16. The deception is that men are enemies and that motivating forces like fame and patriotism are of consequence. But ironically, death by violence is the means of bringing about understanding, reconciliation, and peace.

Line 17. *lie low*: cf. "The Portent" (line 6), "The Armies of the Wilderness" (line 76), "On the Slain Collegians" (line 59), "Presentation . . . by Privates of Colors" (line 14), "A Scout Toward Aldie" (line 16).

Line 19. The biblical Shiloh was a sanctuary town, a resting place of the Ark of the Covenant. The meaning of the word is uncertain, but it is associated with rest and tranquillity and with the Messiah as Prince of Peace (Genesis 49:10). Cf. "The Bell Tower" in *Piazza Tales*: "A silence, as of the expectation of some Shiloh, pervaded the swarming plain." For Melville on aspects of silence, see *Pierre* (Bk. XIV, Chap. 1).

The Battle for the Mississippi

At 2 A.M. on April 24, 1862, Admiral David G. Farragut ran a naval force up the Mississippi past two masonry forts, Jackson and St. Philip, 90 miles downstream from New Orleans. He then annihilated the opposing Confederate fleet with the loss of only the "Varuna," a converted merchantman, and moved on to capture the defenseless city the following day.

Official reports of Union officers published in *The Rebellion Record* (IV, 510–25) provided information for Melville. He appears to have used Porter's report for stanza three (IV, 511); the report of Charles Boggs (IV, 515), commander of the "Varuna," and a statement by Commander David Porter (IV, 522) for stanza four; a letter from Farragut (IV, 522) to G. V. Fox, Assistant Secretary of the Navy, for stanza five; General Benjamin F. Butler's report to the Secretary of War (IV, 517) for the description of the New Orleans mob in stanza six; and Farragut's General Order for prayer and thanksgiving (IV, 524) for stanzs six and seven.

As a former sailor Melville was especially interested in naval operations. He had travelled on the Mississippi 'and Ohio by riverboat in 1840 when he visited his uncle, Thomas Melville, at Galena, Illinois, and on the Ohio again during his lecture tour of 1858.

Lines 1–6. Old Testament references set the mood of the poem, the Union forces being identified with the Israelites hymning praise and thanksgiving by the shores of the Red Sea for their deliverance from Pharaoh's pursuing chariots. Following the victory, Farragut's sailors also pray.

Line 1. Cf. Numbers 33:7 and Exodus 14:2.

Line 3. Cf. "Then sang Moses and the children of Israel unto the Lord, . . . saying, I will sing unto the Lord, for he hath triumphed gloriously: the horse and his rider hath he thrown into the sea" (Exodus 15:1). Also cf. "And Miriam the prophetess, the sister of Aaron, took a timbrel in her hand; and all the women went out after her with timbrels and with dances" (Exodus 15:20).

Line 6. A verbatim quotation from Exodus 15:3.

Line 9. Cf. "A Utilitarian View of the Monitor's Fight," line 1: "Plain be the phrase, yet apt the verse . . ."

Line 21. The Confederate river defense included a chain, supported by floating hulks, which extended east from Fort Jackson. High water had seriously damaged it. Cf. "Bridegroom Dick" (lines 284–85), in *John Marr*: "If Dick was with Farragut on the night-river,/ When the boom-chain we burst in the fire-raft's glare."

Lines 23–34. Cf. "And there was war in heaven: Michael and his angels fought against the dragon; and the dragon fought and his angels, and prevailed not; neither was their place found any more in heaven" (Revelation 12:7–8). Also cf. Milton, *Paradise Lost,* I, 174–75: ". . . the Thunder,/ Wing'd with red Lightning and impetuous rage."

Line 24. The more familiar form is "levin," but Melville was notoriously eccentric in spelling. Jarrard (*Poems . . . Critical Edition,* p. 304) points to the eye rhyme with "driven" (line 22) as justification of Melville's choice.

Line 25. Varuna is the Hindu equivalent of Neptune.

Line 30. In a preliminary action on October 11, 1861, the ram "Manassas" moved down the Mississippi to attack successfully the Union river fleet. Hence it was one of the better known Confederate ships.

Lines 41–42. Melville juxtaposes law and religion, which he sees as twin agencies for the control of wayward man, in "The House-top" (lines 19–21) and elsewhere.

Lines 55–56. Unlike "Shiloh" which precedes and "Malvern Hill" which follows, this poem does not end on a note of reconciliation. Instead, there is a prayer of thanksgiving (cf. lines 1–4) and a hesitant expression of hope in an afterlife.

Malvern Hill

Malvern Hill on July 1, 1862 was the last action of the Seven Days' Battle and ended McClellan's attempt to capture Richmond during the Peninsular campaign. McClellan held a strong natural position and beat off Lee's repeated attacks, inflicting losses greater than his own, but withdrew during the night to Harrison's Landing.

A news story in the Grenada *Appeal* dated Richmond, July 7, 1862 (*Rebellion Record,* V, 266) contains a reference to the elms of Malvern, and may have been Melville's source: "The house at Malvern Hill is a quaint old structure of the last century, built of red brick and stands on a lofty hill a thousand yards from the James River. . . . A fine grove of ancient elms embowers the lawn in grateful shade. . . . It seemed a bitter satire on the wickedness of man, this peaceful, serene, harmonious aspect of nature. . . ."

The time of the poem is a May morning in the spring following the battle. The imagery is mainly visual, a sequence of brief vignettes, but

things cannot be plainly seen. The spires of Richmond are hidden by
"musket-haze" (line 12), and the stars of the flag are "eclipsed" (line 21)
by the gunsmoke. In contrast to the intense and chaotic action of the battle
is the passivity and order of the elm grove. A series of questions addressed
to the elms lead to a resolution: spring is the imperative; time and nature
will prevail.

Early in April 1864 Melville "visited various battle-fields" in Virginia
including Malvern Hill.

When he visited the Virginia battlefields, Melville bought for one dollar a
souvenir brick made from the clay of Malvern Hill.

Line 1. Symbolically and thematically the elms are akin to the "piny wood" in line 2 of "An uninscribed Monument on one of the Battle-fields of the Wilderness."

Line 7. A paper cartridge containing powder and a lead ball was used for some muzzle-loading rifles. The paper was bitten open, the powder emptied into the bore, and the paper rammed in as wadding.

Line 8. *fixed arms*: arms rigid, as in death; guns readied and aimed.

Lines 9–10. The arms are uplifted in an invocation to death, of which the cypress is a traditional symbol and one which Melville uses frequently elsewhere in *Battle-Pieces*.

Line 14. *ways*: roads.

Line 24. See Read, "The Rebel Yell as a Linguistic Problem."

Line 26. McClellan's artillery, some 250 guns, was highly effective.

Line 34. Cf. Shakespeare, *As You Like It*, II, vii, 23: " ' . . . Thus we may see,' quoth he, 'how the world wags. . . .' " Also cf. the uncollected poem located by H. P. Vincent, "In a Nutshell" (line 4) : "Wag the world how it may." The phrase is proverbial (Tilley W879).

The Victor of Antietam

Whatever just military criticism, favorable or otherwise, has at any time been made upon General McClellan's campaigns, will stand. But if, during the excitement of the conflict, aught was spread abroad tending to unmerited disparagement of the man, it must necessarily die out, though not perhaps without leaving some traces, which may or may not prove enduring. Some there are whose votes aided in the re-election of Abraham Lincoln, who yet believed, and retain the belief, that General McClellan, to say the least, always proved himself a patriotic and honorable soldier. The feeling which surviving comrades entertain for their late commander is one which, from its passion, is susceptible of versified representation, and such it receives. [Melville's note]

McClellan succeeded General Winfield Scott as General-in-Chief of the Union army after the defeat of First Manassas but was replaced by General John Pope when the Peninsular campaign failed. In turn he replaced Pope after the Second Manassas defeat (see lines 22 and 39) when Lee moved into Maryland. Outnumbered and faced with mounting opposition, Lee decided to make a stand at Sharpsburg near Antietam Creek on September 17, 1862. Both sides suffered heavy losses, but Lee was forced to retire across the Potomac. When McClellan failed to pursue him, he was relieved for a second time. McClellan was a presidential candidate in 1864.

Line 22. *Arrayed*: disposed in proper military order; *array*: a body of soldiers. For a similar parallelism, see line 30. Cf. "Lee in the Capitol" (line 37) : "Of Pope's impelled retreat in disarray."

Line 33. After the Peninsular campaign and before Antietam McClellan was at Alexandria, Virginia, where he saw unit after unit of his command assigned to others.

Lines 45–46. Melville is capitalizing on the nautical associations of several words. A leadsman takes soundings or measurements of depth with a lead-weighted line; but the primary signification here is the unusual one of a person who leads. This sense is re-enforced by the fact that *leadsman* is a variant of *lodesman,* meaning leader, guide, pilot or steersman (*N.E.D.*) . Sounding is measuring depth for the purpose of safe navigation; but it also suggests dropping down abruptly, and as a whaling term connotes uncertainty and suspense over when or whether the whale will surface. The phrase "in the bay" refers to a body of water and to the state of being held in check, at bay.

Line 55. At Antietam Stonewall Jackson led one wing of Lee's army, consequently sharing that day in whatever may be deemed to have been the fortunes of his superior. [Melville's note]

Battle of Stone River, Tennessee

William S. Rosecrans, commanding the Union Army of the Cumberland, met Braxton Bragg, commanding the Confederate Army of Tennessee, at Stones River near Murfreesboro, Tennessee, on December 30, 1862. The four-day battle which ensued was fought with vigor and gallantry by both sides. Bragg achieved a tactical success but was unable to exploit it because he was outnumbered. He withdrew, and Rosecrans did not pursue or resume the offensive until the following June.

Melville was much impressed by Oxford, which he visited on May 3–4, 1857, just prior to his departure for the United States (*Journal . . . to Europe and the Levant,* p. 260) : "Most interesting spot I have seen in England. Made tour of all colleges. It was here I confessed with gratitude my mother land, & hailed her with pride. . . . Catching rhuematism [*sic*] in Oxford cloisters different from catching it in Rome. Contagion in Pamfili Doria but wholsem [*sic*] beauty in Oxford."

Except for line length the poem is fairly regular, consisting of four stanzas of eight lines, with a couplet refrain which uses the same rhyme throughout and has an incremental character. The refrains alternate between statement and question, and since the poem ends with an interrogative it can hardly be thought of as expressing undue optimism concerning amicable reunion of North and South. The peculiar enjambment of the stanza proper with the refrain builds up a momentum which leads to this final question and gives it emphasis. A departure from the rhyme scheme emphasizes it further. In stanza four Melville substitutes near rhyme for the regular rhyme of the preceding stanzas; he then rhymes line 37 with the first line of the final couplet, again deviating from the established pattern. The effect is to point up the single conventional rhyme, thus stressing the content of the last couplet.

Line 1. Edward IV of York, at Barnet Heath on April 14, 1471 and at Tewksbury on May 3, 1471, crushed Lancastrian opposition and ended the fratricidal Wars of the Roses. Melville found the parallel to the Civil War irresistible. Cf. "rival roses" (line 11).

Line 6. Druids are associated with tree worship and with the distant past. Trees (cf. lines 5, 21, 22) are here also linked with the past and therefore are part of the historical perspective which Melville provides with the reference to the Wars of the Roses. The function of this comparison to the past is to suggest the healing potential of time.

Line 21. One suspects that Melville cherished the coincidence that Rosecrans' name fit in with references to the Wars of the Roses. He similarly played on the name of General Jubal Early in "Sheridan at Cedar Creek" (line 30).

Line 23. John C. Breckinridge commanded with skill the division which covered Bragg's retreat. A former senator from Kentucky and Vice President in the Buchanan administration, he ran against Lincoln for president. He fled south to escape arrest and was declared a traitor.

Line 31-33. Cf. Milton, *Paradise Lost*, IV, 98-99: "For never can true reconcilement grow/ Where wounds of deadly hate have pierc'd so deep."

Lines 13-14. The connotations of "Passion" and "Lent sacred fervor" prepare for the religious imagery which follows (lines 15-18). Melville uses language associated with Easter in "Apathy and Enthusiasm" (lines 25-31) and "The Martyr." He may have known that the battle at Barnet Heath was fought on Easter morning.

Line 17. This line concentrates the religious imagery and wordplay which dominate the stanza. The irony cuts deeply. Monks are members of a religious brotherhood, yet they violate their brotherliness and their priestly office by blessing the weapons of both sides in a war of brothers. The "sisters" (line 18) are nuns. In their weaving of scarves for the warriors, they transform what is normally a process of joining together into one of separation. Melville relates disrupted brotherhood to civil strife in "Apathy and Enthusiasm" (lines 15-16) and provides examples of the misuse of religion in "A Meditation" (lines 11-12) and "On the Slain Collegians" (lines 42-43): "Each went forth with blessing given/ By priests and mothers in the name of Heaven." The interesting thing about this stanza is that Melville progresses to a point beyond irony. Logically only one side is worthy to receive the blessing (cf. lines 11–12). But in a fundamental sense neither side is worthy, or else both are. The paradox thus becomes a basis for reconciliation. Cf. Melville's discussion of the inherent contradiction in the role of the naval chaplain in *White-Jacket* (Chap. 38, "The Chaplain and Chapel in a Man-of-war").

Running the Batteries

On the night of April 16, 1863, Admiral David Dixon Porter ran a flotilla of eleven river boats downstream past the Confederate batteries at Vicksburg, Mississippi, to join Grant who was besieging the city. All the boats were hit and one was sunk, but casualties to personnel were light and the fleet remained fully operational. Vicksburg had blocked the Union attempt to free the Mississippi River which had begun with Grant's victory at Fort Donelson and Farragut's capture of New Orleans. The surrender of Vicksburg on July 4, 1863, combined with the Union success at Gettysburg the day before, was a crushing blow to the Confederate cause.

Melville follows so closely the account in the New York *Tribune* of April 17, 1863 (*Rebellion Record*, VI, 546–48) that the poem is little more than versified narration. The events reported in the *Tribune* were seen from the vantage point of a correspondent aboard the "Steamer Sunny South, above Vicksburgh."

Lines 21–23. Allusions to the three Hebrews who survived the fiery furnace (Daniel 3:12–30) also appear in *Moby-Dick* (Chap. 98, "Stowing Down and Clearing Up") and "The Bell Tower" in *Piazza Tales*. Cf. also the reference to "those children of the furnace" in the "Supplement" to *Battle-Pieces*. The biblical namesake of the spokesman, Lot, also escaped the horrors of fire (Genesis 19:1–26).

Line 41. A cresset is an iron basket for holding a fire for illumination. In this reference Melville is following his newspaper source, but he implies that the glare of the fire is like a force of nature in that it "is nobody's ally" (cf. "The Stone Fleet," line 33).

Line 50. Melville or the printer omitted the apostrophe.

Line 65. The beautiful enchantress Circe changed men into beasts (*Odyssey*, X, 237–40; Sealts no. 278). Melville cautions that the light from the fires of battle—an important source of imagery after stanza three—is "false" in the same way. Cf. "The March into Virginia" (line 34 and note) and "Fair Circe" in *Clarel* (II, iv, 143).

Line 75. Admiral Porter is a son of the late Commodore Porter, commander of the frigate Essex on that Pacific cruise which ended in the desperate fight off Valparaiso with the English frigates Cherub and Phoebe, in the year 1814. [Melville's note]

David Porter (1780–1843), a naval hero of the War of 1812, was the author of *Journal of a Cruise Made to the Pacific Ocean* (1815), which Melville drew upon extensively for *The Encantadas*. See especially the fifth sketch, "The Frigate, ad Ship Flyaway." Porter was based in the Galápagos, Melville's "Enchanted Isles," and preyed on British whalers. In *White-Jacket* (Chap. 74, "The Main-top at Night") Melville praises his valor when he was finally trapped by two British cruisers off Valparaiso, but expresses doubts about his common sense.

Stonewall Jackson

On May 2, 1863, at Chancellorsville, Virginia, as he was returning from the front in the early evening, Jackson was accidentally shot by one of his own men. He had just completed a brilliant maneuver which had led to a successful attack on the Union flank. He died of pneumonia on May 10. There are complimentary references to Jackson in the "Supplement" to *Battle-Pieces*." Mason (*Spirit Above the Dust*, pp. 215–16) suggests that the two poems on Jackson indicate Melville's sense of "the inadequacy of any partisan judgement of Jackson (and implicitly of any partisan judgment on war as a whole)."

Line 14. *low*: for comment see notes on "The Portent" (line 6) and "Shiloh" (line 17).

Stonewall Jackson, Ascribed to a Virginian

Lines 6–7. As used here, *charged* has military as well as electrical connotations.

Lines 8–9. Melville refers to "Seneca and the Stoics" in *Moby-Dick* (Chap. 1, "Loomings") and in *Redburn* (Chap. 26, "A Sailor a Jack of All Trades"). He owned and annotated the L'Estrange edition of Seneca's *Morals by Way of Abstract* (London, 1746) and the Thomas Lodge edition of *The Workes of Lucius Annaeus Seneca* (London, 1620). Cf. Sealts nos. 457, 458. See Braswell, *Melville's Religious Thought*, p. 14.

Line 16. The occupation of Romney, 35 miles west of Winchester, Virginia, on January 10, 1862, was one of Jackson's early successes. His home was not far away.

Line 17. On October 26, 1862, Jackson was sent to Winchester as commander of the Confederate forces in the Shenandoah Valley. His winter campaign, which was designed to split the Union army and open the way for a future offensive into Pennsylvania, was conducted in severe weather.

Line 20. Gaines' Mill on June 27, 1862, was fought the third day of the Seven Days' Battle. It was a costly Confederate victory.

Lines 24–25. The decision to invade Maryland in September 1862 involved political considerations. Lee hoped to rally the border state to the Confederate cause.

Lines 26–27. The words to "Maryland, My Maryland" were written by James Ryder Randall, a journalist and poet, upon hearing of the attack by Baltimore citizens on the Sixth Massachusetts Infantry. The song was extremely popular.

Line 28. McClellan turned back the Confederate invasion near Sharpsburg, Maryland, at Antietam Creek, a branch of the Potomac. See "The Victor of Antietam."

Line 32. Marye's Heights, an almost impregnable position at Fredericksburg, Virginia, was unsuccessfully attacked by General Ambrose E. Burnside on December 11, 1862. See "Inscription for Marye's Heights, Fredericksburg."

Lines 42–46. Jackson's appearance was notoriously casual. Shortly after October 11, 1862, when he was promoted to lieutenant general, J. E. B. Stuart presented him with a handsome coat adorned exuberantly with facings, gilt buttons, and gold lace. Somewhat uneasily, he wore this new finery at Fredericksburg.

Line 53. *South's great war* (revision in Melville's copy).

Gettysburg

Lee's second attempt to invade the North (cf. line 8) was checked at Gettysburg, Pennsylvania, on July 3, 1863 by General George Gordon Meade, after three days of spirited Confederate attacks. The poem was first published in *Harper's New Monthly Magazine*, XXXIII (July 1866), 209.

Line 1. *pride*: foremost, first; but also suggestive of the arrogance of Dagon, principal god of the Philistines.

Lines 3–7. Cf. I Samuel 5:2–3: "When the Philistines took the ark of God, they brought it into the house of Dagon, and set it by Dagon. And when they of Ashdod arose early on the morrow, behold, Dagon was fallen upon his face to the earth before the ark of the Lord." For other examples of Melville's use of the fall of Dagon, see *Moby-Dick* (Chap. 82, "The Honor and Glory of Whaling") and "Naples in the Time of Bomba" (Pt. IX, line 55), a posthumously published poem: "Fell down, like Dagon on his face."

The first stanza of "The Battle for the Mississippi" also has an Old

Testament reference which equates the Union army with the hosts of Israel and the Confederates with their enemies, who in this instance are the Egyptians.

Line 4. *Fell* is also here an adjective meaning fierce or deadly.

Line 14. *screamings, taunts, and yells* (*Harper's*).

Lines 15–16. *the three waves*: may refer to the three divisions which on the third day made the sally known as Pickett's Charge—those of James J. Pettigrew, George E. Pickett, and Isaac R. Trimble. See "trebled" (line 2).

Line 20. Cf. "Misgivings."

Line 31. Among numerous head-stones or monuments on Cemetery Hill, marred or destroyed by the enemy's concentrated fire, was one, somewhat conspicuous, of a Federal officer killed before Richmond in 1862.

On the 4th of July, 1865, the Gettysburg National Cemetery, on the same height with the original burial-ground, was consecrated, and the corner-stone laid of a commemorative pile. [Melville's note]

Line 28. Cemetery Hill was a defensive position and rallying point for Federal troops after their defeat on July 1, the first day of Gettysburg. The hill was successfully defended on the second day and retained on the third.

The House-top

The New York draft riots were precipitated by the publication on July 11, 1863, of the first list of those selected for compulsory military service. Negroes were the principal victims of the rioting. The mob burned a Negro church and orphanage. Other fires caused property losses in the millions. Federal troops put down the disturbance, inflicting an estimated thousand casualties. Less serious riots took place in Boston and other cities.

Lines 3–6. The tiger as a symbol of noble savagery appears frequently in romantic art and literature. Cf. "Charleston" (lines 13–16) by the Confederate poet Henry Timrod, first published in the Charleston *Mercury* of December 13, 1862:

> And down the dunes a thousand guns lie couched
> Unseen beside the flood,
> Like tigers in some Orient jungle crouched,
> That wait and watch for blood.

Also cf. *Moby-Dick* (Chap. 114, "The Gilder"): ". . . beholding the tranquil beauty and brilliancy of the ocean's skin, one forgets the tiger heart that pants beneath it. . . ."

Lines 5–6. Libya was proverbial for heat, drought, and sterility. Cf. Shakespeare, *Troilus and Cressida*, I, iii, 327–28.

Line 8. *roar*: cf. line 3.

Line 9. Sirius in Canis Major, called the Dog Star because it follows its master Orion, is the brightest star in the sky. During "dog days," July 3 to August 11, according to tradition, Sirius rises with the sun, increasing its heat. "Dog days" is supposedly the period when dogs are susceptible to rabies, a disease said to be characterized by madness and fear of water. The star's name is from the Greek adjective *seiros,* meaning hot, scorching.

Lines 12–13. Shakespeare often used the words *charms* and *spells* together in a context which has to do with witchcraft (see *Macbeth,* III, v, 18–19; *Merry Wives of Windsor,* IV, ii, 185; *Midsummer-Night's Dream,* II, ii, 17; *I Henry VI,* V, iii, 2). Melville seems to be conscious of this usage here, in at once calling for the restraints of law and religion and recognizing that they are never totally effective.

Line 13. John J. Hughes, Roman Catholic Bishop of New York, was asked by the city authorities to address the rioters, many of whom were Irish immigrants. His plea for submission to the law contributed largely to the restoration of order. Bishop Hughes, a native of Ireland, had been an early advocate of conscription.

Line 15. Cf. Shakespeare, *Tempest,* IV, i, 148–58.

Line 16. "I dare not write the horrible and inconceivable atrocities committed," says Froissart, in alluding to the remarkable sedition in France during his time. The like may be hinted of some proceedings of the draft-rioters. [Melville's note]

Melville is quoting from Lord Berners' translation of Froissart's *Chronicles* (Chap. 182). The passage concerns the Jacqueries, a peasant uprising, in May 1358, that was accompanied by excesses which Froissart, despite his statement to the contrary, proceeds to detail. The rebellion was crushed by Charles the Bad, King of Navarre, with "violent reprisals upon the peasants." Melville also drew upon Froissart for *Moby-Dick* (Chap. 42, "The Whiteness of the Whale") and *Mardi* (Chap. 24, "Dedicated to the College of Physicians . . .").

Line 18. *drag that jars the wall* (revision in Melville's copy).

Line 19. Cf. "The Martyr" (line 22): "The Avenger wisely stern." Draco codified the unwritten laws of Athens and administered them vigorously. His code was regarded as harsh and its provisions were much modified by Solon. Solon's opinion of the code is known from Plutarch's sketch, which Melville appears to have read. For Melville on Plutarch, see his note to "The Frenzy in the Wake."

Line 21. The poem is alliterative to an extent unusual even for Melville. Alliteration is used to give the unity elsewhere provided by rhyme. But the alliteration of line 21 is especially heavy and is made more obvious by its position in a section of the poem where alliteration is relatively sparse. The line is further stressed because it is bracketed between the phrases "Draco comes" (line 19) and "he comes" (lines 20, 22). Another device which points up line 21 is the relation between the words *Draco* and *code,* normally used together but here separated—a device which gives a jarring effect in the interval of waiting for the set phrase to be completed. This concentration on line 21 serves to emphasize a concept of fundamental importance to Melville: the parallel roles in society of law and religion, both needed by man because of his natural depravity (cf. line 26).

Line 22. *cynic*: pessimistic regarding human motives and behavior; but also etymologically pertaining to the Dog Star (cf. line 9). Necessity demands the cynical exercise of discipline—Melville's justification of the ways of God to man. In "The Apparition," in *Timoleon,* Melville refers to Diogenes, the Cynic philosopher, as one of those "cynic minds" who "barked so much at Man." *The Confidence-Man* (esp. Chap. 22) associates "cynic" with "dog" and "canine," and Plotinus Plinlimmon's famous pamphlet in *Pierre* (Bk. XIV, Chap. 3) refers to "dogmatical teachers" whose students turn "like a mad dog, into atheism."

Line 25. *The grimy slur,*—the need for "cynic tyrannies"—derives ultimately from the doctrine of the natural goodness of man, held by the founders of the Republic and incorporated—to its detriment—into the political structure. In spite of having just been rescued from retrogression by "Draco" and "Calvin," man remains heedless of the power of evil.

Line 27. Acts 16:37–38 and 22:25–29 relate how Paul invoked his right as a Roman citizen to exemption from scourging. Cf. *White-Jacket* (Chap. 34, "Some of the Evil Effects of Flogging"): "Is it lawful for you to scourge a man that is a Roman? asks the intrepid Apostle, well knowing, as a Roman citizen, that it was not. And now, eighteen hundred years after, is it lawful to you, my countrymen, to scourge a man who is an American?" Also cf. *Redburn* (Chap. 40, "Placards, Brass Jewellers, Truck Horses and Steamers"), *Billy Budd* (Chap. 9), and "Bridegroom Dick" (lines 373–429), in *John Marr.*

Melville, as a sailor himself subject to the lash, saw scores of seamen flogged during his service aboard the "United States" (Howard, *Melville,* p. 72).

Look-out Mountain

Lookout Mountain, a plateau 1,100 feet above the Tennessee River, was held during the Chattanooga campaign by two brigades guarding the Confederate flank. Union forces attacked on November 24, 1863. A heavy fog obscured the scene. The Confederates withdrew at night, and early the following morning Union soldiers planted on the heights a flag clearly visible to Grant's army below.

Melville may have used as general background the news account from the Cincinnati *Gazette* of November 23, 1863 (*Rebellion Record,* VIII, 228-36).

Line 1. Cf. Isaiah 57:15: "For thus saith the high and lofty One that inhabiteth eternity, whose name is Holy; I dwell in the high and holy place. . . ." Also cf. Psalms 15:1: "Lord, who shall abide in thy tabernacle? who shall dwell in thy holy hill?"

Lines 1–6. Lookout Mountain is compared to Kaf, a mountain in the Caucasus. Beneath Kaf lay a subterranean palace of fire, the Arabian hell. At its base Kaf had a miraculous emerald-like stone, the reflected rays of which colored the sky (cf. line 2). Melville could have been acquainted with this information from reading the *Arabian Nights, Vathek, an Arabian Tale* by William Beckford (Sealts no. 54) or Byron's *The Giaour* (Sealts no. 112). He owned the latter two books. Cf. "L'envoi," in *Timoleon* (line 5): "Kaf thrusts his snouted crags through fog."

Line 5. Eblis, according to the Koran (Sura 7), was the chief of the fallen angels. When Adam was created, God commanded all the angels to pay homage to him. Eblis refused and was turned into a devil. Cf. *Clarel* (II, x, 111).

Lines 7–8. Cf. Psalms 47:5: "God is gone up with a shout, the Lord with the sound of a trumpet."

Line 10. In *Paradise Lost* (II, 988) the Anarch is identified with Chaos as lord of misrule. Cf. "After the Pleasure Party," in *Timoleon* (line 92).

Lines 15–16. The poetry section of *The Rebellion Record* (VIII, 1) includes "The Storming of Lookout Mountain" by Captain Thomas H. Elliott, which describes Union soldiers praying for victory and watching the mountain top for indications of the outcome of the battle.

Chattanooga

The culminating engagement of the Chattanooga campaign was the assault on the Confederate position at Missionary Ridge on November 25, 1863. Grant had planned to have his men halt and reorganize after taking the first lines up the slope. Instead, because they were able to avoid fire from the crest and found weaknesses in Bragg's defenses, they continued their charge. Bragg retired and Chattanooga fell, leaving the way open for the Atlanta campaign and the march to the sea.

The narrative content of the poem follows the Cincinnati *Gazette* dispatch of November 23, 1863 (*Rebellion Record,* VIII, 228–36).

First published in *Harper's New Monthly Magazine,* XXXIII (June 1866), 44.

Line 2. Although the month was November, the day was in character an October one—cool, clear, bright, intoxicatingly invigorating; one of those days peculiar to the ripest hours of our American autumn. This weather must have had much to do with the spontaneous enthusiasm which seized the troops—an enthusiasm aided, doubtless, by glad thoughts of the victory of Look-out Mountain won the day previous, and also by the elation attending the capture, after a fierce struggle, of the long ranges of rifle-pits at the mountain's base, where orders for the time should have stopped the advance. But there and then it was that the army took the bit between its teeth, and ran away with the generals to the victory commemorated. General Grant, at Culpepper [*sic*], a few weeks prior to crossing the Rapidan for the Wilderness, expressed to a visitor his impression of the impulse and the spectacle: Said he, "I never saw any thing like it": language which seems curiously undertoned, considering its application; but from the taciturn Commander it was equivalent to a superlative or hyperbole from the talkative.

The height of the Ridge, according to the account at hand, varies along its length from six to seven hundred feet above the plain; it slopes at an angle of about forty-five degrees. [Melville's note]

Line 2. *heaven's October air (Harper's)* .
Line 7. *the Mountain then (Harper's)* .
Line 10. *On yestermorn, in (Harper's)* .
Line 11. *Armies, like ghosts, on hills had fought; (Harper's)* .
Line 12. *And, rolled from the cloud, their (Harper's)* .
Line 13. *caught; (Harper's)* .
Line 20. *wall; (Harper's)* .
Line 24. *He from the brink* [no comma] *(Harper's)* .
Line 28. *Yet, here and there, (Harper's)* .
Line 31. *show, (Harper's)* .
Line 41. *color-bearer, with (Harper's)* .
Line 42. *Grant— (Harper's)* .
Line 43. *stump, (Harper's)* .
Line 44. *While, in solicitude, his (Harper's)* .
Line 49. *name. (Harper's)* .
Line 51. *caught; and (Harper's)* .
Line 52. *led: (Harper's)* .
Line 54. *of foemen fled* (revision in Melville's copy) .
Lines 55–63. These lines do not appear in the poem as first published in *Harper's*. Their source is apparently the Cincinnati *Gazette* of November 23, 1863 (*Rebellion Record*, VIII, 235): "The expression upon the faces of our own men who had fallen here, was most touching and remarkable, for not all the pains of dissolution had been able to drive from their features the smile of victory, or the placid look of contentment which

rests upon the countenance of him who feels his work well done. . . . For it was plain as the sun at noonday, that there men had died, not only without mental agony, but that their last earthly feeling was one of calm contentment or triumphant joy."

At the request of Lieutenant Colonel Alexander Bliss, who with John Pendleton Kennedy, the novelist, compiled *Autograph Leaves of Our Country's Authors* (Baltimore, 1864) for the benefit of the Sanitary Commision, Melville supplied a poem entitled "Inscription for the Slain at Fredericksburgh":

> A dreadful glory lights an earnest end;
> In jubilee that patriot ghosts ascend;
> Transfigured at the rapturous height
>   Of their passionate feat of arms,
> Death to the brave's a starry night,—
>   Strewn their vale of death with palms.

This version is Melville's revision from a letter to Bliss dated New York, March 22, 1864 (*Letters*, p. 224).

The Armies of the Wilderness

The Army of the Potomac under Grant met the Army of Northern Virginia under Lee on May 5, 1864, near the Rapidan River in the foothills of the Blue Ridge Mountains. After three days of bloody but indecisive fighting, Grant retired to begin the Spotsylvania campaign. The battleground in Virginia was a dense second-growth forest, cut up by streams. It had been the scene of previous fighting around Chancellorsville, May 1–4, 1863.

If Elizabeth Melville's recollections are correct, Melville saw the Wilderness battlefield when he visited Colonel Henry Gansevoort (Howard, *Melville*, p. 276). This would have been less than a month before the battle.

Although the poem is based upon the Battle of the Wilderness and contains specific references to it, Melville sought to encompass more than narrative. His aim is achieved in several ways. First, the title of the poem is ambiguous. It refers to the battle of May 1864, but the same ground had been fought over before and Melville interweaves references to the earlier fighting (see lines 75–82, 172–79). Second, the word *wilderness* suggests an area of confusion and is associated with a "maze" (line 223) and a "riddle" (line 226) that defies solution. This association constitutes the theme of the final stanza, for which the way has been prepared by a number of questions posed at intervals throughout. Third, the dates of the subtitle are a further indication that the battles of both May 1863 and May

1864 are to be considered, and this inclusiveness suggests a possibility of further extension. Fourth, Melville identifies the Union army with the Israelites (lines 214–19) by an allusion to the pillars of smoke and fire which guided the Children of Israel in their wilderness. By extending the context of the poem and enriching the meaning of the word *wilderness,* Melville is able to make the Battle of the Wilderness a metaphor of the Civil War as a whole, of any war and the puzzling questions that arise with it, and ultimately of the confusion and conflict which are part of the human situation and which only death can resolve.

Nathalia Wright (*Melville's Use of the Bible,* pp. 47–60) found that Melville follows the Bible in his use, exemplified by the pilgrims of *Clarel,* of the wilderness as a place where experiences occur which may bring maturity.

Cf. "The College Colonel" (line 27) and "The Fall of Richmond" (line 19) for possible examples of a similar connotative use of *wilderness.*

The poem consists of nineteen stanzas, each followed by a quatrain which Melville had set in italic type, and is divided into two sections of almost equal length, the first dealing with winter and the second with spring. Each of the stanzas describes a scene, the details of which lead to generalizations made in the accompanying quatrains by a process akin to inductive logic, the quatrains serving as a kind of gnomic commentary on the stanzas. The stanzas could almost stand alone, as could the quatrains, but while Melville takes care to set them apart typographically, he links them logically and by means of the rhyme scheme. For other examples of alternating passages see "The Conflict of Convictions" and "Donelson."

Line 8. *The bravos of* (revision in Melville's copy).

Line 13. *pointed glass*: field glasses.

Line 14. *The foot-ball bounding* (revision in Melville's copy).

Line 17–20. *The reddish soil* and the digging of entrenchments suggest bloodshed and burial.

Lines 33–34. It is said of Belial in *Paradise Lost* (II, 108–15) that "A fairer person lost not Heav'n" and that "his Tongue/ Dropt Manna, and could make the worse appear/ The better reason. . . ." His speech to Satan's host (II, 226) ends: "Thus Belial with words cloth'd in reason's garb."

Lines 37–46. This is the only ten-line stanza. Its length may be attributed to the presence of direct address, but see the preceding stanza. The rhyme scheme is unchanged.

Line 49. Cf. John 12:13.

Lines 65–66. *dole*: sorrow, *amort*: dead. See note on lines 77–80 concerning the influence of Webster.

Line 66. Ishmael "dwelt in the wilderness of Paran," located in the east-central region of the Sinai peninsula. See Genesis 21:21.

Line 74. The cockatrice or basilisk, a fabulous monster hatched by a serpent from the egg of a cock, was said to kill with a glance.

Lines 77–80. Cf. John Webster, *The White Devil*, V, iv, 109–11:

> Call unto his funeral dole
> The ant, the field-mouse and the mole,
> To rear him hillocks that shall keep him warm.

In "Hawthorne and His Mosses" (1850) Melville praises Webster and other Renaissance dramatists. In 1862 he asked Evert Duyckinck to lend him "volumes of Elizabethan dramatists," particularly Dekker and Webster (*Letters*, p. 213).

Line 83. *dust to dust*: cf. Genesis 3:19. The passage is from God's speech to Adam just before the expulsion from Eden. Note Adamic references in lines 86 and 90.

Line 90. See Genesis 4:17. Melville also refers to Cain's city in *The Confidence-Man* (Chap. 24, "A Philanthropist Undertakes to Convert a Misanthrope") and *Billy Budd* (Chap. 3).

Lines 99–105. Melville was at Fairfax Courthouse, Virginia, a divisional headquarters, during his visit to the front. He wrote General Robert O. Tyler on July 21, 1864 (*Letters*, p. 226): ". . . I recalled your hospitality at Fairfax, and the agreeable evening I spent with you there, in company with my cousin, Col. Gansevoort." The town was the scene of a number of minor engagements. The stanza may refer to the depredations of raw Union soldiers who on their way to First Manassas took Fairfax Courthouse from retreating Confederates. Because of their behavior General Irvin McDowell wrote on July 18, 1861: "I am distressed to have to report excesses by our troops" (*War of the Rebellion*, Ser. 1, II, 306). The most notable skirmish at Fairfax Courthouse took place on June 27, 1863, during Stuart's Gettysburg raid, when General Wade Hampton's cavalry captured two companies of the Eleventh New York Cavalry.

Line 111. The Pleiades, seven daughters of Atlas, were transformed into stars by Jupiter when they were pursued by Orion. They turned pale upon beholding the fall of Troy and have so remained.

Line 123. The Battle of the Wilderness took place in May.

Lines 147–54. Grant crossed the Rappahannock River on May 4, 1864.

Lines 155–58. Robinson Crusoe, Alexander Selkirk upon whose life the Defoe novel is based, and Juan Fernandez Island where Selkirk was marooned are all frequently associated by Melville with loneliness, isolation, or incongruity—in *Typee, Omoo, Redburn, Israel Potter, The Encantadas, Clarel, Journal . . . to Europe and the Levant*, and elsewhere. Melville first saw Crusoe's isle on May 7, 1841, while serving on the whaler "Acushnet" (Howard, *Herman Melville*, p. 45). According to an official record of the cruise, the frigate "United States," with Melville aboard as an ordinary seaman, on November 20, 1843, sailed near enough to "the famed Island of Juan Fernandez" to obtain a "remarkable and picturesque view" (Leyda, *Log*, p. 176).

Line 161. Grant's headquarters from March 26 to May 4, 1864, were at Culpeper, Virginia. Here and elsewhere Melville misspells the name of this town.

Lines 165–66. *the Cyclone's core*: the calm eye or axis of a hurricane, about which the winds revolve violently. Cf. *Moby-Dick* (Chap. 87, "The Grand Armada"), where the pursuing boat sails into the center of the herd of whales: "In this central expanse the sea presented that smooth satin-like surface, called a sleek . . . Yes, we were in that enchanted calm which they say lurks at the heart of every commotion. And still in the distracted distance we beheld the tumults of the outer concentric circles, and saw successive pods of whales, eight or ten in each, swiftly going round and round, like multiplied spans of horses in a ring; . . ." For other examples of moving circles controlled by a stable center, see "A Canticle," note on line 24.

Line 170. Orpheus was given a lyre by his father, Apollo. He became so proficient that he could charm wild beasts with his music. Horace explains in the *Art of Poetry* that the legend was symbolic of the refining forces of civilization at work. Pommer (*Milton and Melville*, pp. 22–23) shows how Melville used a phrase from Milton's *Of Education*, "the harp of Orpheus was not more charming," in *White-Jacket* (Chap. 2, "Homeward Bound"). Other references to Orpheus' powers to charm are found in *Redburn, The Confidence-Man, Clarel,* and *Billy Budd.* In the latter (Chap. 23) Captain Vere states that "forms, measured forms are everything; and that is the import couched in the story of Orpheus. . . ."

Line 171. Winfield Scott Hancock's Second Corps bivouacked at Chancellorsville during the Battle of the Wilderness. Here Jackson, after outflanking the Union army, was fatally wounded.

Line 189. This line, with its clumsy internal rhyme, is heavy with wordplay. *Shade* refers to the shadows found in the "jungles" (line 184) of the Wilderness, but also suggests the ghosts residing in Hades, the abode of the dead. The mention of Hades in turn suggests Hell, and hence the hellish nature of the fighting.

Line 210. On May 6, 1864, General James Longstreet sent his troops through an unfinished railroad cut for a successful attack on the Federal flank. The same day, in a situation that recalls Jackson, he was wounded by one of his own men.

Lines 216–18. Cf. Exodus 13:21: "And the Lord went before them by day in a pillar of a cloud, to lead them the way; and by night in a pillar of fire, to give them light; to go by day and night." The pillars of cloud and fire appeared to the Israelites as they entered the Wilderness rather than, as here, when "Right" emerged from it. The flaming ghosts are an indication of the price of victory.

Line 220. The Sabaeans were a Semitic merchant people of southwest Arabia. The reference may be to the riddles put to Solomon by the Queen of Sheba (Saba) in I Kings 10:1-3. See also Job 1:15 for a reference to the Sabaeans' attack on the servants of Job, a passage which provides the epigraph to the "Epilogue" of *Moby-Dick,* the sole such quotation in the novel.

Line 221. *The entangled rhyme* is evidence of Melville's attempt to suit verse form to content. Cf. "A Utilitarian View of the Monitor's Fight" (lines 1–2). Actually the poem is relatively smooth and regular in form, the entanglement deriving from difficulty in describing events and extracting their meaning. The "strife in the pines" can neither be narrated nor explained. It remains a riddle to which only the dead know the answer. The formal order of the poem is in ironic contrast to the obscure and disorderly nature of its subject.

Line 225. *Harper's Weekly* of June 4, 1864, has a vivid sketch by Alfred R. Waud of "Wounded Soldiers Escaping from the Burning Woods of the Wilderness" accompanied by a descriptive text, also by Waud. (Sealts no. 214).

On the Photograph of a Corps Commander

In the Spotsylvania Campaign of May 7–20, 1864, Winfield Scott Hancock commanded the Second Corps; G. K. Warren, then somewhat under a cloud, the Fifth Corps; John Sedgwick the Sixth Corps until May 9, when he was killed and replaced by George Wright; and Ambrose Burnside, who had been so severely beaten at Fredericksburg, the Ninth Corps. Of these officers Hancock was by far the most spectacular. His attack on Richard S. Ewell on May 12 resulted in the capture of most of the famous "Stonewall" brigade, Jackson's former command. *Harper's Weekly* of May 28, 1864 had a heroic three-quarter-length portrait of Hancock as its cover illustration.

Line 5. The usual spelling is "Spotsylvania."

Lines 7–9. This passage seems Emersonian.

Line 15. In 1415 the outnumbered English defeated the French at Agincourt in northern France. English bowmen were particularly effective against the heavily armored French knights.

Line 16. Cf. Shakespeare, *Henry V,* esp. IV, iii, 51–54.

Line 18. The Knights Templars were a religious and military order founded around 1118 at Jerusalem to protect pilgrims visiting the Holy

Land. Melville alludes to the order at length in "The Paradise of Bache-lors," *Clarel* (IV, ii, 111–25), and elsewhere.

Lines 19–24. Melville is concerned with the idea of manliness as it appears outwardly and inwardly in the archetypal figure of the corps com-mander. Unobtrusively at first and later with increasing emphasis, the word *man* and related words appear (see lines 1, 12, 14, 15, 19, 20, 23). The last stanza enhances the significance of the corps commander by show-ing his effect upon others. Its meaning is intensified by repetition (*man, manhood, fellow-man, manly, men,* in lines 19–20, 23) and rhyme, especially the instance of identical rhyme (lines 19–20), the change in rhyme scheme, and the choice of the rhyming words. R. E. Watters ("Melville's 'Sociality,' " p. 37) suggests that in this stanza "manliness is asserted to give more sus-tenance to the human spirit than godliness." He sees in Melville's stress upon "manly greatness" as a device for drawing men together a dissent from the emphasis of the Transcendentalists upon the exaltation of in-dividualism.

The Swamp Angel

The great Parrott gun, planted in the marshes of James Island, and employed in the prolonged, though at times intermitted bombardment of Charleston, was known among our soldiers as the Swamp Angel.

St. Michael's, characterized by its venerable tower, was the historic and aristocratic church of the town. [Melville's note]

On August 22–23, 1863, an eight-inch gun firing a 200-pound in-cendiary shell ineffectively bombarded Charleston from Morris Island at a range of 7,900 yards. It exploded during the firing of its thirty-sixth round.

Verbal parallels and similarities in prefatory material are to be found in "The Swamp Angel" by "T.N.J." in the poetry section of *The Rebel-lion Record* (VIII, 3). Cf. the first sentence of Melville's note above, and the note accompanying the *Rebellion Record* poem: "The large Parrott gun used in bombarding Charleston from the marshes of James Island is called the Swamp Angel—*Soldier's Letter*."

St. Michael's Episcopal Church, begun in 1752, is a Charleston land-mark.

Line 2. Parrott guns, because they were rifled and had to be re-en-forced with wrought-iron bands, had a thick, ungraceful appearance. Mel-ville here and in line 38 identifies the gun with the Negro slave.

Lines 17–19. Cf. I Thessalonians 5:2–3: "For yourselves know perfectly that the day of the Lord so cometh as a thief in the night. For when they shall say, Peace and safety; then sudden destruction cometh upon them, as travail upon a woman with child; and they shall not escape." The quotation concerns Christ's second coming. The word *gloaming* interested Melville. See *Journal . . . to Europe and the Levant,* p. 204.

Lines 20–23. General P. G. T. Beauregard, commanding the Charleston defenses, wrote General Q. A. Gilmore, commanding Federal troops on Morris Island, on August 22, 1863, protesting what he called "the novel measure of turning your guns against the old men, the women and children and the hospitals of a sleeping city" and called the incendiary shells "the most destructive missiles ever used in war . . ." (*War of the Rebellion,* Ser. 1, XXVIII, pt. 2, 59). The shells were filled with "Short's Solidified Greek Fire" and other incendiary charges—the only notable use of incendiaries in the Civil War. Cf. lines 12–13, 31.

Line 38. Southerners "mocked at" both the Negro slave and the siege gun.

Line 39. Melville may have had in mind Isaiah 51:17–22, which concerns the fall of Jerusalem and in which the "cup of fury" symbol appears.

Lines 40–43. In Normandy St. Michael is the patron of mariners, and Mont-Saint-Michel, the medieval Benedictine abbey, is dedicated to him. In first reversing traditional color associations ("a coal-black Angel/ with a thick Afric lip") and then implying that Michael himself ("the white man's seraph") has sided with his black counterpart, Melville suggests a reconciliation between black and white.

The Battle for the Bay

In the early morning of August 5, 1864, Admiral Farragut sailed past Confederate forts guarding Mobile Bay to destroy the Confederate ironclad ram "Tennessee" and three wooden gunboats. Melville's source was Farragut's official report as published in *The Rebellion Record* (VIII, 100–6), which he followed closely in stanzas 10–13 (VIII, 102).

Line 13. In the "Journal of Melville's Voyage in a Clipper Ship" (p. 122) there is this entry for June 27, 1860: *Crossed the Line* last evening. Saw bonetas under the bow." The usual spelling is "bonito," after a Spanish word meaning "pretty." Cf. "Commemorative of a Naval Victory" (lines 26–27): "The shark/ Glides . . ."

Line 19. *breaks, along the* (revision in Melville's copy).

Lines 25–27. Farragut "sailed second" in a line of fourteen wooden ships and four monitors, moving up when the lead ship, the "Tecumseh," hit a mine. His flagship was the "Hartford." See lines 83–85.

Line 29. Farragut climbed aloft to get a better view of the battle and lashed himself to the rigging to prevent falling if he should be wounded.

Cf. "Bridegroom Dick" (lines 287–88), in *John Marr*: "In the *Battle for the Bay* too if Dick had a share,/ And saw one a-piloting the war—"

Lines 29–41. Cf. "On the Photograph of a Corps Commander." The "influence" of Farragut, in this astrological metaphor, is comparable to the function of the manliness of the corps commander.

Line 44. Hekla, an active volcano 70 miles from Reykjavik, Iceland, had last erupted in 1845. Cf. the humorous simile in *Moby-Dick* (Chap. 3, "The Spouter-Inn"): "as cool as Mt. Hecla in a snow storm." Cf. also *Clarel* (II, xxxiv, 10–11): "Like Hecla ice inveined with marl/ And frozen cinders. . . ."

Line 84. Properly "Lackawanna."

Line 96. The Confederate ship is satanic. Cf. II Thessalonians 2:3: "Let no man deceive you by any means: for that day shall not come, except there come a falling away first, and that man of sin be revealed, the son of perdition." See also line 75. The phrase "Man-of-Sin" suggests "man-of-war."

Sheridan at Cedar Creek

Having a clear view of Union dispositions, Jubal Early moved against Philip Sheridan's command, the Middle Military Division, at Cedar Creek, Virginia, on October 19, 1864. He met with initial success, but Sheridan made his famous ride from Winchester, fourteen miles away, and organized an effective counterattack, the last important fighting in the Shenandoah Valley.

Melville pays tribute to the legendary feats of the horse as a means of elevating his master to an epic level. In fact, there is confusion at times as to which is being referred to, horse or rider (see lines 14–15). But the emphasis is first on the horse and later on Sheridan's men (lines 32–40), never on Sheridan himself. That he is spoken of as "Philip, king of riders" (line 25) further indicates his epic stature, as well as the affectionate esteem of his soldiers. In Melville's lecture on "Statues in Rome" as reconstructed by Sealts (*Melville as Lecturer*, p. 146), is this statement: "The horse was idealized by the ancient artists as majestic next to man, and they longed to sculpture them as they did heroes and gods. To the Greeks nature had no brute. Everything was a being with a soul, and the horse idealized the second order of animals just as man did the first." Melville reveals his enthusiasm for horses in *Pierre* (Bk. II, Chap. 1).

In form the poem suggests an ode, and it is regular to the extent that the rhyme scheme and number of verses in each stanza are the same throughout. Another feature of its regularity may be noted in the opening lines of the four stanzas. Each begins with a verb of one syllable in the imperative mood, upon which one of the three trochaic stresses of the line falls. The lines are tightly knit together through alliteration or consonance and internal rhyme. Finally, each of the initial lines is followed, in a quasi-logical way, by an explanation or justification of the opening demand. Opposed to this regularity is variation in meter and line length. Thus Melville obtains organic freedom within the discipline of regularity.

This poem was one of the few in *Battle-Pieces* to receive public attention of any sort during Melville's lifetime. It was first published in *Harper's New Monthly Magazine,* XXXII (April 1866), 640, under the title "Philip," and was reprinted in the New York *Leader* of December 8, 1866, in the Pittsfield *Sun* of June 17, 1867, and in other newspapers (Thorp, *Melville: Selections,* p. 426). Two anthologies included it, namely W. J. Linton's *Poetry of America . . . 1776 to 1876* (London, 1878) and E. C. Stedman's *Library of American Literature* (New York, 1889). Stedman praised the poem in his review of *John Marr,* as did Richard Henry Stoddard in a review of *Clarel* (Leyda, *Log,* pp. 750, 810).

Line 11. *ermine*: the white fur worn by judges as an emblem of purity and honor.

Line 12. Two "foam-flakes epauletting his shoulders" symbolize the submission of the Glendinning colts to *Pierre* (see general notes concerning this poem).

Lines 14–15. The pronoun reference of *he* and *him* is ambiguous, the more so since *Horseman* precedes *horse* in line 16. Cheering the horse alone, with Sheridan mounted on him, would seem a little unreasonable. The ambiguity serves to associate horse and rider more closely so that homage to one, here and elsewhere in the poem, is homage to both.

Line 17. *They faced about, each man*; (*Harper's*).

Line 18. *Faint hearts were strong again*; (*Harper's*).

Lines 21–30. A pattern of change and contrast, appropriate in a poem which celebrates a reversal of fortune, is concentrated in the third stanza. The cypress, symbol of death, is transformed into amaranths, the flowers that never die (lines 22–23). The dead return to life (line 26). The camp is lost at dawn (line 27) and recovered in the evening (line 28). That which was "early" is now late (line 30). For other examples of change see lines 6, 12–13, and the last stanza, where the joy of triumph shifts to "pathos deep."

Line 22. The curious quality of this line stems from the feeling that it is both end-stopped and run-on. As an end-stopped line with a sense of termination from the meter and the relation of "led" to "lead him" (line 21), it explains that the steed deserves a wreath for leading the charge. As a run-on line it shifts the emphasis from the charge to the result of the charge—the transformation of the cypress into a wreath of amaranths.

This in turn makes the steed worthy of a wreath of his own.

Line 24. The dedication of "Weeds and Wildings," a collection of poems which Melville left unpublished, mentions "wild amaranths . . . emblems of immortality" in a passage which recalls *Pierre* (Bk. XXV, Chap. 4), as Vincent notes (*Collected Poems,* p. 482). See *Paradise Lost,* III, 353–55 for the flower that grew "fast by the Tree of Life" and I Peter 5:4 for the flower traditionally in the "crown of glory that fadeth not away."

Line 26. See John 11:1–43 for the story of Lazarus, whom Christ raised from the dead.

Line 30. The laughter of the host (line 29) must have been somewhat strained if it was in response to Melville's onomastic wordplay. Cf. Benjamin Franklin in *Israel Potter* (Chap. 10) whose "frankness" is praised by Captain John Paul Jones, and the winebibbing Captain Claret, "a portly gentleman" in *White-Jacket* ("Some Superior old 'London Dock' from the Wine-coolers of Neptune," Chap. 37).

Line 40. Other poems which end with tributes to the "nameless dead" are "Chattanooga," "The Armies of the Wilderness," and "The Battle for the Bay." Melville was particularly interested in one of the men killed at Cedar Creek, Colonel Charles Russell Lowell, the model for the colonel in "A Scout Toward Aldie" (see Howard, *Melville,* p. 277).

In the Prison Pen

Between 1862 and 1866 there were at least fifty-four books and articles published giving accounts of personal experiences of Union war prisoners in the South, according to W. B. Hesseltine (*Civil War Prisons,* p. 347). The majority of these appeared in 1865 and 1866.

The first recorded use of the phrase "prison pen," according to the *Dictionary of Americanisms* is in Whitman's *Specimen Days,* published in 1882 but in part written perhaps twenty years earlier. This is another example of Melville's proclivity for neologisms, and of the air of immediacy which he gave to *Battle-Pieces.*

Line 9. *plaining*: complaining.

Lines 9–10. Cf. *Aeneid,* VI, 297–316. The passage concerns the unsanctified dead who plead with Charon to be carried across the River Styx.

The College Colonel

Leyda (*Log,* p. 662) quotes from the Pittsfield *Sun* of August 27, 1863 as follows: "The residence of J. R. Morewood, Esq., was handsomely illuminated, and there was a fine display of fireworks on his grounds, on

Saturday evening, in honor of the return of the 49th, and the Colonel of the Regiment, his worthy guests." For this festive occasion, the Melvilles decorated their house with "Flags and festoons."

The "Colonel of the Regiment" was William Francis Bartlett. He enlisted as a private in the Massachusetts Volunteers while a Harvard student but returned to college for a brief period, following which he received a commission as captain in the Twentieth Massachusetts. He lost a leg at Yorktown in the Peninsular campaign and was mustered out in November 1862, but shortly organized and was elected colonel of the Fifty-Ninth Massachusetts. He was twice wounded at Port Hudson, Louisiana, in the operation that completed the opening of the Mississippi River to the Union forces. Upon his recovery, he organized and commanded still another regiment, the Fifty-Seventh Massachusetts, and was wounded in the Wilderness fighting. Promoted to brigadier general of volunteers, he took part in the Petersburg mine assault and was captured. He was mustered out in 1866 after being breveted a major general, and became a business-man in Richmond, Virginia, and Pittsfield.

A copy of *Battle-Pieces* which Melville presented to Bartlett in 1867 has survived.

Line 26. The Seven Days' Battle, June 25 to July 1, 1862, was the final phase of the Peninsular campaign, ending at Malvern Hill. See notes on "Malvern Hill," p. 231.

Line 27. See notes on "Armies of the Wilderness," p. 244.

Line 28. For Bartlett's several wounds, see biographical statement above.

Line 29. The Petersburg Crater was the result of a mine exploded on July 30, 1864 beneath Elliot's Salient during the siege of Petersburg. The mine was a success, but the assault which followed was, in the words of Grant, a "stupendous failure."

Line 30. Libby in Richmond, a warehouse, served as a prison for captured Union officers.

The Eagle of the Blue

Among the Northwestern regiments there would seem to have been more than one which carried a living eagle as an added ensign. The bird commemorated here was, according to the account, borne aloft on a perch beside the standard; went through successive battles and campaigns; was more than once under the surgeon's hands; and at the close of the contest found honorable repose in the capital of Wisconsin, from which state he had gone to the wars. [Melville's note]

Melville's source was an anonymous poem in *The Rebellion Record* (VIII, 59–60), "The Eagle of the Eighth Wisconsin." A footnote to the poem based on information from the Iroqua (Wisconsin) *Times* states that the name of the eagle was Old Abe and that it had been struck twice by bullets. Neither the poem nor the footnote mentions the eagle's being in "honorable repose." Another poem in *The Rebellion Record* (VI, 28–29), "The Eagle of Corinth" by "H. H. B.," confirms Melville's statement that other regiments had eagles as mascots.

On August 18, 1865 Melville bought from Harper a copy of *The Story of the Great March* (New York, 1865) by Major George Ward Nichols, Sherman's aid-de-camp. A sketch of emblematic eagles used as a tailpiece may have suggested details which Melville used in his poem. The artist was probably Theodore R. Davis of *Harper's Weekly,* who accompanied Sherman on the march to the sea.

Tailpiece from *The Story of the Great March* by George Ward Nichols.

Line 12. The eagle had known storm-swept mountain peaks. Cf. Job 39:27–30, esp. 28: "She dwelleth and abideth on the rock, upon the crag of the rock, and the strong place."

Lines 14–16. Cf. "The March into Virginia" (line 34) : "enlightened by the vollied glare."

Line 15. Cf. *Mardi* (Chap. 135, "Babbalanja Discourses in the Dark") : "If eagles gaze at the sun, may not men at the gods?"

Line 24. *Blue* suggests both the natural habitat of the eagle—as do *aloft, brother of the star, the crag*, etc.—and the color of the Union uniform.

A Dirge for McPherson

The late Major General McPherson, commanding the Army of the Tennessee, a native of Ohio and a West Pointer, was one of the foremost spirits of the war. Young, though a veteran; hardy, intrepid, sensitive in honor, full of engaging qualities, with manly beauty; possessed of genius, a favorite with the army, and with Grant and Sherman. Both Generals have generously acknowledged their professional obligations to the able engineer and admirable soldier, their subordinate and junior.

In an informal account written by the Achilles to this Sarpedon, he says:

"On that day we avenged his death. Near twenty-two hundred of the enemy's dead remained on the ground when night closed upon the scene of action."

It is significant of the scale on which the war was waged, that the engagement thus written of goes solely (so far as can be learned) under the vague designation of one of the battles before Atlanta. [Melville's note]

McPherson was 35 when he was killed. The *Dictionary of American Biography* states that "his death was one of the heaviest individual losses ever suffered by the Union forces."

Melville seems to have confused Sarpedon with Patroclus or Achilles with Hector. According to the *Iliad*, Sarpedon, son of Jupiter and Europa, fought on the side of Troy. He was slain by the Greek warrior, Patroclus, friend of Achilles. Hector, the Trojan hero, avenged Sarpedon's death by killing Patroclus. Cf. line 26.

Lines 5–6. Confederate forces defending Atlanta abandoned Lost Mountain on June 17, 1864, for an almost impregnable position at nearby Kennesaw Mountain. Here the terrain, heat, and firm resistance delayed Sherman's advance. Eventually Union troops moved forward to a point close to the Confederate lines where it was as dangerous to retreat as to advance. On June 27 the Confederate forces retired to a new defensive position along the Chattahoochee River before Atlanta.

Line 16. After proper funeral preparations (lines 10–15), the "Lesson"—a part of the funeral service consisting of a passage from Scripture intended for instruction—is read. As Melville presents it, the "Lesson" derived from the death of McPherson is that man's nobility and bravery are as useless and inconsequential as "a weed." This point of view is certainly cynical but Melville had a peculiar tenderness for such plants. In the manuscript poems, "Weeds and Wildings," he is almost Wordsworthian in his affection for goldenrod, clover, dandelion, hardhack, and many another "way-side Weed divine" (see, e.g., "Inscription").

At the Cannon's Mouth

The Confederate ram "Albermarle" at Plymouth, North Carolina, was about to undertake operations endangering the Union fleet. On the night of October 27, 1864, Lieutenant William B. Cushing with a volunteer crew of fifteen sank the ram by means of a torpedo attached to a spar. Only Cushing and one member of the crew escaped death or capture. At the time Cushing was twenty-one years old.

Line. 11 *to stay in the Boy* (revision in Melville's copy).

Line 12. *The martyr-passion?* (revision in Melville's copy).

Line 20. *draw*: appeal, attract. The handsome youth Adonis spurned the love of Venus, goddess of beauty, in order to hunt the boar. His rejection of love like Cushing's of his own safety, is at once puzzling and attractive.

Line 23. *imps*: as a noun, *imp* has the archaic meaning of a child or scion; used as a verb, it refers to the addition, in falconry, of feathers to increase the power of flight.

Lines 23–25. This passage is interrogative, concluding a sequence of questions, begun in line 10, which arise from Cushing's unusual behavior. The modifiers "unfathomable" (line 18), "bafflingly" (line 19), and "strangely" (line 20) call further attention to the complexities which underlie Cushing's bravery.

Lines 29–30. A paradox sets forth the significance of Cushing's accomplishment. Only those prepared to reject without any certainty of reward the good things which life offers can hope to obtain its greatest gifts.

Line 31. Melville suggests that Cushing was born under the influence of a favorable star. In astrology a planet is described as ascendant when it rises above the eastern horizon at the time of birth.

The March to the Sea

On November 17, 1864, Sherman destroyed Atlanta and moved toward Savannah, masking his intentions with feints by his flanking columns. He reached Savannah without serious opposition on December 10, re-establishing his lines of communication and placing his army in a position to support Grant in Virginia by moving north. Sherman's operations deep within enemy territory, with no lines of communication, were unusual but not unprecedented. His devastation of Georgia and South Carolina was excused as military "Necessity" and justified as "Treason's retribution" (lines 91–92).

Melville could have obtained information about Sherman's march to the sea from any number of contemporary sources, but he is known to have owned a copy of *The Story of the Great March* by Major George Ward Nichols (Sealts no. 384a), an extremely popular book which had had more than twenty printings before Melville published his poem. From it he may have taken his title and such details as the allusions to Kennesaw, Allatoona, and "charred Atlanta" (lines 1–5, cf. Nichols, pp. 15–17); the "grand pines" (line 17, cf. Nichols, pp. 70–71); "Kilpatrick's snare of riders" (line 25, cf. Nichols, p. 79); the flocks and herds of animals (lines 39–41, cf. Nichols, p. 151); the numerous slaves who "joined the armies" (line 52, cf. Nichols, pp. 71–72); and the activities of the foragers (lines 61-62, cf. Nichols, pp. 51, 207, *passim*). Almost certainly Melville drew upon Nichols for the description of the gamecocks kept as pets by the Union soldiers. See note on lines 54–56.

Among the paintings shown at the 1865 exhibition of the National Academy of Design, which Melville saw, were two that might have provided background for the poem: "General Sherman's March through Georgia— his Advance arriving at a Plantation" by Thomas Nast, and "Foraging Party" by F. O. C. Darley.

The poem was first published in *Harper's New Monthly Magazine*, XXXII (February 1866), 366–67.

Line 1. *Kenesaw high arching*, (*Harper's*).

Lines 11–12. The light-hearted refrain reflects the mood of Sherman's troops as described by Nichols and by Sherman himself. However, the refrain of the last two stanzas changes incrementally, as though tempered by a recognition of the serious purpose of the march, and in keeping with a shift of attention from the conquering marchers to the defeated.

Line 33. *the marching—* (revision in Mrs. Melville's copy).

Line 34. *Right onward to the sea:* (revision in Mrs. Melville's copy).

Lines 54–56. Cf. Nichols, *The Story of the Great March*, pp. 76–77: "The favorite pet of the camp, however, is the hero of the barn-yard. There

is not a regiment nor a company, not a teamster nor a negro at headquarters, nor an orderly, but has a 'rooster' of one kind or another. When
the column is moving, these haughty game-cocks are seen mounted upon
the breech of a cannon, tied to the pack-saddle of a mule, among pots and
pans, or carried lovingly in the arms of a mounted orderly; crowing with
all his might from the interior of a wagon, or making the woods re-echo
from his triumphant notes. . . . The game-cocks which have come out of
repeated conflicts victorious are honored with such names as 'Bill Sherman,'
'Johnny Logan,' etc.; while the defeated and bepecked victim is saluted
with derisive appellations, such as 'Jeff. Davis,' 'Beauregard,' or 'Bob Lee.' "

Nichols devotes the final part of his chapter to the gamecocks. Immediately following is the tailpiece reproduced below.

Tailpiece from *The Story of the Great March* by George Ward Nichols.

Lines 77–78. Cf. Matthew 24:7: "For nation shall rise against nation, and kingdom against kingdom: and there shall be famines, and pestilences, and earthquakes, in divers places."

Line 91. Cf. *Paradise Lost,* IV, 393–94: "So spake the Fiend, and with necessity,/ The Tyrant's plea, excus'd his devilish deeds." From Melville's Miltonic source and his own revisions it is clear that he took a dim view of military necessity as an excuse for the destruction wrought by Sherman's army, and that his attitude was increasingly conciliatory. See textual variants below and Melville's prefatory note to "The Frenzy in the Wake."

Lines 91–92. In *Harper's* these lines read: "It was Treason's retribution/ (Necessity the plea) ; . . ." The revision in Melville's personal copy is: "Was the havoc, retribution?/ But howsoe'er it be, . . ." The three versions represent a progressive softening in Melville's attitude toward the South.

The Frenzy in the Wake

This piece was written while yet the reports were coming North of Sherman's homeward advance from Savannah. It is needless to point out its purely dramatic character.

Though the sentiment ascribed in the beginning of the second stanza must, in the present reading, suggest the historic tragedy of the 14th of April, nevertheless, as intimated, it was written prior to that event, and without any distinct application in the writer's mind. After consideration, it is allowed to remain.

Few need be reminded that, by the less intelligent classes of the South, Abraham Lincoln, by nature the most kindly of men, was regarded as a monster wantonly warring upon liberty. He stood for the personification of tyrannic power. Each Union soldier was called a Lincolnite.

Undoubtedly Sherman, in the desolation he inflicted after leaving Atlanta, acted not in contravention of orders; and all, in a military point of view, is by military judges deemed to have been expedient, and nothing can abate General Sherman's shining renown; his claims to it rest on no single campaign. Still, there are those who can not but contrast some of the scenes enacted in Georgia and the Carolinas, and also in the Shenandoah, with a circumstance in a great Civil War of heathen antiquity. Plutarch relates that in a military council held by Pompey and the chiefs of that party which stood for the Commonwealth, it was decided that under no plea should any city be sacked that was subject to the people of Rome. There was this difference, however, between the Roman civil conflict and the American one. The war of Pompey and Caesar divided the Roman people promiscuously; that of the North and South ran a frontier line between what for the time were distinct communities or nations. In this circumstance, possibly, and some others, may be found both the cause and the justification of some of the sweeping measures adopted. [Melville's note]

In *White-Jacket* (Chap. 41, "A Man-of-war Library") Melville describe's Plutarch's *Lives* as "super-excellent biographies." References to "our old family Plutarch" occur in *Redburn* (Chap. 14, "He Contemplates a Social Call . . ."). See also "At the Hostlery" (line 43), in the posthumously published miscellaneous poems. See also notes on "The House-top" and "The Surrender at Appomattox."

A companion piece to "The March to the Sea," the poem is a Southern hymn of hate. The victorious North, Melville felt, could afford exuberance and even generosity, while the defeated South had nothing to sustain it but insane fury.

Lines 11–12. Judges 4:2–23: Encouraged by Deborah the prophetess, Barak raised an army and defeated Sisera, general of Jabin, king of Canaan, who held Israel in captivity. Sisera sought refuge in the tent of Jael, who slew him by driving a nail into his temple. Melville refers to Jael and Sisera in "In a Bye-Canal" (lines 5–6), in *Timoleon,* and in "The Bell Tower," in *Piazza Tales.*

Lines 15–16. Cf. Shakespeare, *Hamlet,* I, i, 162: "The nights are wholesome; then no planets strike." Planets were thought to have had a malignant power which was exercised by "striking."

Lines 31–32. Cf. *Paradise Lost,* I, 105–8:

> What though the field be lost?
> All is not lost; the unconquerable Will,
> And study of revenge, immortal hate,
> And courage never to submit or yield.

The Fall of Richmond

Richmond was evacuated on the night of April 2, 1865. Formal surrender of the Confederate capital took place at 8:15 A.M., April 3, at the City Hall. Pommer (*Milton and Melville,* p. 79) sees a relation between this poem and "Apathy and Enthusiasm" in that one deals with the fall of Fort Sumter and the other with the fall of Richmond, i.e. with the first fighting and the last, and that both contain Miltonic imagery.

Line 6. Cf. Jeremiah 51:8: "Babylon is suddenly fallen and destroyed." Cf. also Isaiah 13:19: "And Babylon, the glory of kingdoms, the beauty of the Chaldees' excellency, shall be as when God overthrew Sodom and Gomorrah."

Line 11. Cf. *Paradise Lost,* IV, 985–86: "On th'other side *Satan* alarm'd/

Collecting all his might dilated stood."

Lines 13–14. Grant at Appomattox "wore straps of a lieutenant-general" which were embroidered with three stars (*Personal Memoirs,* II, 490). The constellation Orion rises in the fall, season of tempests, and is comparable to Grant's rise during a stormy period for the Northern cause.

Line 16. Cf. II Timothy 4:7: "I have fought a good fight, I have finished my course, I have kept the faith."

Line 21. Cf. "Pippa's Song" from Browning's *Pippa Passes* (Sealts nos. 107, 109). Montague ("Melville's *Battle-Pieces,*" p. 112) interprets this line as irony, Melville having been "moved to lash out at Northern reactions to Southern suffering."

The Surrender at Appomattox

After his withdrawal from Richmond, Lee attempted to join forces with General Joseph E. Johnston, who was moving northward under pressure from Sherman. Vigorous action by Grant prevented this and brought about Lee's surrender at Appomattox Courthouse, Virginia, on April 9, 1865.

Line 8. The terms of the surrender avoided the embarrassment of accepting swords from Confederate officers. Grant felt that "it would be an unnecessary humiliation to call upon them to deliver their side arms." (*Personal Memoirs,* II, 409)

Line 9. In the context of the lines immediately following, the word *eagles* calls to mind the standards of the Roman legions. Cf. "The Eagle of the Blue," and especially the illustration from Nichols' *Story of the Great March.*

Lines 11–12. Caesar defeated Pompey at Pharsalus, Greece, in 48 B.C. The civil war between Caesar and Pompey is the subject of Lucan's epic, *Pharsalia.* Melville would have recalled the battle from Plutarch's life of Pompey, to which he refers in his note on "The Frenzy in the Wake," or from Plutarch's life of Caesar. See "The Frenzy in the Wake" for notes on Melville's use of Plutarch.

A Canticle

The title and subtitle indicate that Melville sought to compose a hymn of thanksgiving to celebrate the victory of the righteous over an evil foe. This foe is given magnitude through a vague identification with the Fall of Man and several specific associations with the War in Heaven as depicted by Milton. The central image is that of a mighty cataract roaring downward into a deep pool below, where it forms foamy billows and a shimmering rainbow. Hence the word *Fall* (line 2) fuses the concepts of the original Fall and of Milton's fallen angels with what is to become the sustaining image of the poem. See note on lines 50–55. The most famous waterfall in America, Niagara, may have contributed to the imagery.

Howard suggests that Melville visited Niagara Falls in 1840, when he followed the Erie Canal to the Great Lakes on his way to Galena (*Melville*, p. 33). But even though he may not have seen Niagara itself, it was so popular a subject for painters that as a collector of prints and a frequenter of art galleries he would certainly have encountered many representations from which details which appear in the poem could have been taken. Currier and Ives, for example, produced a popular lithograph which meets the specifications. More interesting are two paintings, one of which Melville surely saw and the other of which, whether he saw it or not, he could hardly have escaped hearing about. The first of these is "Sunrise at Niagara" by DeWitt Clinton Boutelle. It was displayed in the 1865 exhibition of the National Academy of Design, in the same room with Vedder's "Jane Jackson," which inspired the poem, "Formerly a Slave." The second is "The Great Fall, Niagara" by Frederick Church. Widely acclaimed in 1857, when it was first shown, it received an award at the Paris Exposition before being bought for the Corcoran Gallery. Charles M. Dow's *Anthology and Bibliography of Niagara Falls* (II, 906–12) reprints several newspaper articles from this period which show its great popularity. Melville appears to have known Church. On February 24, 1865, at the time he was writing his Civil War poems, he received an invitation from Bayard Taylor to meet with "The Travellers," a club of artists, writers, and musicians. Taylor wrote: "Many of the members are no doubt old friends of yours— [F. O. C.] Darley, Church, [Albert] Bierstadt, [Louis] Gottschalk . . ." (Leyda, *Log*, p. 762).

A New York *Daily Times* article (as quoted by Dow), after describing Church's success in capturing the grandeur of Niagara, states that in the painting "vaporous white veils of mingling spray and mist float lightly and tenderly up, smitten through and through with the glory of the glittering rainbow" (cf. lines 24–29).

Melville may have had in mind still another connotation of his key word namely the fall of Richmond. Evidence of the importance of this event to him is his statement that *Battle-Pieces* "originated in an impulse imparted by the fall of Richmond." His poem on the subject, which further indicates this concern, contains references to the defeat of Lucifer (lines 10–11).

Line 2. Cf. "The Conflict of Convictions" (line 6): "man's latter fall." Both poems contain Miltonic allusions and possess similarities of subject matter, theme, and texture. Pommer (*Milton and Melville*, pp.

78–79) sees them as a framing device in the structural organization of the collection.

Line 10. In the juxtaposition of the solid (static) and the surging (kinetic) Melville prepares the way for a resolution in line 24. See also line 53.

Lines 17–23. Cf. lines 56–62, which are identical except for line 57 and together form a *Laus Deo* chorus to the hymn.

Line 24. The concept of a stable harmony transcending any material foundation, here suggested by the arching rainbow, is similar to that implicit in the orbit metaphor of "Dupont's Round Fight," which envisions a unity of esthetics, nature, and law. Cf. "The Armies of the Wilderness" (lines 164–65), where the furious activity of war proceeds according to a plan like the "calm" at "the cyclone's core." Also cf. *Mardi* (Chap. 119, "Dreams"): ". . . I and all mine revolve around a great central Truth, sun-like, fixed and luminous forever in the foundationless firmament."

Line 26. Iris, a personification of the rainbow, was an attendant and messenger of Juno. The rainbow as a symbol of God's covenant that "the waters shall no more become a flood to destroy all flesh" (Genesis 9:15) becomes in *White-Jacket* (Chap. 65, "A Man-of-war Race") "God's token that no more would he make war on earth." The rainbow also appears as a symbol of peace in "Iris," an elegy on a Southern girl and her Northern lovers, dated 1865, in the posthumously published "Weeds and Wildings." In *Clarel* (II, xxix, 120–59) the significance of the rainbow over the Dead Sea is much debated by the pilgrims. In *Mardi* the iris signifies a message. See Davis, "Flower Symbolism in *Mardi*," p. 637.

Lines 30–35. The opposition of snow as a symbol of desolation and the rainbow as a symbol of hope also occurs in *Moby-Dick* (Chap. 42, "The Whiteness of the Whale"): "Not so the sailor, beholding the scenery of the Antarctic seas . . . [who] instead of rainbows speaking hope and solace to his misery, views what seems a boundless church-yard grinning upon him with its lean ice monuments and splintered crosses."

Lines 40–45. A passage from *The Encantadas* (Sketch First, "The Isles at Large") contains comparable details, equates the setting with the infernal regions, and sets up an opposition between "repose" or "calm" above and turbulence below. Cf.: "In many places the coast is rock-bound . . . forming dark clefts and caves here and there, into which a ceaseless sea pours a fury of foam; overhanging them with a swirl of grey, haggard mist, amidst which sail screaming flights of unearthly birds. . . . However calm the sea without, there is no rest for these swells and those rocks; they lash and are lashed, even when the outer ocean is at peace . . . dark and vitrified masses, many of which raise themselves among the white whirlpools and breakers . . . present a most Plutonian sight. In no world but a fallen one could such lands exist."

Line 41. Cf. *Paradise Lost,* I, 177: "To bellow through the vast and boundless Deep."

Lines 44–45. Cf. Daniel 7:9: "I beheld till the thrones were cast down, and the Ancient of days did sit, whose garment was white as snow, and the hair of his head like the pure wool."

Lines 46–47. Cf. *Paradise Lost,* I, 192–97, esp. 192–93: "Thus Satan talking to his nearest Mate/ With Head up-lift above the wave." Like Satan, although cast down into the deep the Giant remains a threat.

Lines 50–55. Cf. *Paradise Lost,* XII, 470–585, esp. 548–50:

> From the conflagrant mass, purg'd and refin'd,
> New Heav'ns, new Earth, ages of endless date
> Founded in righteousness and peace and love.

The quotation is from the speech of Michael to Adam before the expulsion from Eden. Adam has just expressed his understanding of the significance of his experience in the crucial passage on the Fortunate Fall, and Michael is describing the promise of the future. The parallel between Milton and Melville is significant in view of the lapsarian theme in "A Canticle," here as elsewhere in the context of waterfall imagery. See general comments on this poem.

Lines 53. *steadfast State:* the latter word is used in the sense both of a condition and of a political entity. The phrase is embedded in imagery of motion, the whole constituting a restatement of the concept expressed in lines 10 and 24.

Lines 54–55. The uncharacteristic note of optimism which appears here is almost inevitable since the poem is an ode of thanksgiving "to the Lord of hosts,/ The hosts of human kind." But the two poems which follow manifest a dampening of this elation.

The Martyr

In his personal copy of *Battle-Pieces,* Melville struck a line through the title, perhaps because he feared it might be inflammatory. For similar second thoughts, see his revisions of "The March to the Sea" (lines 91–92).

Melville was apparently moved by the significance of the unprecedented demonstration of national grief that followed Lincoln's assassination, for the poem is less concerned with the death of Lincoln than with the reactions of "the people" to it. (See subtitle and lines 14, 16, 31, 33.) The real subject is forces, not personalities. If Lincoln is depersonalized, so are "the people" who mourn and threaten, the "they" who killed him, and "The Avenger" who succeeds him.

The opening lines of the poem suggest a convention of the traditional ballad of which at least a dozen examples can be found in Child's collection. Much interested in the ballad genre, Melville in 1859 acquired Child's *English and Scottish Ballads* (Sealts no. 143); he portrayed Jack Chase of *White-Jacket* as a singer of Sir Patrick Spens and of "other salt-sea ballads and ditties" (Chap. 74, "The Main-top at Night"); he recounted with relish, in *Redburn,* the career of a British ballad-monger (Chap. 39, "The Booble Alleys of the Town"); and he tried his own hand at the broadside ballad with "Billy in the Darbies" (*Billy Budd,* Chap. 31) and the sea ballad with "Tom Deadlight" (*John Marr*). The suggestion of ballad form at the beginning of the poem serves to infuse it with the depth and power of folk utterance. The almost sacramental nature of the event, however, forced a shift to a more elevated form, the choric dirge, which is also an appropriate expression of the mass psyche. For another example of Melville's use of ballad conventions see "The Scout Toward Aldie," and the notes thereto.

Line 1. Lincoln was shot by John Wilkes Booth on Good Friday, April 14, 1865, and died the next morning. Melville subtly exploits this coincidence in the subtitle, identifying Lincoln with Christ through the responsive "passion of the people" which his martyr death arouses, and subsequently in descriptions of Lincoln as a redeemer (line 7) and "Forgiver" (line 20). See note on lines 31–34.

Line 9. The phrase "killed with kindness" is proverbial (Tilley K51).

Lines 16–17. Cf. *White-Jacket* (Chap. 44, "A Knave in Office in a Man-of-war"): ". . . *the people* of a man-of-war have been guilty of the maddest vengeance."

Line 19. Lincoln's office and his personality caused him to be affectionately known as "Father Abraham" (e.g., in the Union recruiting song, "We are Coming, Father Abr'am" by James Sloan Gibbons), echoing the phrase used by Christ in speaking of the Old Testament patriach (Luke 16:30). Cf. Genesis 17:5: "Neither shall thy name any more be called Abram, but thy name shall be Abraham; for a father of many nations have I made thee." For another association of Lincoln with the biblical Abraham, see "The Muster" (lines 1–2). Lincoln's murderers are called "parricides" (line 25).

Line 20. Cf. "The Swamp Angel" (line 47).

Line 21. At this period of excitement the thought was by some passionately welcomed that the Presidential successor had been raised up by heaven to wreak vengeance on the South. The idea originated in the remembrance that Andrew Johnson by birth belonged to that class of Southern whites who never cherished love for the dominant one; that he was a citizen of Tennessee, where the contest at times and in places had been close and bitter as a Middle-Age feud; that himself and family had been hardly treated by the Secessionists.

But the expectations built hereon (if, indeed, ever soberly entertained), happily for the country, have not been verified.

Likewise the feeling which would have held the entire South chargeable with the crime of one exceptional assassin, this too has died away with the natural excitement of the hour. [Melville's note]

Line 28. God addressed Cain (Genesis 4:11): "And now art thou cursed from the earth, which hath opened her mouth to receive thy brother's blood from thy hand."

Lines 31–34. The irony of the association of Lincoln's death with the sacrificial death of Christ is that the result is not peace and redemption but an impulse toward revenge. Thus Melville warns of the difficulties which beset the advocates of forgiveness, specifically those who favor lenient treatment of the defeated South.

"The Coming Storm"

Sandford Robinson Gifford (1823–80) exhibited "The Coming Storm" at the fortieth annual exhibition of the National Academy of Design. He has been confused by Melville scholars (e.g. Vincent, p. 456; Leyda, p. 674; Kaplan, p. xix) with Robert Swain Gifford (1840–1905), who also painted landscapes, was likewise a member of the National Academy, and participated in the 1865 show. The present owner, through whose courtesy the painting is reproduced, is Robert Wilkinson of Poughkeepsie, New York.

"The Coming Storm," by Sandford R. Gifford.

The subject of the painting was not an unusual one for the period. George Inness, for example, painted at least six such landscapes, including one dated 1878 which bears the same title (Albright Gallery, Buffalo, New York). Melville takes the simple contrast of calm and storm and extends its symbolic application to represent the Civil War, itself for Melville a symbol of the eternal war between the powers of light and darkness and of the inherent uncertainties of human existence.

The exhibition catalogue lists Edwin Booth, the most noted actor of Shakespearean tragedy in his generation, as the owner of the painting. He was the brother of John Wilkes Booth, who assassinated Lincoln. On March 24, 1865 he completed an unprecedented New York run of one hundred nights as Hamlet, and he was in Boston playing the same role when he learned of his brother's part in Lincoln's death. The shock and his fear, which proved to be unfounded, of an unfavorable public reaction, caused him to go into retirement. He returned to the stage, once more as Hamlet, on January 3, 1866. The order of the poems suggests that Melville attended the exhibition shortly after the death of Lincoln. If so, he would hardly have failed to think of Edwin Booth without recalling his relation to the Lincoln tragedy, his association with the role of Hamlet, and the appropriateness of his ownership of Gifford's prophetic picture.

Although he does not mention the Booth connection, Kaplan (ed. Battle-Pieces, p. xix) sees the poem as "really a commentary on the assassination of Lincoln" and therefore "properly placed" immediately following "The Martyr." While all this is true, "The Coming Storm" also harks back to the storm of "Misgivings" which initiates the collection and likewise is related thematically to "The Apparition" near the end. As one of the terminal poems, it is a summary comment on the significance of the insights and experiences which are the subjects of the preceding poems.

Pierre, on his way to the meeting with Isabel which will mark the end of his Adamic innocence, sees a darkening landscape with lake and mountains which seems to anticipate Gifford's painting: "On both sides, in the remoter distance, and far beyond the mild lake's further shore, rose the long, mysterious mountain masses . . ." (Pierre, Bk. VI, Chap. 1).

Line 1. That the poem has as its subject the individual "Who felt this picture," presumably Edwin Booth, as well as the picture itself, is evident from the references to "him" (esp. lines 1, 13) and from the epithet, "Shakespeare's pensive child" (line 8). Moreover, the position of him at the end of the first line of the first and last stanzas and the manner in which it is embedded in parallel phrases ("feel for him/ Who" and "come to him/ Who") give it particular importance.

Cf. "I and My Chimney," in Piazza Tales: "All feeling hearts will sympathize. . . ."

Lines 1–2. The kind of repetition exemplified by the use of *feeling, feel,* and *felt* (polyptoton) is characteristic of Melville. Cf. the variations played on *man* in "On the Photograph of a Corps Commander" (lines 19–23). It contributes a sense of control and regularity to lines which are irregular in terms of syllable count.

Lines 2–3. *dim*: owing to its position this modifier of *Presage* functions as a link with the next line, where repetition serves to intensify its effect.

Line 4. Cf. Melville's essay, "Hawthorne and His Mosses": "Now it is that blackness in Hawthorne . . . that so fixes and fascinates me." Note color connotation of *Dim inklings* and *shadowy* (line 3).

Lines 5-7. The passive, protectively enclosed, and orderly landscape becomes the victim of the dynamic "demon-cloud," as though Satan were once again invading Eden. Cf. "The Apparition," where a volcanic upheaval cracks the surface of the "pastoral green" fields. In "Misgivings" the autumnal tempest provokes "horror" but it is, after all, a part of the orderly progress of the seasons. In "The Coming Storm" horror is compounded by the juxtaposition of storm and peaceful landscape, and a hint that it is a desecration of the repose of the dead (see note on line 7).

Line 7. *home of the shades*: a shady place, a protected retreat; but also the habitation of ghosts, the dead. The words *spirit* (line 6) and *urned* are associated with death.

Line 9. "The lines" were not "lightly scanned," but scanned in an opposite way—darkly; and the depth of their dark import was comprehended.

Lines 10–11. Hamlet-hearted persons like Edwin Booth are receptive to this picture, and their "feeling hearts" (line 1) share the artist's tragic awareness of all that the intrusion of the storm cloud into the idyllic valley signifies. For one gifted with such penetration there can be no surprises (lines 13–16).

Lines 11–12. *antedate*: foresee. The Hamlet-hearted are seers. Cf. lines 2–3 for an earlier suggestion of their perceptiveness.

Lines 13–16. Matthiessen (*Selected Poems*, p. 7) called this quatrain "perhaps the best poetry Melville ever wrote . . . one of the most profound recognitions of the value of tragedy ever to have been made."

Line 14. Cf. "Hawthorne and His Mosses": "But it is those deep faraway things in him; those occasional flashings forth of the intuitive Truth in him; those short, quick probings at the very axis of reality;—these are the things that make Shakespeare Shakespeare. Through the mouths of the dark characters of Hamlet, Timon, Lear, and Iago, he craftily says, or sometimes insinuates, the things which we feel to be so terrifically true that it were all but madness for any good man, in his own proper character, to utter, or even hint of them." Cf. "The Apparition" (lines 11–12) : "So, then, Solidity's a crust—/ The core of fire below."

Rebel Color-bearers at Shiloh

The incident on which this piece is based is narrated in a newspaper account of the battle to be found in the "Rebellion Record." During the disaster to the national forces on the first day, a brigade on the extreme left found itself isolated. The perils it encountered are given in detail. Among others, the following sentences occur:

"Under cover of the fire from the bluffs, the rebels rushed down, crossed the ford, and in a moment were seen forming this side the creek in open fields, and within close musket-range. Their color-bearers stepped defiantly to the front as the engagement opened furiously; the rebels pouring in sharp, quick volleys of musketry, and their batteries above continuing to support them with a destructive fire. Our sharpshooters wanted to pick off the audacious rebel color-bearers, but Colonel Stuart interposed: 'No, no, they're too brave fellows to be killed.' " [Melville's note]

The quotation is from the Cincinnati *Gazette* of April 9, 1862 (*Rebellion Record,* IV, 391). Except for Stuart's military title, abbreviated in *The Rebellion Record,* it is exact. Melville's mention of *The Rebellion Record* revealed a profitable area for source study, first exploited by Thorp (*Selections,* p. 425) and most recently by Day ("Melville's Use of the Rebellion Record," unpublished thesis).

Line 24. See notes on "Shiloh," p. 228.

Line 26. The Confederates under Braxton Bragg won a tactical victory at Chickamauga, September 19–20, 1863, forcing Rosecrans to seek refuge in nearby Chattanooga. However, Confederate losses were extremely severe.

Line 27. See notes on "The Armies of the Wilderness," p. 244.

Line 35. The surrender discussions between Grant and Lee were distinguished by magnanimity on the part of Grant.

The Muster

According to a report of the Secretary of War, there were on the first day of March, 1865, 965,000 men on the army pay-rolls. Of these, some 200,000—artillery, cavalry, and infantry—made up from the larger portion of the veterans of Grant and Sherman, marched by the President. The total number of Union troops enlisted during the war was 2,668,000. [Melville's note]

A "Grand Review" of veterans from the Armies of the Potomac, Tennessee, and Georgia paraded before the President and the commanding generals in Washington on May 23–24, 1865.

Montague ("Melville's *Battle-Pieces*," p. 107) uses "The Muster" to support his charge that Melville's "failure to see a poem as an organic unit led him . . . to interpose in a poem which admirably sustains a basic river image another series of images whose connection is so tenuous as to cripple the poem." The poem is not, of course, a single extended image; rather, it is a structure controlled by the first and last stanzas, which focus upon the river and which enclose four related quatrains. While these quatrains move gradually away from the river imagery, which itself blends in with imagery of the sea, they are verbally linked to each other (e.g. "hazy," line 19, to "nebulously," line 20, to "Milky Way," line 21) and to the enclosing frame (e.g. "waves," line 10, to "surf," line 16, to "sea-wide," line 26). The "Milky Way" image, seemingly the one most remote from "the basic river image," is linked in its turn to the reference to the starry banners carried by the stream of soldiers (lines 21-24).

Lines 1–4. The epithet "Abrahamic" recalls the patriarchal aspect of Lincoln (cf. "The Martyr," note on line 19) and relates him as a national myth to the Mississippi River, "Father of Waters," a natural phenomenon of mythic proportions. Leyda (*Log*, p. 518) quotes from a discarded chapter of *The Confidence-Man*: "As the word Abraham means father of a great multitude of men so the word Mississippi means the father of a great multitude of waters. His tribes stream in from east & west, exceeding fruitful the lands they enrich." Cf. *Israel Potter* (Chap. 4, "Further Wanderings . . .") : ". . . the patriarchal demeanor of this true Abrahamic gentleman. . . ."

Line 3. Cf. *Iliad*, Bk. II, where rivers are introduced into the catalogues to indicate the origin of various contingents of the army. The roll call of the streams is also a convention of the classical elegy and of neo-classical topographical poetry. Like the identification of the marchers with Lincoln and the Mississippi, it is an effort to enhance magnitude. For possible wordplay on "roll," see quotation below.

Lines 9–11. Cf. *Mardi* (Chap. 119, "Dreams") : "And as the great Mississippi musters his watery nations: Ohio, with all his leagued streams; Missouri, bringing down the torrents the clans from the highlands; Arkansas, his Tartar rivers from the plains; so, with all the past pouring in me, I will roll down my billows from afar."

Lines 20–21. Cf. *Mardi* (Chap. 15, "Dreams") : "Shoals, like nebulous vapors, shoring the white reef of the Milky Way. . . ."

Lines 20–21. Cf. *Mardi* (Chap. 119, "Dreams") : "Shoals, like nebulous produced with the notes to "The Eagle and the Blue." This illustration accompanies the short concluding section "Going Home," which chiefly concerns the review. Note stars, banner, and eagles.

Aurora-Borealis

The wavering display of the aurora borealis, the northern lights, is a symbol of the Northern army and its varied fortunes. It "gives way" to another Aurora, the goddess of the new day. Melville, an admirer of the paintings of Guido Reni (Leyda, *Log,* pp. 330, 349, 577), had seen Guido's ceiling fresco, "Aurora," which "floats overhead like sun-dyed clouds" (*Journal . . . to Europe and the Levant,* p. 204) and refers to it in *Redburn* (Chap. 46, "A Mysterious Night in London"). He may also have heard of a most widely commented-upon display of the aurora borealis which took place near Fredericksburg, Virginia, in mid-December 1862, just after the defeat of the Union forces there. Many contemporary accounts survive. A Union staff officer wrote in his journal on December 14 that a "fine auroral display took place at night—one of the finest I have ever seen here" (Jedediah Hotchkiss Papers, Library of Congress), and a Confederate veteran recalled how his comrades "felt that the heavens were hanging out banners and streamers and setting off fireworks in honor of our victory" (Robert Stiles, *Four Years Under Marse Robert,* p. 137). In *Harper's Weekly* of May 25, 1861, Melville would have seen a cartoon on Union mobilization which depicted "A Rebel General startled in his Camp by the Beautiful and Unexpected Display of NORTHERN LIGHT." The comparison was inescapable. Thus the informing image of the poem would appear to be an alternation between the aurora borealis, a phenomenon of night, and the phenomenon of dawn personified in the Guido painting. There is a further hint of shifts and reversals, analogous with the character of the lights themselves, in the coinciding of the aurora borealis with a Southern victory which was in turn to be followed by defeat. In all this the associational values of the words *northern lights* and *aurora* play a part. Melville makes the point that the aurora borealis with its "Splendor and Terror" occurs in times of darkness and is overcome eventually by "pale, meek Dawn." But both are manifestations of divinity (lines 16–19).

Line 2. *steely play*: the flashing rays of the northern lights; but also the reflection of light on the steel weapons (cf. line 20) and their use in battle. In *Moby-Dick* (Chap. 56, "Of the Less Erroneous Pictures of Whales . . .") Melville described paintings at Versailles of the "great battles of France; where every sword seems a flash of the Northern Lights. . . ."

Line 3. *feels a creeping awe* (revision in Melville's copy).

The Released Rebel Prisoner

For a month or two after the completion of peace, some thousands of released captives from the military prisons of the North, natives of all parts of the South, passed through the city of New York, sometimes waiting farther transportation for days, during which interval they wandered penniless about the streets, or lay in their worn and patched gray uniforms under the trees of the Battery, near the barracks where they were lodged and fed. They were transported and provided for at the charge of government. [Melville's note]

Melville had probably seen released war prisoners in New York, where he was living in June, 1865.

Line 3. From his note above, one assumes that Melville had New York in mind. In *Redburn* (Chap. 30, "Redburn Grows Intolerably Flat and Stupid over Some Outlandish Old Guide-Books") he associates Nineveh with a New York of the future, but most of his references to Nineveh are in connection with the Jonah story. Cf. Jonah 4:11: "And should I not spare Nineveh, that great city, wherein are more than sixscore thousand persons . . . ."

Line 11. *Gulf-weed*: a species of seaweed found floating in large masses in the Gulf Stream and the Sargasso Sea.

Line 17. General A. P. Hill was killed on April 2, 1865, in the final phase of the Confederate defense of Petersburg, Virginia.

Line 18. General Turner Ashby was killed on June 6, 1862, while covering a Confederate retreat near Harrisonburg, Virginia.

Line 19. General J. E. B. Stuart was mortally wounded at Yellow Tavern, Virginia, on May 11, 1864. A spectacular cavalry leader, he manifested his fondness for the dramatic by wearing a plumed, cocked hat of the kind affected by Prince Rupert, the general of horse of Charles I. In *Redburn* Melville referred to Prince Rupert as "that mad nephew of King Charles . . ." (Chap. 36, "The Old Church of St. Nicholas . . .").

Lines 26–27. Cf. "The Returned Volunteer to his Rifle."

Lines 33–34. The gray festoons of Spanish moss trailing from the trees are a somber detail of the Southern landscape. The cypress, once again, is suggestive of death.

Line 35. *As drear, from* (revision in Melville's copy). *Weird* is spelled "wierd" in the original edition.

Line 40. In a poem containing lines as poor as any Melville ever wrote, one would scarcely expect to find grounds for arguing the success of his manipulation of language. Yet it is typical of Melville's unevenness that such is precisely the situation here. For example, the subject of the verb *go* may be either the prisoner himself or his "countrymen." On the surface the prisoner, with his listless wandering, demands primary attention. However, there is a contrast between his aimless lingering and the behavior of his "cousins and his countrymen" who, aware of him but preoccupied with their own affairs, remain indifferent to his lot. Melville seeks to arouse pity for the defeated and to score the victor-kinsman who lacks compassion.

A Grave near Petersburg, Virginia

Shortly prior to the evacuation of Petersburg, the enemy, with a view to ultimate repossession, interred some of his heavy guns in the same field with his dead, and with every circumstance calculated to deceive. Subsequently the negroes exposed the stratagem. [Melville's note]

"Formerly a Slave"

The painting is listed in the catalogue of the 1865 exhibition of the National Academy of Design as "Jane Jackson, formerly a Slave—Drawing in oil-color" by Elihu Vedder. In his memoirs Vedder relates how he came to paint it (*Digressions,* p. 236) : "At the time I had my studio . . . on Broadway; I used to pass frequently a near corner, where an old negro woman sold peanuts. Her meekly bowed head and a look of patient endurance and resignation touched my heart. . . . She had been a slave down South, and had at that time a son, a fine tall fellow, she said, fighting in the Union Army. I finally persuaded her to sit to me and made a drawing of her head and also had her photograph taken. Having been elected associate of the National Academy, according to custom I had to send in a painting to add to the permanent collection, so I sent in this study of her head and called it simply by her name—which was Jane Jackson."

Vedder later used this drawing as the basis for his more pretentious painting, "The Cumaean Sibyl," but Melville sensed the sibylline qualities in the prototype.

Melville seems never to have met Vedder, but he held him in such esteem as to dedicate *Timoleon,* printed in 1891, to him. Vedder acknowledged the compliment in a letter written to Elizabeth Melville after her husband's death: "I may not have been very successful in a wordly way—but the knowledge that my art has gained me so many friends—even if unknown to me—makes ample amends" (Metcalf, *Melville: Cycle and Epicycle,* p. 288) .

Jane Jackson is like Hunilla of *The Encantadas* (Sketch Eighth, "Norfolk Isle and the Chola Widow") in her prolonged suffering and in the

Jane Jackson - War Time - Studio in Gibson building Bway -

An old negro Woman - the origin of many Sibyls by V, see Jane Jackson "the Struggle".

Preliminary sketch for "Jane Jackson, Formerly a Slave," by Elihu Vedder.

nature of her ultimate deliverance. Her "idealized Portrait" becomes in the poem a symbol of man who suffers and endures, sustained by a vision that his offspring will prosper. But this limited optimism is still further qualified by the grim implications of "The Apparition" immediately following.

Line 1. Cf. Shakespeare, *Merchant of Venice,* I, iii, 111: " For sufferance is the badge of all our tribe."

Line 10. *revel*: revelatory? Not in *N.E.D.* in this sense.

Line 12. Melville visited the Sistine Chapel where he saw Michelangelo's frescoes, among them the famous series of sibyls (*Journal . . . to Europe and the Levant,* pp. 200, 211). He may have noticed Guido's "Cumaean Sibyl" when he visited the Uffizi collection of Florence (*ibid.,* pp. 218, 222). He also visited the legendary cave of the Cumaean Sibyl near Naples (*ibid.,* p. 186).

The Apparition

Here the theme of "The Coming Storm" recurs, a volcanic eruption replacing the tempest as the force which desolates an idyllic, pastoral scene. The poem is more obviously related to the Civil War and, as Fogle states, "the blighting hand of war upon the landscape becomes a revelation of the fiery hell beneath all agreeable surfaces" ("Melville and the Civil War," p. 79). The logical argument of the poem is inductive, the first two stanzas providing evidence from which a conclusion is drawn in the third.

In *Mardi* (Chap. 122, "Babbalanja Regales the Company with Some Sandwiches") Melville has Babbalanja expound the "Plutonian" theory of the formation of the earth's surface, drawing some conclusions therefrom: "The coral wall which circumscribes the isles but continues upward the deep buried crater of primal chaos. In the first times this crucible was charged with vapours nebulous, boiling over fires upthrew the ancient rocks; . . . Thus Nature works, at random warring, chaos a crater, and the world a shell."

For another reminder of the frailty of orderly systems and of the uncertainty of their survival when confronted with disorder, see the quotation from *The Encantadas* in the note to lines 40–45 of "A Canticle."

Lines 1–6. Cf. "Supplement" to *Battle-Pieces*: "Wherefore in a clear sky do we still turn our eyes toward the South, as the Neapolitan, months after the eruption, turns his toward Vesuvius? Do we dread lest the repose may be deceptive? In the recent convulsion has the crater but shifted?"

Magnanimity Baffled

While advocating a policy of magnanimity toward the South, Melville was aware of obstacles to its implementation. In this verse parable, he hints that reconciliation may not be a simple matter of good will and good works. Defeat is represented as death. The dead cannot participate in a reconciliation, and those who killed them are guilty of murder. The very process of rooting out evil creates a situation in which magnanimity is impossible. For another statement on the limitations of victory see "The Conflict of Convictions," note on line 79. The word *baffled* means both frustrated and perplexed.

On the Slain Collegians

The records of Northern colleges attest what numbers of our noblest youth went from them to the battle-field. Southern members of the same classes arrayed themselves on the side of Secession; while Southern seminaries contributed large quotas. Of all these, what numbers marched who never returned except on the shield. [Melville's note]

Thematically the poem bears a curious relation to "The March into Virginia," which, appearing near the beginning of the collection, also deals with youth and war. In "The March into Virginia," the boy soldiers "die experienced" (line 33) and "Perish, enlightened" (line 34). In "On the Slain Collegians," they die untouched by any kind of enlightening experience. References to a golden age, youth, spring, and budding flowers reveal a yearning for innocence in a world glutted with experience and recall similar imagery in *Billy Budd*, as well as the response of both Vere and Claggart to the prelapsarian innocence of Billy.

Lines 5–6. The veneration by youth of womanhood and duty can be subverted to a murderous purpose.

Line 19. *troops*: any large group; but also a military force.

Line 21. *Saturnians* refers to the golden age of the gods; but also to the baleful influence of the planet Saturn. The Vale of Tempe, in Greece, was so famed for its beauty that its name became the generic one for a beautiful valley. As such it is mentioned in the writings of Wordsworth, Shelley, Keats, and other romantic poets. The sacrilege of bloodshed in Tempe occurs in *Clarel* (II, v, 46). As noted by Horsford, the source is Melville's journal entry about the Englishman who had been "shooting in the Vale of Tempe" (*Journal . . . to Europe and the Levant*, p. 72).

Lines 33–34. The famous statue in the Vatican known as the Apollo Belvedere portrays the god just after he has slain the Python, a monstrous serpent bred in the slime of the receding Flood. The Pythian games were in honor of this feat. Melville saw the statue when he visited the Vatican Museum in 1857, and he owned Robert Macpherson's *Vatican Sculptures . . .* (London, 1863), which had been sent to him from Rome by the author on May 4, 1866 (Sealts no. 344). When he lectured in 1857 on "Statues in Rome" he praised the Apollo extravagantly and made repeated references to it. Sealts points out that this was in keeping with the taste of the period, following the lead of Winckelmann and Byron's description in the fourth canto of *Childe Harold* (*Melville as Lecturer*, p. 136).

Melville owned a reproduction of "Apollo Killing the Python" by Turner, the original of which he probably saw at the National Gallery in London in 1857. This print is now in the collection of the Berkshire Athenaeum.

The reference to Apollo and the Python is related to Tempe (line 21), for it was here that Apollo purified himself after he killed the monster.

Lines 42–43. Cf. "Battle of Stone River" (lines 15–16) and "A Meditation" (lines 11–12).

Line 44. *in all was* (revision in Melville's copy).

Line 46. *So put it* (revision in Melville's copy).

Lines 54-60. The imagery of the concluding lines is of spring flowers which have been killed before they have lost their bloom. Similarly, the boy soldiers have retained their bloom, and are dead without having reached maturity.

America

The concluding poem in the first section of *Battle-Pieces* reviews major themes from the preceding poems and orders them into a progression which through the experience of the allegorical mother goddess, America, reveals the meaning of the Civil War. Stanza one depicts the pleasure of the mother goddess as she beholds the innocent happiness of her children; stanza two is devoted to her agony as she watches them turn in fury upon each other; stanza three portrays her death-like sleep and her dream vision of the underlying evil which is a part of existence; and stanza four shows her awakening to the knowledge, brought by experience, of the need for law. Once she has undergone the archetypal journey from childlike innocence to mature experience, from death to resurrection, and from the depths of the foundations to the heights of the mountain, her initiation is complete and she faces the future gravely but serenely.

It is not surprising that Melville should have thought of his "America" as a statuesque allegorical figure, for the concept was popular with American sculptors of the period. In Italy he had seen Thomas Crawford's "America," commissioned for the pediment of the Capitol, and Hiram Powers' "America," afterwards destroyed in a fire. Horsford (*Journal . . . to Europe and the Levant*, p. 222n.) quotes from a contemporary description of the latter: "It is a female figure, with a loose, flowing sash thrown about her person, a serene and placid countenance, one hand lifted and fingers pointing to heaven . . . the other hand placed upon a bundle of rods, representing the states of our confederacy, and the feet standing on the broken emblems of tyranny and oppression." The theme of the death-like sleep was likewise popular. For example, the motto "The Union is not dead but sleeping," adopted for the flag of a New York regiment, is the subject of a poem in *Harper's Weekly* of May 25, 1861. Entitled "Not Dead," it describes a personification of the Union "who is not dead, but sleeping for a while." There are "watchers" during her sleep and the "Earth trembles," but eventually, "Crowned with the Stars . . ./ Bearing the Stripes aloft," she can be expected to awaken.

Line 1. See "The Conflict of Convictions," note on line 44, for the dome as a symbol of the state. Here it is used, more conventionally, in reference to the sky.

Line 3. The constellation Coma Berenices is named for Berenice, the Egyptian queen who pledged her hair to Venus for the safe return of her husband from war. Cf. Pope, "The Rape of the Lock," V, 129. In *Mardi* (Chap. 188, "Babbalanja Relates to them a Vision") Melville refers to "spangled Berenice's Locks."

Line 15. The lightning is ambiguous, Chase observes, because it may be either creative or destructive (*Melville,* p. 237).

Lines 17-19. Cf. *Paradise Lost,* II, 44-45: "Stood up, the strongest and fiercest Spirit/ That fought in Heaven; now fiercer by despair." See also *Paradise Lost,* IV, 115: "Thrice chang'd with pale, ire, envy and despair." Melville used this quotation as the epigraph to Chapter 13 of *Billy Budd.*

Line 25. Jarrard (*Poems . . . Critical Edition,* p. 310) suggests that quotation marks should enclose this line.

Line 29. For an earlier use of this phrase see "The Conflict of Convictions," line 65.

Line 30. The Gorgons, three snake-haired sisters, were so terrible to behold that whoever looked upon them was turned to stone. Melville associated the Gorgons with "The Maldive Shark" (line 8), in *John Marr,* and in *Mardi* (Chap. 18, "My Lord Shark and his Pages"), where "The shark swims sluggishly; creating no sign of a ripple; but ever and anon shaking his Medusa locks, writhing and curling with horrible life." For other sharks which symbolize the ultimate terror see "Commemorative of a Naval Victory," note on lines 26-27.

Line 32. Cf. "The Scout Toward Aldie," note on line 430.

On the Home Guards

Union forces surrendered Lexington, Missouri, to General Sterling Price on September 20, 1861, after three days of fighting. Contrary to the impression given by Melville, the Home Guard was severely criticized for cowardice and inefficiency (e.g. in *Harper's Weekly,* October 12, 1861).

Inscription for Graves at Pea Ridge, Arkansas

Melville pays tribute to Arkansas Unionists who died in the defense of Pea Ridge on March 7–8, 1862, when the Union Army of the Southwest under General Sam Curtis drove Confederates under General Earl Van Dorn from the field. This defeat ultimately resulted in Van Dorn's receiving orders to withdraw from Arkansas.

The Fortitude of the North

Lee, newly appointed as commander of the Army of Northern Virginia, defeated but was unable to destroy the much larger Union Army of Virginia under General John Pope on August 29–30, 1862, at Manassas Junction, site of an earlier Southern victory. The defeat of Pope followed upon Lee's success in turning back McClellan's march on Richmond from the Peninsula.

Line 1. *No shame they take for* (revision in Melville's copy).

Lines 5–9. Cape Horn, which survives the battering of sea and storm, is described in detail in *White-Jacket* (esp. Chaps. 21, 25, 26, 28). See "Misgivings," note on lines 11–13. On September 1, 1860, while aboard the "Meteor" Melville wrote to his son Malcolm: "The next day we were off Cape Horn, the Southernmost point of all America. Now it was very bad weather, and was dark at about three o'clock in the afternoon. The wind blew terribly. We had hail-storms, and snow and sleet, and often the spray froze as it touched the deck" (*Letters,* p. 202).

On the Men of Maine

A Confederate expedition against Baton Rouge on August 5, 1862 met with success until the ram "Arkansas" developed engine trouble and could not provide naval support. Repelling the attack were elements of seven Union regiments, including the Fourteenth Maine.

Melville, as his introductory note to the collection indicates, was sensitive to the implications of "the geographical area covered by the war." Cf. "The Frenzy in the Wake" (lines 17–18).

Inscription for Marye's Heights, Fredericksburg

General Ambrose E. Burnside, commanding the Army of the Potomac, advanced toward Fredericksburg, Virginia, while Lee, taking advantage of the terrain, drew up his army on Marye's Heights west of the town. To attack, Burnside had to cross the Rappahannock River, drive through the town, and breast a stone wall in front of a sunken road at the base of Marye's Heights. He had 12,700 men killed or wounded in repeated attemps to drive Lee from the hill. Lee's losses were 5,300. On December 15, 1862 Burnside withdrew.

Line 6. The word *erect* is the principal verb, but it also functions as an adjective modifying *Stone* and as such contrasts with *overthrown*.

On the Slain at Chickamauga

Some eight months after Bragg and Rosecrans fought an inconclusive battle at Stones River near Murfreesboro, Tennessee, they met again. The Federals forced Bragg out of Chattanooga only to be trapped there by him temporarily as a result of the battle on September 19–20, 1863 at Chickamauga.

Line 12. Those whose eyes were closed by death persisted in spite of having seen only defeat.

An Uninscribed Monument

See general comment on "The Armies of the Wilderness."

On Sherman's Men

At Kennesaw Mountain on June 27, 1865, General Joseph E. Johnston took up a strong defensive position in an effort to block Sherman's march on Atlanta. He withstood Sherman's assault but when threatened by envelopment withdrew to a line along the Chattahoochee River before Atlanta.

On the Grave

This poem has the tightly knit, epigrammatic quality of an epitaph from the Greek Anthology. Melville, who was often heavy-handed in such matters, maintains control gracefully through the connotation of three words ("Gold," "unenriched," "fortune") which suggest that the young soldier, though rich in life, was even richer in his death.

Line 3. According to the floral dictionaries, violets signify modesty. Melville used "the language of flowers," notably in *Mardi* but also elsewhere. The violet is a low-growing plant.

A Requiem

Lines 1–2. Cf. "Misgivings" (lines 1–3).

Line 15. Jarrard (*Poems . . . Critical Edition,* p. 312) suggests the plural, "Frolics," on the grounds that Melville's final *s* is frequently indistinct in manuscript.

Lines 19–22. Matthiessen (*American Renaissance,* p. 494) was perhaps referring to these lines when he wrote that the poem "seems to echo 'Lycidas' in some of its undersea images." Cf. line 19 to "Lycidas," 164: "And, O ye *Dolphins,* waft the hapless youth"; lines 20–21 to "Lycidas," 63–64: "His gory visage down the stream was sent,/ Down the swift Hebrus to the Lesbian shore"; and lines 20–22 to "Lycidas," 154–60, esp. 154–55: "Whilst thee the shores, and sounding Seas/ Wash far away, where'er thy bones are hurl'd."

Line 23. Melville may have been thinking of Milton's Invocation to Light, with which Book III of *Paradise Lost* begins. For Melville's reaction to the Invocation to Light, see *Redburn* (Chap. 29, "The Booble Alleys of the Town").

Lines 25–26. Fogle ("Melville and the Civil War," p. 80) sees in the poem "Melville's sense of the isolation, the utter abandonment, of a death at sea." He finds lines 25–26 "reminiscent of the end of the *Pequod,* with the seahawk, the sinking flag, and the lonely, eternal surges of the Pacific." See *Moby-Dick* (Chap. 135, "The Chase—Third Day").

On a Natural Monument

Written prior to the founding of the National Cemetery at Andersonville, where 15,000 of the reinterred captives now sleep, each beneath his personal head-board, inscribed from records found in the prison-hospital. Some hundreds rest apart and without name. A glance at the published pamphlet containing the list of the buried at Andersonville conveys a feeling mournfully impressive. Seventy-four large double-columned pages in fine print. Looking through them is like getting lost among the old turbaned head-stones and cypresses in the interminable Black Forest of Scutari, over against Constantinople. [Melville's note]

In July 1865, Clara Barton led an expedition to Andersonville, Georgia, "for the purpose of identifying the graves and enclosing the grounds of a cemetery created there during the occupation of that place as a prison for Union soldiers in Rebel hands"—to quote from her preface to the pamphlet cited below. Accompanying her was Dorence Atwater, a former prisoner at Andersonville. While serving as a clerk Atwater secretly copied an official record of those who had died there. Clara Barton interested

Horace Greeley in this list, and Greeley had it published as a pamphlet bearing the *Tribune* imprint. Entitled *A List of the Union Soldiers Buried at Andersonville,* it carries Atwater's signature. An editorial in the *Tribune* for February 14, 1866, indicates that the pamphlet was completed by that date. As Melville states, the list consists of 74 pages of fine print in double columns.

Melville's statement that his poem on a "natural" monument was written before the Barton mission placed "head-boards" on the Andersonville graves provides a means of determining the date of its composition. On August 17, 1865, after Miss Barton had completed her work, she conducted a flag-raising and dedication ceremony at the National Cemetery.

Melville visited several cemeteries while he was in Contantinople in 1856. According to entries in the *Journal . . . to Europe and the Levant,* on December 13 he "saw cemeteries, where they dumped garbage. Forrests [*sic*] of cemeteries" (p. 79). On December 14 he "went toward cemeteries at Pera" (p. 89). On December 18 he visited Scutari, the most Oriental of the suburbs, with "Cemeteries like Black Forrest" (p. 104). It was customary to plant cypresses in Moslem cemeteries.

Line 12. *In horror they choked the* (revision in Melville's copy).
Line 16. Cf. *Moby-Dick* (Chap. 23, "The Lee Shore").

Commemorative of a Naval Victory

Melville may have had in mind his first cousin, Guert Gansevoort, when he wrote this poem. In 1842, as a lieutenant aboard the brig "Somers," Gansevoort had been in charge of the court martial which condemned to death for mutiny a midshipman, Philip Spencer, and two seamen under circumstances which remain subject to controversy. Although cleared by an official inquiry, his life was marked by the strain and mystery attached to this event. He distinguished himself for bravery at Vera Cruz in 1847, during the Mexican War, and in 1851 he led a naval expedition in the defense of Seattle against an attack of some 2,000 Indians. On May 25, 1862 Melville wrote to his brother Tom: "Guert has recently been appointed to the command of a fine new sloop of war. He is brave as a lion, a good seaman, a natural-born officer, & I hope he will turn out the hero of a brilliant victory" (*Letters,* p. 215). In October 1864 he was assigned to the Brooklyn Navy Yard, where Melville could have seen him often. (Leyda, *Log,* pp. 157–63, 238, 511, 671).

The most significant recollection of Guert Gansevoort and the "Somers" affair is to be found in *Billy Budd.* He also appears in "Bridegroom Dick," in *John Marr,* as "Guert Gan," hero of the Vera Cruz beach (lines 82–94), as "Tom Tight" who was "lieutenant in the brig-o'-war famed/ When an officer was hung for an arch-mutineer" (lines 315–16), and perhaps as "Dainty Dave" whose career was clouded by "some sad disaster" (lines 52–61).

Lines 1–3. The "simple nature" of sailors and the refining influence of "continuous martial discipline and repeated presence in battle" are described in *Billy Budd* (Chap. 2).

Lines 3–5. *damasked blade*: a highly refined steel sword made in Damascus, characteristically ornamented with a wavy or watered pattern; *The discipline of arms*: a refining process, here applied equally to making steel weapons and to training sailors; *wave*: refers both to the "tempering" experience of the sea on sailors and to the watered pattern of the blade. In *White-Jacket* (Chap. 39, "The Frigate in Harbour") Melville compares American sailors to " slender Damascus blades, nimble and flexible," and tells the familiar story of how "Richard clove an anvil . . . and Saladin elegantly severed a cushion" in a contest between broadsword and Damascus blade. A related conceit appears in *Mardi* (Chap. 32, "Xiphius Playtypterus") where Melville describes the bill of the swordfish which, "though tempered not in Tagus or Guadalquiver, it yet revealed upon its surface that wavy grain and watery fleckiness peculiar to tried blades of Spain." Note that the man in Titian's painting (line 8) carries a sword.

Line 6. The blade provides a last touch of sedate graciousness. However, the words *last grave grace* have funereal connotations, and Melville might also have meant that the "refined" life, which the blade represents, receives an accolade at the time of burial, when the beam of the blade above the dead hero is symbolic of a state of grace.

Lines 7–9. The painting by Titian which best fits Melville's description is "The Man with a Falcon" (Joslyn Art Museum, Omaha, Nebraska). It was exhibited by the British Institute in 1844 and an engraving of it was made in 1811. Titian was closely associated with Emperor Charles V and painted a number of portraits of him. Melville may have been thinking of the account in Vasari's biography (Sealts no. 534) of Titian's gift to Charles V of an "Annunciation" which greatly pleased his patron. Melville described Titian (in "Daniel Orme") as "a profound portrait-painter."

Line 19. Laurel crowns were awarded by the Greeks and Romans to those who excelled in poetry and war.

Line 20. From the popular floral dictionaries, one of which Elizabeth Melville owned (Sealts no. 353), Melville would have known the etymological connection with the French word *pensée,* thought. Cf. Shakespeare, *Hamlet,* IV, v, 176: "There is pansies, that's for thoughts." Montague ("Melville's *Battle-Pieces*," p. 107) adds this example of wordplay to his list of Melville's shortcomings as a poet: "Faulty diction—such alliterative

"The Man with a Falcon," by Titian.

(and semantically redundant) eccentricities as 'pensive pansies'—mars essentially strong poems."

Lines 26–27. Melville had read Schiller's "The Diver, a Ballad" (Sealts nos. 437, 439) in 1860, marking the stanza on the shark (Leyda, *Log*, p. 626) :

> Dark-crawl'd—glided dark the unspeakable swarms, . . .
> And with teeth grinning white, and a menacing motion,
> Went the terrible Shark—the Hyaena of Ocean.

White sharks glide through a number of Melville's poems and novels, including "America" (line 30 and "The Scout Toward Aldie (line 13). In *Mardi* (Chap. 13, "Of the Chondropterygii . . .") the "ghastly White Shark . . . Timon-like" pursues his malevolent way; in *White-Jacket* (Chap. 92, "The Last of the Jacket") , the jacket, symbol of that which protects and destroys, is mistaken for a white shark as it floats in the sea; in *Moby-Dick* (Chap. 42, "The Whiteness of the Whale") "the white gliding ghostliness of repose in that creature" provokes a particular horror. "The Maldive Shark," in *John Marr,* has been seen as a warning "that the individual must condition himself to those very forces which, at a whim, can destroy him" (Stein, "Melville's Poetry," p. 22), and as "the Fate symbol" (Warren, "Melville the Poet," p. 218) . "In a Bye-Canal," in *Timoleon,* Warren describes the poet as having undergone an initiation " 'Twixt the whale's black flukes and the white shark's fin." Generally, the white shark represents, by a typical inversion of imagery, a meaningful venture into what Melville calls in *Moby-Dick* the "blackness of darkness." In this dark depth lies possible destruction but also the only possibility of ripeness. For other references to the shark, see "America," note on line 30.

Although the poem is about a naval hero its context is the Civil War. The "light and shadow on every man" which applies to the individual also applies to the war, an inextricable mixture of good and evil.

The Returned Volunteer to His Rifle

Cf. "The Released Rebel Prisoner" (lines 26–27) .

The Scout Toward Aldie

The Partisan Raiders were organized by Colonel John S. Mosby in January 1863. They consisted originally of cavalry detached from Stuart's command in Loudon County, located in northeastern Virginia, with the mission of diverting attention from the main Confederate force. Union troops spent much time and effort in unsuccessful attempts to put an end to the Raiders' activities. The unit was disbanded on April 21, 1865.

Aldie is situated in Loudon County, about ten miles south of Lees-burg, the county seat. Loudon Valley lies between the Bull Run Mountains on the east and the Blue Ridge on the west. A sharp skirmish took place at Aldie during the preliminary phase of the Gettysburg campaign.

The format of the original edition indicates that Melville considered "The Scout Toward Aldie" as standing apart from the rest of *Battle-Pieces,* for the title appears in the table of contents in a different type face and separation pages set it off from the memorial verses which precede and from "Lee in the Capitol" which follows. In addition to its length it is unusual in its origin and its form. Melville was not rehashing *The Rebellion Record* but was creating from personal experience and from events described to him by soldiers he had met, and he had chosen a genre, the literary ballad, which he had not previously attempted. The poem is autobiographical in that it came out of Melville's visit to the battlefront, where he participated in a cavalry scout into the Mosby country southwest of Washington. Of this visit Elizabeth Melville years later wrote in her notebook (Berkshire Athenaeum MSS.) : "Herman went to Virginia with Allen in April 1864. Visited various battle-fields & called on General Grant. Henry Gansevoort then in the service in camp at Vienna, Virginia."

On April 8, 1864 Melville obtained a pass from the Secretary of War to "visit the Army of the Potomac & return" (Leyda, *Log,* p. 666). With his brother. Allen he set out to see a cousin, Colonel Henry Gansevoort, stationed with the Thirteenth New York Cavalry at Vienna, which was then assigned to operate against Mosby's Partisans. On April 14 he was allowed to go along on a cavalry raid into the wilderness where Mosby was known to be ranging. This military expedition was brief and trivial, lasting less than two days and resulting merely in the capture of a half-dozen guerrillas who were planning to burn a bridge (Howard, *Melville,* p. 276). However, Melville was provided with literary capital. He received a few sharp impressions which could be turned into tropes such as that of the almost mythic Mosby gliding about in the shadows of the spring foliage, a pervasive malevolence like the shark with which he is compared (lines 13–14). He also heard stories and witnessed scenes which could serve germinally for plot, character, setting, and tone. Especially important was his acquaintance with the dashing Charles Russell Lowell, a nephew of the poet. Another "college colonel," he had graduated with first honors from Harvard. Lowell, whose bride had made a memorable visit to the camp a few months before, had rejoined his regiment after recovering from a wound (Howard, *Melville,* p. 277). He was to die at Cedar Creek the following October, having been repeatedly wounded but still refusing to leave his command.

Like many another writer of the Romantic period, Melville sought to inform his poem with the authority of folk expression. His setting is a land of enchantment, an "Eerie Land" (line 29). His characters and situations fit the ballad pattern. He introduces shape-shifters (lines 18, 700) and haunted houses (line 198); much talk of spells, charms, elves, fairies, and ghosts; and an invisible personage who ravages the countryside, invulnerable to lead bullets but perhaps not to silver ones (line 728). Cf. "The Martyr," prefatory note.

The use of the refrain Melville justified partly on the grounds of the associations of Mosby's name in "the popular mind" (see note on line 238), or the folk mind, as contemporary usage has it. A second and likewise folkloristic reason for the refrain was Melville's belief in its power as incantation. This notion, which he got from reading Madame de Staël in 1862, appears in a passage which he marked: "The ancients, and the poets of the middle ages, were acquainted with the kind of terror caused in certain circumstances by the repetition of the same words; it seems to awaken the sentiment of inflexible necessity" (Leyda, *Log,* p. 647). The poem cannot sustain the frequent repetition of Mosby's name, but the idea that this repetition should arouse terror and represent necessity is interesting in terms of the "blithe" colonel's death through his heedlessness and his contempt of magic, and the major's survival because of his respect for danger and for that which he cannot understand.

Lines 13–14. For other symbolic sharks, see "Commemorative of a Naval Victory," note on lines 26–27. This couplet attracts particular attention because of initial as well as end rhyme and the break in rhythm due to the length of the sound in *green,* especially noticeable in relation to the brevity of *dark.*

Lines 32–35. For the dome as a national symbol, see "The Conflict of Convictions," note on line 44. Aldie is some 30 miles from Washington.

Line 36. *A ride toward* (revision in Melville's copy).

Line 38. Cf. Shakespeare, *Romeo and Juliet,* I, i, 141: ". . . so soon as the all-cheering sun . . ."

Lines 41–42. The ironical contrast between the bridal bed and the grave is a foreshadowing device. Cf. lines 669–70.

Line 70. Cf. Psalms 90:5–6: "In the morning they are like grass which groweth up. . . . in the evening it is cut down, and withereth."

Line 100. *a dreary place* (revision in Melville's copy).

Line 115. In one of Kilpatrick's earlier cavalry fights near Aldie, a Colonel who, being under arrest, had been temporarily deprived of his sword, nevertheless, unarmed, insisted upon charging at the head of his men, which he did, and the onset proved victorious. [Melville's note]

The officer was Colonel Louis Di Cesnola, Fourth New York. General Judson Kilpatrick returned his sword in tribute to his bravery. He was later wounded and captured. (*War of the Rebellion*, Ser. 1, XXVII, Pt. 2, 742).

Line 147. *A spell-bound land* (revision in Melville's copy).

Line 160. *dead-man's-hand*: a local name for various species of orchis (*N.E.D.*).

Line 162. *The road they leave and* (revision in Melville's copy).

Line 200. *we deemed* (revision in Melville's copy).

Line 206. *The pool they skirt, avoid* (revision in Melville's copy).

Line 238. Certain of Mosby's followers, on the charge of being unlicensed foragers or fighters, being hung by order of a Union cavalry commander, the Partisan promptly retaliated in the woods. In turn, this also was retaliated, it is said. To what extent such deplorable proceedings were carried, it is not easy to learn.

South of the Potomac in Virginia, and within a gallop of the Long Bridge at Washington, is the confine of a country, in some places wild, which throughout the war it was unsafe for a Union man to traverse except with an armed escort. This was the chase of Mosby, the scene of many of his exploits or those of his men. In the heart of this region at least one fortified camp was maintained by our cavalry, and from time to time expeditions were made therefrom. Owing to the nature of the country and the embittered feeling of its inhabitants, many of these expeditions ended disastrously. Such results were helped by the exceeding cunning of the enemy, born of his wood-craft, and, in some instances, by undue confidence on the part of our men. A body of cavalry, starting from camp with the view of breaking up a nest of rangers, and absent say three days, would return with a number of their own forces killed and wounded (ambushed), without being able to retaliate farther than by foraging on the country, destroying a house or two reported to be haunts of the guerrillas, or capturing non-combatants accused of being secretly active in their behalf.

In the verse the name of Mosby is invested with some of those associations with which the popular mind is familiar. But facts do not warrant the belief that every clandestine attack of men who passed for Mosby's was made under his eye, or even by his knowledge.

In partisan warfare he proved himself shrewd, able, and enterprising, and always a wary fighter. He stood well in the confidence of his superior officers, and was employed by them at times in furtherance of important movements. To our wounded on more than one occasion he showed considerate kindness. Officers and civilians captured by forces under his immediate command were, so long as remaining under his orders, treated with civility. These things are well known to those personally familiar with the irregular fighting in Virginia. [Melville's note]

In his personal copy Melville partially corrected the tense sequence of the last sentence of the second paragraph of the above note.

Line 241. Bull Run Mountains.

Line 266. *time for thought* (revision in Melville's copy).

Line 307. For other references to hanging, see lines 232–38, 309, and note on line 238.

Line 387. A week after the scout in which Melville participated, another party captured some of Mosby's partisans who were attending a wedding at Leesburg. Howard suggests that Melville may have heard of this raid through Colonel Gansevoort (*Melville,* p. 277). For other references to Leesburg and to an attempt to surprise Mosby there, see lines 410, 606–9.

Line 409. *Cuff*: a proper name of African origin, sometimes a generic name for a Negro. See line 461 where he is addressed as "Garry" by his mistress.

Line 430. Cf. Shakespeare, *Macbeth,* I, i, 11: "Fair is foul, and foul is fair." This echo from the witches' scene contributes to the haunted atmosphere and suggests a witch-like quality in the girl, who is said to "mystify" and who disappears under strange circumstances. Cf. "Misgivings" (line 7) and "America" (line 32).

Lines 507-9. Cf. "Supplement," *Battle-Pieces,* p. 196.

Line 518. In the singing contest, the "bluebirds" are the Northern soldiers and the "butternuts" are the Southerners. The nicknames are from the color of their uniforms. This is confirmed by Melville's revision of the Union sergeant's speech, note on line 540.

Lines 525-26. Cf. lines 672, 685–86, and "The March into Virginia" (line 21).

Line 537. During the Gettysburg campaign the Confederates under Stuart were under serious pressure after engagements at Aldie and nearby Upperville. Stuart took up a defensive position at Ashby's Gap eighteen miles west of Aldie, on June 21, 1863.

Line 540. *Comrades, you* (revision in Melville's copy).

Lines 543–53. Another song using the butternut conceit is "Babylon Is Fallen," written by Henry C. Work in 1863. After explaining that their master is now a colonel in the Confederate army, his slaves sing:

> We will be de Massa,
> He will be de sarvant,
> Try him how he like it for a spell;
> So we crack de Butt'nuts,
> So we take de Kernel,
> So de cannon carry back de shell.

It is unlikely that this minstrel song was Melville's source; however, such songs interested him, for in *White-Jacket* (Chap. 41, "A Man-of-war Library") the sailors find pleasure in "a negro song-book."

Line 604. Proverbial as early as c.1220. "To do brown" is slang for thoroughly, perhaps suggested by roasting (*N.E.D.*).

Line 644. *This gold-lace gleams—does* (revision in Melville's copy).

Line 684. *come astray on* (revision in Melville's copy).

Lines 685–86. *confederates*: Confederate soldiers are suggested, but the trees assist Mosby by providing cover for his ambush. Cf. note on lines 525–26.

Line 698. *skurry*: rush.

Line 700. Cf. lines 17–18.

Lee in the Capitol

Among those summoned during the spring just passed to appear before the Reconstruction Committee of Congress was Robert E. Lee. His testimony is deeply interesting, both in itself and as coming from him. After various questions had been put and briefly answered, these words were addressed to him:

"If there be any other matter about which you wish to speak on this occasion, do so freely." Waiving this invitation, he responded by a short personal explanation of some point in a previous answer, and, after a few more brief questions and replies, the interview closed.

In the verse a poetical liberty has been ventured. Lee is not only represented as responding to the invitation, but also as at last renouncing his cold reserve, doubtless the cloak to feelings more or less poignant. If for such freedom warrant be necessary, the speeches in ancient histories, not to speak of those in Shakespeare's historic plays, may not unfitly perhaps be cited.

The character of the original measures proposed about this time in the National Legislature for the treatment of the (as yet) Congressionally excluded South, and the spirit in which those measures were advocated— these are circumstances which it is fairly supposable would have deeply influenced the thoughts, whether spoken or withheld, of a Southerner placed in the position of Lee before the Reconstruction Committee. [Melville's note]

The date in the subtitle is incorrect. The fact that Melville was accurate in his dating in all previous subtitles suggests that the error may have been deliberate. If it is indeed not simply due to inadvertence, the cause may be that Melville attached a value to the first anniversary of the surrender and changed the date accordingly, or else that he wished to make his book appear as timely as possible. In any case, he protected himself by claiming "poetical liberty."

Lee arrived in Washington on February 16, 1866 and left on February 20. He came at the summons of a sub-committee for the states of Virginia, North Carolina, and South Carolina of the joint Congressional Committee created to investigate "the conditions of the states which formed the so-called Confederate States . . . and report whether they, or any of them, are entitled to be represented in either house of Congress." Lee's testimony was printed in the *Report of the Joint Committee on Reconstruction . . . 39th Congress* (Pt. II, pp. 129–36). A full account was published in the New York *Tribune* of Feburary 19, 1866, and this could have been Melville's source. Other New York newspapers, the *Herald* for example, also gave coverage to the story.

Line 9. Aside from the alliterative convenience they afford in this line, Stuart and Stonewall Jackson were probably the two among his general officers whose loss Lee felt most, both personally and for the sake of their military value.

Freeman (*Lee,* IV, 256) states that the story about Lee's going to Arlington to visit the Custis mansion, where he was married and lived from 1834 to 1861, is not true. He found the source of the legend in a newspaper article by the Washington correspondent of the New York *Tribune* which was reprinted in the *National Intelligencer*: "A gentleman of this city having occasion to pass through Arlington at dusk on Saturday saw a lonely figure standing with folded arms at the foot of a tree. Struck with the sorrowful attitude of the person, he walked past him, and saw that it was Robert E. Lee standing in the street that passes through the middle of his old estate. Mrs. Lee had applied to the President for a return of this estate, which has virtually become a National Union cemetery. The expectation is general that the President will order its restoration."

Lines 26–27. The Arlington estate went by "forfeit" for delinquent taxes, in consequence of a law taxing real estate "in the insurrectionary districts," when the commissioners refused to accept payment from anyone but the owners in person.

Line 37. Cf. "The Victor of Antietam," note on line 22.

Line 54. Cf. *Paradise Lost,* III, 345–46: "The multitude of Angels with a shout/ Loud as from numbers without number, sweet."

Lines 55–56. Cf. "The Muster" for another parade described in terms of a river.

Line 60. Cf. note to "The Muster."

Lines 67–69. Lee married Mary Ann Randolph Custis in 1831. She was the daughter of George Washington Parke Custis, grandson of Martha Washington.

Lines 74–88. Lee appeared before the Congressional Committee for two hours on February 17. He did not wish to testify, but he answered questions politely, if briefly, and conducted himself with dignity. The chairman, Jacob M. Howard of Michigan, inquired about the Southern attitude toward the North and the future of the freedmen. He also asked his pet question: "In the event of war between the United States and any foreign power, such as England or France, if there should be held out to the secession portion of the people of Virginia, or the other recently rebel states, a fair prospect of gaining their independence . . . is it, or is it not, your opinion that they would avail themselves of the opportunity?" (*Report,* p. 130)

Line 107. According to Freeman, Lee meticulously observed his parole in deed and spirit.

Line 133. *from those charnel-fields* (revision in Melville's copy).

Line 152. *intermeddlers and malign* (revision in Melville's copy).

Line 187. Sulla, the Roman leader of the aristocratic party, was noted for instituting bloody proscriptions of his enemies. Melville would have read his life in Plutarch.

Line 200. *Forbear to wreak the ill you* (revision in Melville's copy).

Lines 210–13. The cheery note with which this poem ends is a strange turnabout. Lee's earnest argument for the "magnanimity" which could result in "re-established law" (line 145) has not convinced the committee. If the evidence he offered has validity, and if it represents, as it appears to, Melville's own opinion, then the lame substitute of "Instinct" for logic is a serious defect. However, Melville may have sensed the irony of the Northern substitution of instinct for logic and stood apart from it.

A Meditation

In the original edition the poem is preceded by a separation page with a full title as follows:

ATTRIBUTED TO A NORTHERNER AFTER ATTENDING THE LAST OF TWO FUNERALS FROM THE SAME HOMESTEAD—THOSE OF A NATIONAL AND A CONFEDERATE OFFICER (BROTHERS), HIS KINSMEN, WHO HAD DIED FROM THE EFFECTS OF WOUNDS RECEIVED IN THE CLOSING BATTLES.

Lines 11–12. Cf. "Battle for Stone River," note on line 17.

Line 30. Many of the soldiers, both Union and Confederate were veterans of the Mexican War, 1847–48.

Lines 41–42. Cf. "Donelson" (lines 254–55).

Lines 43–48. Among "The great Captains on both sides" were a number who had been classmates at West Point on the Hudson River.

Line 54. See Christ's denunciation of the Pharisees for hypocrisy, Mark 7:6, and the parable of the Pharisee and the publican (Luke 18:10–14), to which Melville also refers in *Clarel* (IV, x, 77).

Supplement

The urgency of the times, which Melville considered reasonable grounds for appending a political tract to a volume of verses, was apparent in the controversy centering about the Fourteenth Amendment which Congress had passed in June 1866, and the impending congressional elections, the first since the end of the war. Carefully reasoned and restrained, his political views as he stated them in the "Supplement" are consistent with the themes of the war poems. He inclined in his political sympathies toward the Democrats and the moderate wing of the Republican party, and one of the few reviews of any length devoted to *Battle-Pieces* was in a newspaper of this persuasion (New York *Herald,* September 3, 1866). As Fogle points out in his excellent analysis of the "Supplement" ("Melville and the Civil War," pp. 85-89), he is in the Romantic tradition in that he used "poetry in public affairs and wrote good prose to supplement it." At a time of shouting and tumult, his soft-spoken words went almost unheard. Indeed, so mild was the response that his views did not prove a stumbling block to the political appointment he was then seeking, that of customs inspector in New York.

[1]Melville substituted "fairmindedness" for "impartiality" in his own copy.
[2]Melville in his own copy eliminated the phrase "out of the graceful instinct of a gentleman" and the commas which enclosed it.
[3]On March 8, 1857 Melville, in Rome, wrote (*Journal . . . to Europe and the Levant,* p. 207): "To St. Peters—tour of interior—Stuarts' tomb." As Horsford notes, these monuments were to the descendants of James II, who lost his throne in the Glorious Revolution of 1688. Much of the cost for constructing them was paid by George IV.
[4]James Hogg (1770–1835), Scottish poet and novelist.
[5]Cf. Milton, "To the Lord General Cromwell," line 3: "Guided by faith and matchless fortitude."
[6]Edmund Ruffin, an ardent secessionist, fired the first shot from Morris Island against Fort Sumter. He killed himself on June 18, 1865. Although

67 years old at the time, he served as a volunteer with the Palmetto Guard at Charleston and was a "temporary" private at First Manassas. (*D.A.B.*).

[7]Cf. "The Scout Toward Aldie" (lines 507–9).

[8]The Fourteenth Amendment disqualified from office those who had sworn to support the Constitution but afterwards "engaged in insurrection or rebellion against the same, or given aid or comfort to the enemies thereof."

[9]Cf. "Running the Batteries," note on lines 21–23.

[10]Melville substituted "great" for "terrible" in his own copy.

[11]This echo from Aristotle's discussion of the drama suggests that Melville saw the experience of the Civil War as possessing the same nature and function as Greek tragedy. In his note to "The Frenzy in the Wake," Melville, referring to Lincoln's death, had used the phrase, "historic tragedy."

Works Cited

Barrett, Laurence. "The Differences in Melville's Poetry," *PMLA*, LXX (1955), 606–23.

Berlind, Bruce. "Notes on Melville's Shorter Poems," *Hopkins Review*, III (1942), 24–35.

Bernstein, John. *Pacifism and Rebellion in the Writings of Melville*. University of Pennsylvania dissertation, 1961.

Braswell, William. *Melville's Religious Thought: An Essay in Interpretation*. Durham, N. C., 1943.

Chase, Richard. *Herman Melville: A Critical Study*. New York, 1949.

The Civil War: A Centennial Exhibition of Eyewitness Drawings. Washington, 1961.

Davis, Merrell R. "The Flower Symbolism in *Mardi*," *Modern Language Quarterly*, II (1942), 625–38.

Day, Frank L. *Herman Melville's Use of* The Rebellion Record *in His Poetry*. University of Tennessee thesis, 1959.

Dow, Charles Mason. *Anthology and Bibliography of Niagara Falls*. Albany, 1921. 2 vols.

Fogle, Richard Harter. "Melville and the Civil War," *Tulane Studies in English*, IX (1959), 61–89.

Freeman, Douglas Southall. *R. E. Lee: A Biography*. New York, 1934–35. 4 vols.

Harper's New Monthly Magazine, XXXII–XXXIII (1866).

Harper's Weekly, V–IX (1861–65).

Hesseltine, William Best. *Civil War Prisons: A Study in War Psychology*. Columbus, Ohio, 1930.

Howard, Leon. *Herman Melville: A Biography*. Berkeley and Los Angeles, 1951.

Leyda, Jay. *The Melville Log: A Documentary Life of Herman Melville*. New York, 1951. 2 vols.

Mason, Ronald. *The Spirit Above the Dust: A Study of Herman Melville*. London, 1951.

Melville, Herman. *Battle-Pieces and Aspects of the War.* Ed. Sidney Kaplan. Gainesville, Fla., 1960.

——*Collected Poems of Herman Melville.* Ed. Howard P. Vincent. Chicago, 1947.

——*Clarel.* Ed. Walter E. Bezanson. New York, 1960.

——*The Letters of Herman Melville.* Ed. Merrell R. Davis and William H. Gilman. New Haven, 1960.

——*Journal of a Visit to Europe and the Levant.* Ed. Howard C. Horsford. Princeton, 1955.

——*Journal of a Visit to London and the Continent, 1849–1850.* Ed. Eleanor Melville Metcalf. Cambridge, Mass., 1948.

——"Journal of Melville's Voyage in a Clipper Ship," *New England Quarterly,* II (1929), 120–25.

——*Poems by Herman Melville: A Critical Edition of the Published Verse.* Ed. Norman Eugene Jarrard. University of Texas dissertation, 1960.

——*Herman Melville: Representative Selections.* Ed. Willard Thorp. New York, 1938.

——*Herman Melville: Selected Poems.* Ed. F. O. Matthiessen. Norfolk, Conn., 1944.

Metcalf, Eleanor Melville. *Herman Melville: Cycle and Epicycle.* Cambridge, Mass., 1953.

Montague, Gene B. "Melville's *Battle-Pieces,*" *University of Texas Studies in English,* XXXV (1956), 106–15.

National Academy of Design . . . Catalogue of the Fortieth Annual Exhibition. New York, [1865].

Nichols, George Ward. *The Story of the Great March.* New York, 1866.

Pommer, Henry F. *Milton and Melville.* Pittsburgh, 1950.

Read, Allen Walker. "The Rebel Yell as a Linguistic Problem," *American Speech,* XXXVI (1961), 83–92.

The Rebellion Record. Ed. Frank Moore. Vols. I–VIII (1862–65) and Supplement (1864). [Each volumes is divided into three parts with separately numbered pages. Unless otherwise specified, all page numbers cited are from the section entitled "Documents and Narratives."]

Report of the Joint Committee on Reconstruction, 39th Congress, Pt. II. Washington, 1866.

Sala, G. A. *My Diary in America in the Midst of War.* London, 1865.

Sealts, Merton M. *Melville as Lecturer.* Cambridge, Mass., 1957.

——"Melville's Reading: A Check List of Books Owned and Borrowed," *Harvard Library Bulletin,* II–IV (1948–50); VI (1952). [Books mentioned in the notes to this edition of *Battle-Pieces* are identified by the numbers given in Sealts' check list.]

Stein, William B. "Melville's Poetry: Its Symbols of Individuation," *Literature and Psychology*, VII (1957), 21–26.

Taft, Robert, *Artists and Illustrators of the Old West: 1800–1900*. New York, 1953.

Thompson, W. Fletcher. *The Image of War*. New York and London, 1960.

Tilley, Morris Palmer. *A Dictionary of Proverbs in England in the Sixteenth and Seventeenth Centuries*. Ann Arbor, Mich., 1950.

Personal Memoir of U. S. Grant. New York, 1885–86. 2 vols.

Vedder, Elihu. *The Digressions of V*. London, 1910.

Vogel, Dan. *Melville's Shorter Published Poetry: A Critical Study of the Lyrics in* Mardi, *of* Battle-Pieces, John Marr, *and* Timoleon. New York University dissertation, 1956. [Although not cited, this study was useful and provocative.]

The War of the Rebellion: A Compilation of the Official Records . . . Ser. I, Vol. II, Washington, 1880; Ser. I, Vol. XXVIII, Pt. 2, Washington, 1890.

Warren, Robert Penn. "Melville the Poet," *Kenyon Review*, VIII (1946), 208–23.

Watters, R. E. "Melville's 'Sociality,' " *American Literature*, XVII (1945), 33–49.

Williams Jr., Hermann Warner. *The Civil War: The Artists' Record*. Boston, 1961.

Wright, Nathalia. *Melville's Use of the Bible*. Durham, N. C., 1949.

Index of First Lines